Frontline Women

D0872710

Many young women are struggling to find an appropriate place in today's mission world. This helpful book is honest and realistic, showing how "women's issues" are not a side-light in mission, but are genuinely everyone's concern. I want to give a copy to a friend who is grappling with some of these matters.

Elizabeth S. Brewster
Associate Professor, School of Intercultural Studies,
Fuller Theological Seminary

This unique book realistically describes the personal and spiritual problems that women encounter when caught up in the cross-cultural and spiritual task of proclaiming and demonstrating the good news of the Kingdom.

the late Arthur F. Glasser
Dean Emeritus, School of Intercultural Studies,
Fuller Theological Seminary

Years of pain will be skipped when women read *Frontline Women*. With the frank disclosures and clear suggestions in this book, women will be prepared before they get to the field. Mission agencies will be equipped to bless the women on their team.

Miriam Adeney
Associate Professor, Seattle Pacific University
Teaching Fellow, Regent College

Women need to read this book to be encouraged. Men need to read it and wake up.

Darrell L. Whiteman, *from the Foreword*

FRONTLINE WOMEN

Negotiating Cross-Cultural Issues in Ministry

edited by *Marguerite G. Kraft*

revised edition

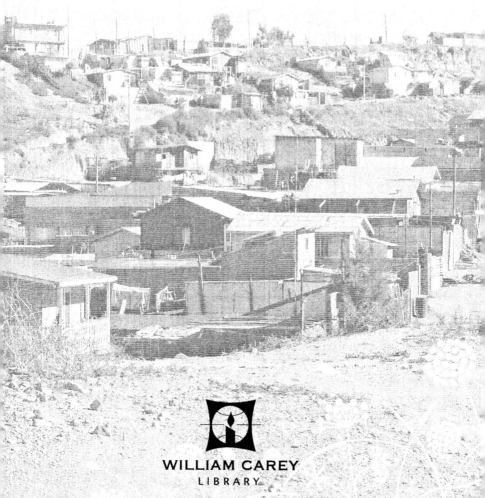

WILLIAM CAREY
LIBRARY

Published by William Carey Library
1605 E. Elizabeth Street
Pasadena, CA 91104 | www.missionbooks.org

Kelley K. Wolfe, editor
Cheryl Warner, copyeditor
Alyssa E. Force, cover and interior design
Rose Lee-Norman, indexing
Cover photo copyright © by Fotosearch.com. All rights reserved.

William Carey Library is a ministry of the
U.S. Center for World Mission
Pasadena, CA | www.uscwm.org

Printed in the United States of America

16 15 14 13 12   6 5 4 3 2 BP800

Library of Congress Cataloging-in-Publication Data

Frontline women : negotiating cross-cultural issues in ministry / Marguerite G. Kraft, editor.
    p. cm.
  Includes bibliographical references and index.
  ISBN 978-0-87808-399-2
  1. Women in missionary work. 2. Women missionaries.
  3. Christianity and culture. I. Kraft, Marguerite G.
  BV2610.F76 2012
  266.0082--dc23

                                               2012024071

CONTENTS

Foreword to the Revised Edition vii

Foreword... xi

Preface xv

Acknowledgments...xvii

Contributors xix

Introduction
Marguerite G. Kraft...xxv

ONE   **Distinctly Female**
Marguerite G. Kraft 1

TWO   **Created to Serve**
Marla Campbell 21

THREE   **Making Adjustments Favorably**
Marla Campbell 33

FOUR   **Constraints and Opportunities**
Laurel A. (Cocks) McAllister 65

FIVE   **Dealing with Loss**
Dianne B. Collard..91

SIX   **Negotiating Reality Single**
Sharon E. Soper..101

SEVEN   **Negotiating Female Missionary Roles Cross-culturally**
Donna Downes...125

EIGHT   **Emotional Straight Talk**
Ruth Ann Graybill...155

NINE   **Combating Chronic Stress by Restoring God's Image**
Sheryl Takagi Silzer.. 207

TEN   **Helping Finishers Bridge the Gap**
Dianne B. Collard...221

ELEVEN   **High Alert to Enemy Attacks**
Marguerite G. and Charles H. Kraft..................................231

TWELVE   **In the Line of Fire**
Steve Hoke and Judith E. Lingenfelter 259

Scripture Index 277

Index.. 279

FOREWORD
TO THE REVISED EDITION

"Men do not ask the question, 'Can I be a leader?'…They assume they can be a leader without even questioning this assumption" (p. 73). "Men may ask the guidance questions of where and how, but they assume they can be leaders. Women, however, begin with a prior question about the very possibility of their involvement in ministry as a leader, a question men do not have to ask" (*Leadership Development for Women in Christian Ministry*, Elizabeth Glanville, Dissertation, 2000, 278).

I grew up as an MK in Latin America and I was blessed with some healthy and godly role models of women in cross-cultural ministry, and some men who were not threatened by strong women with leadership gifts. Although working within a culture where there was considerable *machismo*, and in a theologically conservative organization where women's roles were very carefully proscribed, these women ministered within the opportunities they were given, and often carved roles that stretched the limits of the gender-role definitions. Due to the lack of workers on the field the women's gifts were needed and utilized, but ironically when they were on furlough they were at times not even allowed to report on their ministry, while the men were invited into the pulpit to share their heart and their ministry experiences.

One of my colleagues, Dr. Bobby Clinton has noted,

In all the case studies we have done with males no male has been refused a leadership position because of his gender. If they are refused some leadership position it is because of lack of experience, giftedness, fit for ministry, or political reasons. Not so with women. Perfectly gifted women with good experience and who are fit for a given leadership position have often not even been considered for such a position just because of gender. (Class notes for ML530)

The authors in *Frontline Women* address the assumptions, the experience, and the challenges of women in cross-cultural ministry. As Donna Downes points out (p. 125), a woman's gender at times interferes with ministry not because of anything inherent in her, but because of cultural or organizational constraints. In my own experience I have watched women missionaries struggle in a very male-oriented agency in a male-oriented society, at times becoming frustrated, but often finding ways to "fly under the radar" and accomplish ministry goals without raising too many hackles. To borrow from Sharon Soper's analogy, these women had to be chameleons "of changing colors...adapt[ing] to unpredictable circumstances, diverse social environments, and leadership authorities, forming a natural camouflage to ensure...survival and success on the mission field" (p. 101).

Yet this survival and success often comes at considerable personal cost. The various authors in this book have helped raise awareness of some of the issues surrounding the cost for women in cross-cultural ministry, and have given many practical suggestions for dealing with the barriers that women face—suggestions for changing the systems as well as for ways to work and thrive within the systems.

The themes raised in this book can provide a basis for women and men in ministry to listen to one another and to dialogue regarding the barriers and opportunities that they face—issues such as role deprivation, undefined roles, male dominance, need for women's voices to be heard in decision-making, differing experiences of men versus women in culture shock and cross-cultural settings, cultural gender factors, and theological presuppositions regarding gender roles. Hoke and Lingenfelter suggest: "It would also help if the men on a mission team were aware of how they can be good brothers to the women on the team and help be a buffer and protect them" (p. 264).

The research, case studies, anecdotes, and practical suggestions in this book will prove helpful for:

- Women considering mission to help them realistically face what may lie before them
- Women missionaries struggling to find their role
- Women missionaries and their male colleagues to dialogue on these issues
- Sending agencies and sending churches in considering how their structure and policies can facilitate or hinder ministry
- Field supervisors
- Pre-field trainers
- Counselors of missionaries and of returning missionaries

This book carefully addresses the experiences of American women. I trust that this book will also set an example that will stimulate women from other cultures to write about the situations women face in their respective cultures and ministries.

The goal is to better fulfill the call of God in and through the lives of both women and men. As Meg Kraft writes, "As the genders work together and listen to each other, we can better accomplish God's work" (p. 18).

Elizabeth Brewster

retired associate professor of language and culture learning and mission
Fuller Theological Seminary, School of World Mission, Pasadena, CA

FOREWORD

"While it is possible to be a missionary, and possible to be a woman, it is impossible to be both at the same time." This was the solemn conclusion of my colleague Eunice Irwin at a consultation in which Dana Robert's (1996) important book, *American Women in Mission*, was discussed. Irwin based her conclusion that she couldn't simultaneously be a woman and a missionary on twelve years of cross-cultural ministry in the Philippines, and even more years in dealing with the male-dominated hierarchy of her mission sending organization.

Unfortunately, my colleague Eunice is not alone in her assessment of what it means to be a woman in mission today. Women in mission have often felt, and been, marginalized, isolated, and ignored. And yet, since the first two American women missionaries were appointed in 1812, women have played a very significant role in spreading the Good News of Jesus Christ around the world. But that role has often been fraught with ambiguity, and as Meg Kraft notes in her introduction, "For too long missionary women have struggled silently."

This book through a dozen chapters gives voice to that frustration and to the many things about which they are legitimately angry, but it does so without an angry, strident, feminist agenda. And for that reason, it will be taken more seriously by both women and men in mission. Women need to read this book to be encouraged. Men need to read it and wake up.

For a long time we have needed a book that helps us get in touch with and understand how significant is gender in mission. What are the different personal, emotional needs and perspectives that women missionaries have and how are they different from those of their male counterparts? What are the challenges of crossing cultural barriers, building relationships, and communicating the gospel that are unique to women, both married and single? How can women missionaries negotiate satisfying roles in ministry when working in male-dominated societies or with North American mission boards that are likewise dominated by men? How can women develop deep meaningful relationships in cross-cultural ministry when working in such task-oriented, goal-driven, left-brained mission bodies? These are the kinds of issues women are raising about being in mission today.

Fortunately, *Frontline Women* raises and answers these questions and more. The reader will come away greatly encouraged, knowing that, "Yes, one can be a woman and a missionary at the same time."

This book is refreshing and contemporary. The authors of the various chapters speak from personal mission experience, and tell compelling stories of their challenges and opportunities in cross-cultural ministry, more than they develop abstract missiological theory. Nevertheless, there is a crying need for developing missiological theory that wrestles with the issue of gender equality. We find here frank, honest discussion of emotional needs and concerns which are not dismissed by being overly spiritualized. The chapters are full of common sense and practical suggestions for coping.

The differences between married and single women in mission are addressed in several chapters, and we learn how they deal differently with their identity and with tensions in status, gender, and authority. Role frustration, depression, identity crises, and self-doubt are issues that both married and single women missionaries struggle with. If that isn't enough, not only do women missionaries often have to confront the cultural bias against women in the culture of their host society, they also confront it in the Christian world of church and mission.

It is time for this paradigm to change and to cease endorsing patriarchal church and mission structures as God given.

The thorny biblical issue of women in ministry is addressed head-on, and comes to the conclusion that the Bible fully supports and encourages women in ministry as illustrated in many contexts. We learn that all missionaries experience some form of culture shock, but women experience it differently than do men. I don't think many of us men know that.

It is not enough, however, to understand the world of different cultures in developing effective cross-cultural ministry. We also have to be aware of the often hidden but crucial dimension of spiritual warfare that missionaries continually bump up against, often without knowing it. In Chapter 11, Chuck and Meg Kraft bring their considerable experience of ministry in this realm when they address how women missionaries also face matters that require the intervention of spiritual warfare.

The women writing this book are deeply concerned about the problems women face in mission, but there is no anger coming through in these pages. Instead, we get helpful stories and hopeful, practical suggestions. Laurel McAllister in Chapter 4 captures the situation we are in today when she notes "that women make important contributions to the cause of world mission and evangelism. However, further action needs to be taken so that all women can be encouraged, empowered, and released for ministries to which God is calling them." What would this mean?

There is desperate need for gender reconciliation in mission today, and this book will become a landmark on the path that will someday lead to cooperation and equality between genders. We have needed this book for a long time—first, to get these unvoiced issues on the table so we can talk about them, second to offer hope and encouragement to women in mission, and third to wake up the slumbering men in mission who are often oblivious to the difference gender makes and who then take their positions of power and authority for granted.

The missiological world and the world of mission will be better off because of the insights expressed in this book. Now my prayer is that we together, as men and women in mission, will have the courage to act on what we will learn here.

Darrell L. Whiteman
former professor of cultural anthropology
Dean E. Stanley Jones School of World Mission and Evangelism
Asbury Theological Seminary
Wilmore, Kentucky, 2003

PREFACE

I have been pleased that this book has proved useful to both women and the men who serve with them cross-culturally. It has also been a helpful training tool for mission agencies and academic courses on women's issues. Since times are constantly changing as well as the people who work in and with cross-cultural workers, it is time to update and rework the materials on the various issues dealt with in the first edition. Each author has cooperated and carefully made improvements in her/his chapter. I trust that the changes will make this new edition even more valuable in facing the issues of the day. Although progress is being made in the attitude and treatment of women in Christian circles, women still need to be understood and assisted in finding their rightful place in God's work. This book will help women better understand themselves, their gender distinctives, their needs, and their goals, especially in a different cultural setting.

The original idea behind this book was born when Marla Campbell as a graduate student researched the field to discover the most urgent topics that needed attention regarding women in missions. We then worked together to find qualified authors to write on these subjects. We found these authors working in many parts of the world, and all were concerned that women's issues in cross-cultural work be addressed. I had been teaching a university course on Women in Missions and deeply sensed the need for a book that would focus specifically on women's adjustment to a new cultural setting, finding meaning and value in a new location, and dealing with the everyday pressures in living cross-culturally.

The textbooks available at that time were focused on women's historical contribution to the missionary cause. Clearly it has been great. And female historians have begun to help us see clearly and appreciate the efforts of women that have been so central to mission work. So often it has been the women who have begun the medical, educational, and social reform that have greatly influenced the mission endeavor. Dana Robert writes in her book *Gospel Bearers, Gender Barriers:* "With estimates that at least two-thirds of the new Christians in the global church are women, it is a scandal in mission studies to ignore the socio-political and cultural realities particular to the female gender" (Robert 2002, xi).[1]

Since women's perspective, their strengths, and their gifts have been ignored/overlooked in the past, we believe a book such as this is essential. We have chosen to focus on reality as experienced by women and the issues they face. Among the issues are the male-female dynamics in our home society and in the indigenous church, as well as relationships with supporting churches and the sending mission agencies. These pages not only contain a wealth of sound information but also give wise advice on how to live our faith in Christ well.

Marguerite G. Kraft
South Pasadena, California, 2012

---

1   Dana Robert edited this book published in Maryknoll, New York, by Orbis Books.

ACKNOWLEDGMENTS

Many thanks to Dr. Marla Campbell, who originally initiated and organized the material for the book itself. The energy she put into contacting people and gathering information was most valuable. Actual publication of these materials can be credited to Dr. Sharon Soper, who spent endless hours preparing the manuscript and taking care of minute details. Her organizational gifts and skills along with her constant encouragement are greatly appreciated.

I am grateful to the Brethren Church who first made it possible for me to experience being a woman on the mission field. The wonderful village women in Mbororo, Nigeria, taught me so much about life and God's faithfulness. I had the privilege of reevaluating life, discovering my own identity as a Christian American woman, and gaining great insight into the values, goals, and views of those in a different society who love and follow Jesus, too.

Special thanks to each of the authors for taking valuable time to share from your ministries and from your hearts so that we all might better understand ourselves and others as we actively serve God. I also thank you for patiently waiting to see the fruit of your efforts materialize. I especially appreciate your willingness to update and rework your chapter for the revision based on continued personal experience in the field.

Parts of Chapter 8 authored by Graybill have previously appeared in *Enhancing Missionary Vitality,* pages 147–152 (2002). Permission from the publisher, Mission Training International, to use this material is gratefully acknowledged.

I have felt support and encouragement from my colleagues in the School of Intercultural Studies at Biola University. The acceptance I have experienced as a female scholar along with the privilege to be working together on the cutting edge of missions has been most valuable. I have been given the opportunity to teach several courses that help students better understand gender issues they will face in cross-cultural work. I also want to thank the students in my Women in Missions classes (both at Biola and Morling College in Sydney, Australia) who have given me much appreciated feedback as I have tested the original manuscript with them.

Finally, thanks to my husband, Chuck, who continues to support and encourage me in my writing endeavors and all areas of life. He is truly a gift from God as we are able to work together as a team extending God's kingdom on earth.

CONTRIBUTORS

Marla Campbell serves currently as a faculty member in the Cook School of Intercultural Studies at Biola University. Her focus includes Intercultural Education and Communication and Women in Cross-cultural Ministry. Formerly she served as dean of students at Bethany College in California where she was involved in short-term mission trips. She lived as a missionary for several years in the Balkans of Eastern Europe and has also worked as a missionary for Asia-Pacific Education. Abroad she designed and revised curriculum, did teacher training, and developed ESL and other educational programs. She holds a BA in English and Speech Communications/Pathology from Cal State University, and an MA and PhD from Biola University. Marla enjoys working with women's ministries, missions, and being a seminar or retreat speaker.

Dianne B. Collard and her husband have served as missionaries for twenty-five years in vocational Christian ministry throughout their forty-six years of marriage. As an intercultural trainer, she has worked with hundreds of missionaries serving around the world. Dianne is the Europe Ministries director for Artists in Christian Testimony International. She has an active speaking ministry in North America and Europe. She and her husband have three children and five granddaughters. She holds a BA in Speech/Communications from San Francisco State University, an MA in Intercultural Studies and a Doctor of Missiology degree from Biola University, La Mirada, California. Dianne lives in North Carolina.

Donna Downes is an associate professor of Global Leadership in the School of Intercultural Studies at Fuller Theological Seminary. Prior to joining Fuller in 2008, she and her husband served as missionaries with OC International for twenty-four years—twelve in Kenya and twelve in Romania. She taught Communications and Research at Daystar University in Kenya. In Romania, she taught missions courses in the Romanian language at the Baptist Seminary in Bucharest. Donna holds a Doctor of Missiology degree from Biola University specializing in cross-cultural leadership. Her husband, Stan, continues mission work as OC's Europe Director and Donna teaches in Fuller's innovative Master of Arts in Global Leadership program. They reside in Colorado Springs, Colorado.

Ruth Ann Graybill served as a missionary in Japan for three years and has been active in counseling, crisis intervention, and debriefing for missionaries and missionary children since then. She is a licensed therapist at Biola Counseling Center (Biola University), counseling adolescents, individual adults, couples, and families. She serves as advisor to Biola's chapter of Mu Kappa, a national organization for missionary "kids" on college campuses. Ruth Ann frequently travels to various countries to lead seminars and counsel missionaries. She was formerly an adjunct professor at Rosemead School of Psychology (Biola University) and at The King's College.

Steve Hoke is a Third Culture Adult who grew up in Tokyo, Japan. He holds an MA from Wheaton College Graduate School, an MDiv from Trinity Evangelical Divinity School, and a PhD in Non-formal Adult Education from Michigan State University. Formerly he served as associate director of field training for World Vision International and President of LIFE Ministries (now Asian Access). From 1991–2000 he served as vice president for People Development for Church Resource Ministries (CRM; Anaheim, California), and was a member of the Staff Development and Care Team, developing systemic approaches to helping missionary individuals and families make a more effective adaptation to their cross-cultural home. He now focuses on working with mission organizations around the world in leader development and providing strategic life coaching for missionaries and mission leaders. His passion is to equip and encourage frontline mission leaders to minister in the power of the Spirit and with spiritual authority in the difficult places of the world. Steve is the author of over one hundred articles on missionary training, and is coauthor with Bill Taylor of *Global Mission Handbook:Your Guide for Cross-cultural Service* (InterVarsity Press, 2009).

Charles H. Kraft has trained missionaries as a professor at Fuller Seminary, School of Intercultural Studies, for over forty years. He has served as a missionary in Nigeria planting churches and translating the Bible. He holds a Bachelor of Divinity degree from Ashland Theological Seminary, and a PhD in Anthropology/Linguistics from the Kennedy School of Missions, Hartford Seminary Foundation. He has also taught African languages at both Michigan State University and UCLA. He is author of many articles and thirty books on missions, culture, and spiritual warfare. As founder and president of Deep Healing Ministries, he actively conducts seminars worldwide. His recent books include *I Give You Authority, Confronting Powerless Christianity* and *Two Hours to Freedom*.

Marguerite G. Kraft holds an MA in Linguistics from Kennedy School of Mission, Hartford Seminary Foundation, a Doctor of Missiology and a PhD in Intercultural Studies from Fuller Theological Seminary. She and her husband have served as pioneer missionaries in Nigeria.

She served for thirty years in missionary training as a professor at the School of Intercultural Studies, Biola University. Her research has taken her to several countries. She has authored mission-related books and articles, focusing on women's issues, language learning, spiritual power, and intercultural communication. In retirement, besides occasional teaching, writing, and traveling with her husband, she enjoys her family—four children, fifteen grandchildren, and three great-grandchildren.

Judith E. Lingenfelter holds a PhD in Educational Anthropology from the University of Pittsburgh, and an MLS in Library Science. She and her husband have done extended research in the South Pacific. For twenty-three years she taught at Biola University in the School of Intercultural Studies, and currently serves as affiliate faculty at Fuller Theological Seminary. She has served as a consultant to several mission agencies and holds workshops internationally. In addition to writing many mission-related articles she has coauthored *Teaching Cross-Culturally: An Incarnational Model for Learning Teaching* (2003).

Laurel A. (Cocks) McAllister, educator and trainer, has ministered in secondary school education, missionary training and staff development. She holds a PhD in Educational Studies from Trinity International University and has taught courses in cross-cultural ministry. She has also facilitated member care training and interpersonal skills workshops for missionaries. In retirement, Laurel is a resource person in member care and participates in such activities as missionary debriefing. A friend and mentor to women in ministry, she also serves on several boards and is active in her church missions committee.

Sheryl Takagi Silzer has had twenty-five years of field experience in Colombia, Indonesia, Australia, and Papua New Guinea with a nondenominational mission agency. She holds an MA from Talbot Theological Seminary, and an MA from the School of Intercultural

Studies at Biola University. She holds a PhD from Fuller Theological Seminary. Her mission experience includes serving as both a single and married woman. She is a multicultural consultant and runs Cultural Self-Discovery workshops for mission agencies. Her workshop is based on her book, *Biblical Multicultural Teams: Applying Biblical Truth to Cultural Difference* (William Carey International University Press, 2011).

Sharon E. Soper served sixteen years in Bolivia as a single mission-ary nurse/church planter with the Evangelical Mennonite Mission Conference. She developed a program to combat malnutrition us-ing soybeans and wrote *Soybeans and the Kingdom of God: An Approach to Holistic Mission*. Before leaving Bolivia, the Theological Education by Extension program she developed was fully transitioned to na-tional directorship. Sharon holds a BS in nursing, and both the MA and Doctor of Missiology degrees from the School of Intercultural Studies, Biola University. Presently, she works at QueensCare Health and Faith Partnership in Los Angeles supervising nurses and community health workers who are part of the health ministry team in churches and other faith-based groups.

INTRODUCTION

Marguerite G. Kraft

I n contemporary gender sensitive society, a keen awareness exists regarding the differences between men and women. Their needs and responses to working and living situations, relationships, and environment often seem worlds apart even when functioning in their own culture in comfortable surroundings. It has been said that the differences between male and female are greater than the differences between two totally distinct cultures. What happens then when they are placed in foreign cultures virtually void of traditional support systems? Missionary men and women know well the effects.

Listen to two women's comments:

> In our area of the world, it is a man's world and men are highly esteemed whereas women have no value. This causes a bigger adjustment for women.

> Men hit the ground running and get involved in their work to find validity during times of insecurity or transitions. Women are lost to identify their place and purpose on the field.

Men and women both face adjustments and difficulties when moving to a foreign country. How does that experience vary from male to female? "Men bury themselves in their work...Women bury themselves in the home and family." How does it vary from single to married? "I feel so isolated. I had close friends at home. The other women here have their families." From expatriate to missionary? "My expatriate friends who are not missionaries have all the comforts of home and don't get involved with the culture. Besides they can fly back to the States whenever they want!"

These all present arenas for careful consideration when attempting to avert missionary attrition. A greater concern, however, lies in the fact that examining these factors early enough could better prepare individuals for working on the field. For those already on the field, support and assistance offers the opportunity for personal growth and adjustment. Research has shown that women missionaries suffer a greater degree of unaddressed needs than do their male counterparts and even more so than other female expatriates.

In recent years I have been working with graduate students returning from the mission field for additional study and also training young people for cross-cultural work. I am constantly hearing of specific adjustments that must be faced depending heavily on gender differences. As my husband and I travel overseas teaching and continuing to learn, many women have expressed feelings that often find no audience. Missionaries, especially women, are seeking answers, solutions, and assistance, while mission agencies need assistance in providing training, intervention, and remediation for their members. In my estimation, as both men and women move to understand basic gender differences it will greatly assist in field adjustment, more stable marriages, retention on the field, and further success in mission work. Sending agencies, the missionary team, and the family overseas all need to be aware of the male-female dynamics at work, including those same dynamics at work in the host culture.

The purposes of this collection of writings are to develop a deeper awareness of the difficulties women face in cross-cultural settings, to provide encouragement and hope for women serving God on the frontlines, and to provide helpful insights for the men with whom these women live and work. For too long, missionary women have struggled silently. Hopefully these writings will slow down the attrition rate and woundedness that often result from a lack of understanding and dealing with gender distinctives.

The typical issues that women face in mission work are also often the same ones faced by women pastors and other women in leadership positions in their home countries. When women follow the call of God it often brings change of location and a new environment. Women's instincts, needs, and responses can be better understood through the chapters that follow. It is my prayer that all women in leadership will be encouraged and enriched.

The struggle for equality between the genders has often hidden the differences. Chapter 1 deals with the differences in the realms of biology, communication, culture, and spirituality. I develop an awareness of differences with the perception that the female strengths are meant to complement those of the male. The female approach to life and vision is neither better nor worse, inferior nor superior, right nor wrong, just different and needing to be understood, recognized, and incorporated.

Women have responded to God's call and have historically made up over half to two thirds of the missionary force even when there was great resistance to women's involvement. In Chapter 2 Campbell focuses on the biblical base for equipping, assisting, and releasing women to carry out the Great Commission. The central cause for women in leadership is advancing the gospel as they respond to God's call.

The distance between cultures is usually greater for women to bridge than for men. Since the coping mechanisms differ for men and women, tension is created in the adaptation process. Campbell deals in Chapter 3 with self-worth, loss of relationships, and the struggle for belonging that are seen as specific, expressed female needs. The practical suggestions given to help control missionary attrition and family breakup involve women themselves, the men they live and work with, and the sending agencies.

Based on ethnographic interviews with experienced missionaries, McAllister deals in Chapter 4 with constraints on women, including the influences of culture, marital status and role, gender, children, interpersonal relationships, and the sending organizations. The focus is on coping strategies and new ways for the agencies to affirm and challenge women.

The need to deal effectively with loss is something every missionary woman faces. Again men and women tend to respond differently. Grief and its accompanying emotions are a part of the many adjustments required for serving overseas away from meaningful relationships and things. In Chapter 5 Collard explains some individual differences in responding to loss and presents specific suggestions for resolution to the problem of loss.

Soper deals in Chapter 6 with issues singles often confront in finding a meaningful spot for service in a new cultural environment. The way they negotiate reality involves the mission family on the field, the local leaders, and the supporting agency. The issues of marginality, identity crisis and transitions, sexuality and celibacy, and authority relationships are discussed.

Today there exist a wide variety of mission-related ministries in which women work and interact with national pastors. Whether single or married, it is imperative for women to understand what is culturally appropriate both for conduct and for ministry, title, and position. In Chapter 7, Downes presents ways women respond when they feel restricted or limited in use of their expertise in a new location. Cultural differences in the attitude toward gender status and role may cause women to be regarded differently and require unexpected adaptations on their part.

No matter how committed we are to serving God it does not exempt us from emotional needs. Graybill in Chapter 8 presents the most commonly identified emotional needs of both married and single women in missionary work. She then carefully considers many healthy, appropriate, and realistic ways to get these needs met, emphasizing the fact that each woman is ultimately responsible for assessing and dealing with her own personal emotional needs. A consciousness of what these needs are and being proactive in organizing her life/schedule for emotional health avoids a raft of potential problems.

Chapter 9 is a case study that shows the relationship between stress and physical health. Silzer analyzes her own experiences as a long-term missionary woman facing many typical female stresses on the field. She shows how her life history affected her concept of God and mission work and how this intertwined with her health situation. She gives spiritual insights in dealing with stress, self-image, and being made in the image of God.

Today the missionary workforce includes people becoming missionaries in the second-half stage of life. Early retirement, increased financial stability, and a generation searching for significance brings these people to the mission field. In Chapter 10, Collard explains how these older missionaries are often seen as more respected and knowledgeable about life in the eyes of the local society. She deals with specific issues they face in mission work. Their specific difficulties and needs are discussed by Collard in Chapter 10. These women have varied life experiences, deeper roots, and more home obligations that affect their service.

Women's sensitivity to the spirit realm along with their key position in nurturing often makes them the focus of Satan's attack. Chapter 11 deals with the spiritual battles found on the front lines of mission, especially in relation to women's vulnerabilities. My husband and I deal with demonic activity from without and within based on problems like self-worth, self-rejection, shame, fear, insecurity, unforgiveness, and loneliness. The biblical basis for understanding the activities in the spirit world and ways to assure victory through the power of the Holy Spirit are included. Specific suggestions are given for doing spiritual warfare and helping people to be free from Satan's power to distract their focus on God and sap their energy.

Today's missionary women live and work in countries where political instability creates constant feelings of uncertainty and fear.

Women often find themselves in situations where they must respond to conflicting decisions made without their input by field leaders and distant mission agency leadership. In Chapter 12 Lingenfelter and Hoke identify the problems and tensions women face in such situations, and suggest ways in which both churches and mission agencies can assist in preparation that averts attrition, while working with women in a way that is more just, humane, loving, and caring.

All of the authors have had field experience and through that experience have a strong desire to provide a new depth of understanding to women's issues in today's mission world. It is our desire to bring awareness, improvement, and challenge to both men and women involved in sending, supporting, or actually serving on the front lines carrying out the Great Commission. We trust that the information contained in this book will bring about reflection, discussion, and new strategies for mission.

ONE

Distinctly Female
Marguerite G. Kraft

Today is a time when we are being made more conscious of eradicating sexual discrimination and searching for equality and justice between the sexes. However, it is also a time when research and writing in the social sciences are expanding our appreciation of all human beings by looking at what makes each sex unique. Many are treating men and women as distinct subcultures within each society. In this era of shifting and reforming relationships between men and women, it is important to recognize real gender differences.

Because I am an American, I am writing from an American perspective. Much of the research recently done on gender differences is from the West. I trust that in the future more study will be done on gender differences in non-Western societies. I recognize that today a growing number of cross-cultural workers are from Korea, Latin America, Africa, and other places. If you are from one of these other societies, then some of what I say may not apply directly to you. However, being female and probably trained in Western-type schools causes this material to be food for thought and analysis. Men, who definitely work alongside women, will also benefit from better understanding gender differences.

In today's world, mission teams are often made up of people from different cultures working together. So hopefully this discussion of female distinctives (even though America-based) will be beneficial.

Since Walter Goldschmidt has said, "People are more alike than [their] cultures" (1966, 134), we may be uncovering something basic to humanity rather than simply Western. It is my hope that the distinctive aspects discussed here will alert the reader to a better understanding of self and a consciousness of the cultural influences that cause us to feel and act as we do. Also this material is intended to create an interest and openness to investigate, understand, and appreciate the male-female dynamics at work in someone else's society.

WE LIVE AND WORK IN A MAN'S WORLD

For many years history was viewed only through men's eyes. Even until recently research in the medical field has been done mostly on men and then assumed to be as effective when used for women. Diagnostic tests, prescription medications, surgical techniques, and laboratory values were first developed with the male in mind (Hales 1999, 98–99). Early ethnographies presenting life in various societies around the world were written from the male perspective. In fact, the whole philosophy behind formal education is male-based, and women have to learn to think and reason like a man to do well. It is very evident that standards in society have been regimented and preserved by males. Carol Gilligan (1982, 6) refers to this as implicitly adopting the male life as the norm, and then trying to fashion women out of a masculine cloth.

Male domination looks different in various societies. Boys and girls grow up with different role prescriptions. In most societies men's work is more prestigious than women's. Authority for society-level decisions is most often in male hands. Control of the institutions—e.g., religion, political and legal systems, and economics—is more often than not men's domain. Women's main responsibilities universally seem most closely tied to the home, where they often have more authority. Other dimensions of this dominance will be discussed later.

Too often the emphasis on equality in America is thought of in the framework of sameness. To be equal means same in opportunity, salary, visibility, education, freedom, etc. Our American concept of assuming sameness can be very destructive. To my amazement, in talking with someone from another country where I saw little equality between the sexes, I was informed that there was equality but the definition was different from mine: equal before God, equally valuable in the family, and equal importance to the whole society. Equality is given definition by each society.

WE ARE DISTINCT BIOLOGICALLY FROM MEN

History has often made women wary of their biology. Through past years women have been seen as the weaker sex, dependent on males, temptresses, unclean due to the menstrual cycle, unintelligent, the second sex, and dangerous religiously and sexually. Men have made their gender the model, the standard of achievement, and the center of scholarly attention. It is not unusual for a woman who has done a job well to hear, "You handled it just like a man."

Hales in her research in gender science urges women to reclaim their bodies with pride in their distinctiveness as she writes:

While biology is no longer destiny, it remains a crucial part of our reality. In affirming our femaleness, we are not diminishing or discrediting our mental ability or essential equality. Rather we are recognizing a fundamental source of strength and sustenance. One of the gifts of gender science and of the recent revelations in reproductive biology…is that they allow women to reclaim their bodies with true pride in their distinctiveness, their evolution- ary resilience, their physiological stamina, and their remarkable capacity for renewal and lifelong growth. (1999, xi)

As Christians we recognize that both male and female are created in God's image (Gen 1:26–27). Mary Stewart Van Leeuwen explains:

> Our bodily limits—including our maleness and femaleness—were given to us as the media in which to develop the gift of God's image. They are the forms within which to practice the freedoms of creativity, dominion, sociability, moral choice and the fruits of the Holy Spirit. With the rest of creation, God pronounced those bodily forms "very good." (1990, 76)

Being female is God's gift, and it includes the stamina and characteristics that he intended to complement the male. He approved of our differences and was pleased with his creation.

Let us now look at some of the physiological differences. It is important, however, to recognize that biological differences are not signs of superiority or inferiority, normalcy or deviation, or rightness or wrongness.

Female and male bodies are sculpted in the womb by the mix of estrogens and androgens, different in males and females, developing the fetus in ways that are similar but not identical. The male has a powerful sex drive with a high rate of sperm production to ensure reproduction, and a body large, strong, and fast to provide protection. The female body is equipped for multiple functions, including bearing and caring for children, strong energy, and long-term endurance.

Research has shown that the left hemisphere of the brain is more specialized for language, logical analysis, and mathematics. The right hemisphere is more specialized for artistic and spatial abilities, and for an emotional and nonanalytic approach to reality. Some evidence shows that men's brain hemispheres are more strongly specialized than women's, being either right- or left-brained, for their respective functions. The female brain draws more equally from both sides, and some researchers claim that the fibers running down the center of the brain and linking the two hemispheres are thicker in females, possibly allowing more "cross talk" between the right and left hemispheres. It may be because of this that a woman's intuition and fundamentally holistic organization give her an advantage in remembering and organizing, but also a tendency to be weighed down by trying to handle too many things at once. Women tend to look at the totality of what they do, seeing not just a single task, but rather where it fits in the overall scheme of things. Men, with a more specialized brain, tend to be better at focusing on one thing at a time even to the point of forgetting all else in life during the time of that focus.

Medical science has shown that the body of a woman does not feel, look, or function exactly like a man's. On the average, the body of a woman is shorter than a man's. Her bones are smaller with shoulders narrower and pelvis wider. A woman's liver handles drugs differently, her heart is smaller and beats at a different rate, and her immune system responds more vigorously to common infection, giving extra protection from bacteria, viruses, and parasites. The list goes on and on showing women's biological distinctiveness.

WE COMMUNICATE DIFFERENTLY FROM MEN

Beginning in the 1970s scholars noticed that distinctive speech communities existed, and these were labeled communication cultures. Within a communication culture members embrace similar understandings of how to use talk and what purposes it serves. Since then, feminine and masculine communication cultures have been more clearly defined. For the most part, females are socialized into feminine culture and males into masculine culture. This results in men and women communicating for different reasons and in different ways.

Boys and girls grow up in different worlds of words. Others talk to them differently and expect them to respond in a way suitable to each gender. Both parents and peers are involved in children learning to talk and have conversations. Part of this socialization is also carried out in the games children play. A study done in the United States by two anthropologists, Maltz and Borker (1982), identified different goals, strategies, and relationships in girls' and boys' play. This play then contributes to socializing children into masculine and feminine communication cultures. Girls' games usually require just two or three people, so they promote personal relationships. Girls learn from unstructured, cooperative play to be cooperative and inclusive and to pay attention to other's feelings and needs. Boys tend to play in larger groups and with fixed rules and goals, and these games allow for individual stars. So they learn to be assertive and competitive, and to focus on achievement. Masculine socialization stresses independence, power, and attention to outcomes, while feminine socialization emphasizes intimacy in relationships, sensitivity to people, and the process of interaction.

In adulthood then we find women use talk to build and sustain relationships with others, while men use talk to assert themselves and their ideas and to establish status and power. Independence is the key to the male approach to the world, and conversations are negotiations in which people try to achieve and maintain the upper hand, to protect themselves from being put down and pushed around by others. The female approach to the world is characterized by intimacy, and conversations are negotiations for closeness and the avoidance of isolation. Tannen, a linguist who has analyzed language and gender in the US, captures these differences by using the terms report-talk and rapport-talk.

> For most women, the language of conversation is primarily a language of rapport: a way of establishing connections and negotiating relationships. Emphasis has been placed on displaying similarities and matching experiences. From childhood, girls criticize peers who try to stand out or appear better than others...

> For most men, talk is primarily a means to preserve independence and negotiate and maintain status in a hierarchical social order. This is done by exhibiting knowledge and skill, and by holding

center stage through verbal performance such as storytelling, joking, or imparting information. From childhood, men learn to use talking as a way to get and keep attention…But even the most private situations can be approached like public speaking, more like giving a report than establishing rapport. (1990, 77)

Women in supporting others will show understanding of their feelings and show empathy. Men in supporting others will do something helpful—give advice or solve a problem for them. Women see talking as a human interaction in which details and interesting side comments enhance the depth of the relationship. Men see talking as a linear sequence that should carry information and accomplish goals. For women, talking is a way to express and expand closeness in a relationship; for men doing something other than talking is a more common way of strengthening a relationship. It is no wonder that there is frequent misunderstanding in cross-gender interaction.

Tannen also describes the difference in male/female communication at home:

For everyone, home is a place to be offstage. But the comfort of home can have opposite and incompatible meanings for women and men. For many men, the comfort of home means freedom from having to prove themselves and impress through verbal display. At last, they are in a situation where talk is not required. They are free to remain silent. But for women, home is a place where they are free to talk, and where they feel the greatest need for talk, with those they are closest to. For them, the comfort of home means the freedom to talk without worrying about how their talk will be judged. (1990, 86)

A common problem arises when one gender judges the other based on his/her own conversational style. Although each style is valid on its own terms, much misunderstanding arises because the styles are different.

Nonverbal communication is also affected by gender. Through socialization we learn whether we can show our emotions or how we should sit. Girls are taught to smile more, to be attractive, and to please others. Women are socialized to take up less space and to give space to men. Boys often are encouraged to play outdoors, while girls are more frequently centered within the home. Research has shown that women are significantly better in decoding nonverbal cues than are men. There is no agreement on why this is so; some say it is influenced by their subordinate place in the social structure, and others say it is due to motherhood and related responsibilities. Many of our notions of masculinity and femininity rest on the nonverbal messages we display and those we decode.

WE ARE CULTURALLY CONDITIONED TO BE DIFFERENT FROM MEN

Most differences between the genders are cultural and are learned after birth. The social structure of each society defines male and female status and role. Hierarchical structure in a society most often places men above women in status, power, and authority. Some anthropologists have concluded that male domination is universal. It varies from total control over the women and their movements in society to the accepted standards which are male-oriented in a society and underlie the entire system. In such societies female strengths are often not recognized or utilized. Egalitarian structure in Western society works toward equality/sameness between the genders with both men and women working in jobs as well as in the home. Male dominance is seen in America where skills in relationships are not valued as much as visible task achievements.

In the cross-cultural setting the feminine emphasis on relationships is obvious. While men from outside a culture may be seen by the local men as a threat to their position and power in society, women from outside usually find it natural and easy to develop relationships with the local women. They find things they have in common: family, household responsibilities, cooking, and hanging out with other women while enjoying their company. It is natural to share joys, hurts, and challenges with other women who are eager to build relationships. Getting into a "coffee hour" or Bible study where this can happen provides opportunity for such relationships to develop.

In many societies males are openly considered superior and females are perceived as vulnerable, needing to be cared for, and dependent on males. Often, though, male dominance is more subtle, with males basically making societal decisions and the values of the society reflecting mainly male values. To illustrate, American values of self-reliance and independence are culturally conditioned male values, and a woman pursuing these values is often labeled (at least by the more conservative) as disruptive, aggressive, or manipulative. "Men's work" is found universally to have higher status than that of women. In societies where women gather food and men hunt, even though most of the food is produced by the women, hunting is given higher status. In societies where the women build the houses and the men make baskets, basket-making has the higher social status. In the Western world higher status is given to work outside the home than to homemaking.

Security vs. Freedom Orientation

A basic distinction in types of male/female dynamics in a society is the difference between a security-oriented system and a freedom-oriented system. In the security-oriented system children are seen as the most vulnerable part of society, and they hold the center of a concentric circle arrangement. The women are seen as the circle around them since they are responsible for the protection and care of the children. Often this responsibility is seen in society when the mother is blamed for a child's death or continued illness. In this system women need to be protected and provided for, and men form that circle around the women. For instance, men are the warriors, the ones who set the rules, the providers of food and shelter. This becomes obvious as the man representing each household sits together with male relatives making decisions that affect them all. Men, then, are given support and protection by the kin. The outer circle is the supernatural that provides security for the men who provide security and protection for the women who provide security and protection for the children.

In the freedom-oriented system the individual and his/her rights are most important. One must be free at all costs. So the mother and father are struggling to establish and hang on to their separate identities, and the children are encouraged to develop and become self-reliant as soon as possible. All adults are responsible to themselves first, and individual freedom is in focus. One's security in life depends on how well each person can provide it. Since all are mostly unaware of their orientation, when these two systems (freedom-oriented and security-oriented) come into contact, those involved are apt to lack understanding of each other, misjudge each other, and even lack respect for each other. Understanding this difference in orientation helps make it possible to work more effectively together.

Public vs. Private Sphere

In studying the male/female dynamics of culture there is often a distinction made between the public and private spheres. Women, due to their involvement with children, are the center of the private or domestic sphere. Child care keeps them necessarily closer to home, and they carry greater responsibility in bringing up the children. The father does tasks that take him further from home in order to be the provider and protector for the family. He also represents the entire family in community and business matters. The cultural rules vary as to whether a wife and mother can be away from the domestic sphere. In some societies the permission of the husband and even being accompanied by an assigned male is required for her to be in the public sphere. At one point when an international organization flew a woman leader of a local women's project to another area to start a new work, it almost broke up her marriage. Her husband needed to give permission, and possibly he or a male he assigned should have been included in the trip. When I was learning Hausa in Nigeria and spending a lot of time with the women, a 12-year-old boy was assigned to accompany the wives in a polygamous household when they left their home if their husband was not available.

In Focus vs. Out of Focus

Another cultural distinction in gender relations is the concept relating to power and visibility. It is helpful to think of this as being *in focus* and *out of focus,* or power of authority vs. power of influence. In many societies it is the male who is expected to be in focus, and the power that he exerts is quite visible. The wife's role would be considered out of focus, but it is a very satisfying role. She gains importance in society through her husband's work and status. She also may have great influence in the decisions he makes. In non-Western society it is often the mother and older sister who are listened to more than the wife, so there is increased influence when one becomes a mother-in-law. Out of focus power exercised by women within the kin group often has significant implications for public affairs. It is common in many societies that when a wife begins to work outside the home, people continue to judge her by her performance at home, not by her performance at her outside job. In societies where being in focus is important for all individuals (i.e., in the United States), competition often replaces cooperation as everyone strives to establish their position in the societal system.

Social Differences

Gender identity development is experienced differently by the sexes. From very early, girls come to experience themselves as more continuous, experiencing themselves as being like their mothers. Boys, however, go through separation since the primary parenting is usually by a person of the opposite gender.

Relationships, and particularly issues of dependency, are experienced differently by women and men. For boys and men, separation and individuation are critically tied to gender identity since separation from the mother is essential for the development of masculinity. For girls and women, issues of femininity or feminine identity do not depend on the achievement of separation from the mother or on the progress of individuation. Since masculinity is defined through separation while femininity is defined through attachment, male gender identity is threatened by intimacy while female gender identity is threatened by separation. Thus males tend to have difficulty with relationships, while females tend to have problems with individuation. (Gilligan 1982, 8)

Because women nearly universally are largely responsible for early child care, these basic gender differences recur in personality development.

This separation required in the socialization process for boys is observed in a variety of customs in different cultures. In the Kamwe village where we lived and worked in Nigeria, the boys would be separated from the mother at the age of six or seven by providing a sleeping hut for them on the father's side of the compound. They would then begin spending more time with the father so they could learn the role of men. Girls would stay with their mothers learning the female role until they married.

Gilmore (1990) presents manhood as something that in many societies must be achieved and maintained. Whereas women move naturally into womanhood through marriage and motherhood, men must prove themselves capable of being a man through whatever the society prescribes (e.g., wrestling, drinking, killing an animal, raiding, circumcision rites, whipping ceremony). Achieving manhood involves disassociating oneself from the female world and protecting oneself from female control.

In many societies, women's status is considered ascribed, something that just naturally happens as a girl becomes a woman by following in her mother's footsteps. "Femininity" is seen more as a biological given that is culturally refined:

Something achieved by women who seek social approval…It usually involves questions of body ornament or sexual allure, or other essentially cosmetic behaviors that enhance, rather than create, an inherent quality of character. An authentic femininity rarely involves tests or proofs of action, or confrontations with dangerous foes: win-or-lose contests dramatically played out on the public stage. (Gilmore 1990, 11–12)

Society often values women mainly for their reproductive potential. When a woman's reproductive capacities are limited through barrenness, illness, celibacy, infant mortality, or menopause, she often rechannels her energies into helping others by becoming a midwife or healer or spirit medium. This, then, provides status for her in society.

The world is viewed quite differently by men and women. Barbara Johnstone compared fifty-eight conversational narratives recorded by her students in an American setting, and her study revealed that

men live in a world where they see power as coming from an individual acting in opposition to others and to natural forces. For them, life is a contest in which they are constantly tested and must perform, in order to avoid the risk of failure. For women…the community is the source of power. If men see life in terms of contest, a struggle against nature and other men, for women life is a struggle against the danger of being cut off from their community. (Tannen 1990, 178)

Men's stories were about physical and social contests, while the women's stories were about the norms of the community and the interpersonal activities of the group. The setting for her study was America, but others have written of societies where men must prove themselves by conquering and then be sure they hold themselves apart from the women's activities.

WOMEN CHANGED BY FORMAL EDUCATION

When girls are able to get formal education and become more career-focused, they also get the masculine socialization referred to previously. Schooling emphasizes independence, assertiveness, and achievement goals. Bifurcation results with life becoming a struggle between the natural feminine traits and those masculine traits required in the work world. Recognizing this combination of traits in the socializing process helps women adjust more effectively in the cross-cultural setting.

These changes are perceived differently in different societies. In the US women in the workforce are valued by how well they perform in the workplace, and their status in society is set accordingly. In some other societies women are valued not by their workforce performance, but by how well they carry their family and home responsibilities. There are also societies where the educated woman is allowed to work only in non-male organizations, e.g., banks and businesses. In many societies changes brought about by formal education of women has come so quickly that women face great pressures.

Even though women are changed by schooling, we find women seek after meaningful relationships and have a deep sensitivity to people. If allowed, they can bring a rich quality to the workplace that makes it a better place.

DIFFERENCES IN RELATION TO THE SPIRITUAL

A common cultural perception is the belief that women are the embodiment of evil or at least have long-standing ties with it. "Female sexuality is seen as a disruptive, chaotic force that must be controlled or co-opted by men, periodically purified, and at times destroyed" (Hoch-Smith and Spring 1978, 3). Some cultural forms that express this are the witch, the overpowering mother, the prostitute, the evil seductress, and the nagging wife. Mythology in various parts of the world affirms this concept of feminine evil with the belief that female sexuality is polluting and contaminating to all things male. When women are seen as a source of evil, guilt, shame, and temptation, there is need for rigid control by numerous social structures. It is not unusual for a woman to be blamed for a man's failure.

Men in many societies are seen as masters of their fates, and they do not tend to seek the supernatural as much as women do. It has been found that men are often perceived as having great strength in themselves, and women as having great spiritual power. Women's status and acceptance by the family is related to successful reproduction, and since they tend to be blamed for barrenness and the death of children, they tend to be intimately involved with spiritual powers. In some societies the cultural assignment of mystic powers to female sexuality assists women in countering the power of males. For instance, a *marianismo* concept in Latin America suggests women are semi-divine, morally superior to, and spiritually stronger than men (Stevens 1973).

Women often counter the authority and power of males (assigned by society) with the use of spiritual power. When unacceptable things seem to be on the horizon, they often obtain a charm, contact a spirit, or go to a shrine in order to mobilize power beyond their human power to influence the situation. For example, if a husband is having an affair with another woman, or threatens to marry a second wife or divorce, the wife may go to a diviner or spirit medium for assistance. She often doesn't have as many options for solving her problems as men in the society do, nor does she have as much control over her own life. Stephens, in her research on the socialization of children through Hausa narratives in West Africa, describes how women challenge their husbands through the use of spiritual power.

> Women are most often portrayed in traditional roles as cook and mother. But far from playing dependent wives, many of these heroines consistently challenge and best their husbands. Moreover, oppositions recur, aligning female antagonists with natural and supernatural powers against husbands who represent worldly,

political authority. Conflicts occur between these counterforces and are mediated by women with supernatural abilities to nurture and produce life. If anyone must acknowledge dependency, it is a husband, whose political power is no match for his wife's supernatural power and whose cultural role is sustained by her culinary and reproductive abilities. (Coles and Mack 1991, 223)

A male's seeking after spiritual power is likely to be related to achieving or maintaining manhood, e.g., success in hunting or fishing, protection from female pollution, physical risks, or protection from unknown powers when away from home. However, women, because of their lower status in society and their lack of involvement in decision-making at the societal level, tend to seek spiritual power more frequently.

All in all, women are more sensitive to the spiritual than men. Women are found to be the majority in the practice of a variety of the world religions—in temples, at shrines, and consulting those who administer spiritual power. Among missionary women, the wife is usually the first to recognize the spiritual dimension of existing problems. Not only is she more aware, but there is a willingness to admit human weakness and a desire to get spiritual help. Women are also more apt to recognize that family problems often have spiritual roots. Women in the Christian church worldwide outnumber men in seeing the need for spiritual help and the stimulus and excitement of interacting with God.

CONCLUSION

I have been able to suggest only a few of the many ways the male/female dynamics of society are shaped. Gender affects one's purpose for living and the way a society works. Living in a society different from the one we are raised in causes us to be aware of our own gender distinctives and their cultural variations. I have presented specific Western research and cultural variations with the hope of stimulating your own research. Much more analysis needs to be done which will affect our cross-cultural interactions, training, and strategies.

We have focused on differences between the sexes and gender formation as well as the cultural influences shaping the genders. We might ask why such differences exist. I believe that God gave males and females strengths and weaknesses with the intent that they complement each other. If we could learn to focus on cooperation and not competition, this variability could become a strength for both. Dianne Hales, a health writer who researched in anthropology, physiology, psychology, neuroscience, endocrinology, and medicine, writes:

> Imagine the possibilities such a combination might create: strength working in tandem with stamina, the male's laserlike focus expanding to take in the female's embrace of big-picture context, the female's quest for meaningful connections enriching the male's determination to get things done. In theology, business, education, and communications, there is an emerging recognition of a different vision, a different voice, a different viewpoint—a female one, neither inferior nor superior, neither right nor wrong, neither better nor worse, but one that may open up new and unexplored possibilities for both sexes. (2000, 337)

Gender science is now clearly demonstrating that women are not an inferior or second sex, but a separate sex, unique in body, mind, and spirit.

This same challenge comes to the church today with new and unexplored possibilities for both sexes. God has made us and formed us in our mothers' wombs (Ps 139:13). Women were made distinctly female, and ideas from the past (e.g., women being subhuman, inferior in reasoning power, unable to lead, less valuable than men) should not be used to keep them captive and to quench God's Spirit in them. Loren Cunningham (2000, 42–43), the cofounder of YWAM, writes concerning men and women based on Scripture, showing clearly

God's heart and plan for equality between the genders. He presents the need to release women with God's blessing to be all that God has called them to be. God gifted both male and female that we might do his will. Women and their special gifts must be included as we mobilize for completing the Great Commission. As the genders work together and listen to each other, we can better accomplish God's work.

REFERENCES

Coles, C., and B. Mack, eds. 1991. *Hausa Women in the Twentieth Century.* Madison: The University of Wisconsin Press.

Cunningham, L., and D. J. Hamilton. 2000. *Why Not Women? A Biblical Study of Women in Missions, Ministry and Leadership.* Seattle, WA: YWAM Publishing.

Gilligan, C. 1982. *In a Different Voice: Psychological Theory and Women's Development.* Cambridge, MA: Harvard University Press.

Gilmore, D. D. 1990. *Manhood in the Making: Cultural Concepts of Masculinity.* New Haven, CT: Yale University Press.

Goldschmidt, W. 1966. *Comparative Functionalism.* Berkeley, CA: University of California Press.

Hales, D. 1999. *Just Like a Woman: How Gender Science Is Redefining What Makes Us Female.* New York: Bantam Books.

Hoch-Smith, J., and A. Spring, eds. 1978. *Women in Ritual and Symbolic Roles.* New York: Plenum Press.

Maltz, D. N., and R. A. Borker. 1982. A Cultural Approach to Male and Female Miscommunication. In *Language and Social Identity,* ed. J. J. Gumperz, 196–216. Cambridge, MA: Cambridge University Press.

Stephens, C. 1991. Marriage in the Hausa Tatsuniya Tradition: A Cultural and Cosmic Balance. In *Hausa Women in the Twentieth Century,* ed. C. Coles and B. Mack, 221–231. Madison: The University of Wisconsin Press.

Stevens, E. 1973. Marianismo: The Other Face of Machismo in Latin America. In *Female and Male in Latin America,* ed. A. Pescatello, 89–101. Pittsburgh, PA: University of Pittsburgh Press.

Tannen, D. 1990. *You Just Don't Understand: Women and Men in Conversation.* New York: Ballantine Books.

Van Leeuwen, M. S. 1990. *Gender and Grace: Love, Work and Parenting in a Changing World.* Downers Grove, IL: InterVarsity Press.

TWO

Created to Serve
Marla Campbell

T he age-old question of whether women should be involved in ministry still surfaces today. In this chapter I will explore briefly, according to biblical teaching, whether and to what extent women should serve in ministry and mission. The Bible supports spiritual equality and a non-gender "calling" for all people to spread the gospel (Van Leeuwen 1990). In fact, involvement in Kingdom work goes back to Genesis1:26–27, which establishes that "mankind," both male and female, are made *Imago Dei*—"in God's image." "The word translated 'man' does not represent a male person in this instance. The word is better understood as meaning humankind or human beings" (Gill and Cavaness 2004). As both are also joint heirs with Jesus Christ through his shed blood, it seems clear that both genders are in his plan of partnership and service. Understanding this created origin and purpose clarifies why resistance to the involvement of women on the foreign field is discouraging at best and traumatically damaging at its worst to women desiring to serve. Equality came through the created order, whereas inequality is a result of the Fall. A closer look at Scripture gives a solid platform for the future involvement of women in ministry.

Loren Cunningham, cofounder of Youth With A Mission and a leader in missions for five decades, envisions a new generation taking a fresh look at God's Word and seeing that women can fulfill all of the potential God has put within them. This current generation will simply ask, "Who is it that God wants?" without regard to race, color, or gender (Cunningham and Hamilton 2000, 14). Cunningham, from the perspective of one who ministers in many lands each year, sees the issue of women in ministry as a major crisis in the church for the twenty-first century. If, as he claims, two-thirds of the body of Christ are women, then a huge segment of the evangelical workforce would be eliminated if women were restricted to doing only support tasks.

There is strong evidence that women experience the psychological and emotional effects of missionary involvement at a deeper level than men do. As Dr. Nancy Crawford explains in *Enhancing Missionary Vitality*, "Women in direct achievement roles versus supportive roles are more likely to have job satisfactions, and thus organizational commitment" (Powell and Bowers 2002, 144). This is crucial to the body of Christ and thus to mission agencies. Eenigenburg and Bliss go into extensive detail on this concept in *Expectations and Burnout* (2010).

Many Christians are now addressing this issue, with authors increasingly discovering that the biblical perspective is a complementary approach rather than egalitarian or one of superiority. Reference after reference in the Word of God indicates that men and women need each other in relationship as well as in ministry to fulfill God's purposes. Both genders possess strengths, and it is a wise Christian who embraces the strength in someone else as an enhancement rather than a threat to completing one's own God-directed ministry (Saucy and TenElshof 2001). An examination of some biblical models of this might clarify the topic of complementarianism and purpose.

BIBLICAL PERSPECTIVE OF WOMEN IN MINISTRY

In her book *All of the Women of the Bible* (1955), Edith Deen records the stories of over one hundred noteworthy biblical women. Some of these women are named, some are not, but all of them had an impact within Scripture. There were wives, mothers, missionaries, prophetesses, judges, queens, intercessors, daughters, daughters-in-law, teachers, pastors, deaconesses, grandmothers, and more. Each woman had her own unique gifts. Each was called and used by God. God esteemed women from the point of creation and appointed them to many tasks—not in competition with men but complementing one another as they work in cooperative harmony, so that God's work could be accomplished, furthering his kingdom to his glory.

Throughout Paul's letters one can read a gender inclusive position. "There is neither Jew nor Greek, slave nor free, male nor female, for you are all one in Christ Jesus" (Gal 3:28). Dr. Robert Saucy (2001) devotes an entire chapter in the book *Women in Ministry* to the newness of relationship in Christ, clarifying the intent of this passage in context as it relates to gender roles. Paul continues in this vein in other passages. "Now if we are children, then we are heirs—heirs of God and co-heirs with Christ" (Rom 8:17).

In 1 Corinthians 12:11–27 there is no gender separation in the explanation of God giving gifts to each of us as he determines. The whole of Christ's body fits together and should work as one as we cooperatively function together in a spirit of unity. We likewise are to encourage each other in whatever gifts God chooses for us in order to accomplish his purpose. "We are equally saved, equally spirit-filled, equally sent" (Van Leeuwen 1990, 33). Many contemporary authors (see references) have reexamined traditional interpretations of Scripture to discover that both male and female are, clearly, equally a part of a plan for reaching the lost and discipling the saved.

As Peter addressed a gender inclusive crowd at Pentecost he proclaimed,

In the last days, God says,
  I will pour out my Spirit on all people.
Your sons and daughters will prophesy,
  your young men will see visions,
  your old men will dream dreams.

Even on my servants, both men and women,
I will pour out my Spirit in those days,
and they will prophesy. (Acts 2:17–18)

Both the Old and New Testaments give examples of great women chosen by God, such as Esther, the queen; Deborah, the judge and prophetess; Priscilla, the leader/teacher of home study groups; and Phoebe, the deaconess or pastor. In fact, when Phoebe is spoken of as a "minister," it is the same word used to describe male ministers (Adeney et al. 1996, 15). The first two chapters of Acts clearly number women among the apostles, and they, along with the men present, received the gift of languages and the ordination to the "priesthood of Jesus" as the Holy Spirit descended as tongues of fire (Ide 1984, 69).

Proverbs 6:20–23 admonishes us to heed the teaching of a wise mother. "Possibly the most important teaching ministry is also the most overlooked—the teaching ministry of mothers" (Joyner 1998, 5). Few people would refute the importance of a mother's place in teaching. Missionary mothers can be encouraged in this, the most vital part of their ministry, whether at home or abroad. However, Rick Joyner, in his article "The Greatest Teaching Ministry," goes on to say that the Bible does not qualify gender ministries. He specifies that there were cultural parameters precluding some instances, but the norm was to be a cooperative, mutually supportive functioning of each gender as God appointed them (ibid., 5–7). This, then, would allow for other types of ministry and teaching beyond a domestic setting.

The topic of women in ministry and the biblical teaching on it is clearly a very large and deep issue. For the purposes herein it is important for women missionaries to know in their own hearts between themselves and God that he truly does call and equip women to minister in a variety of ways. Then women should seek the Lord to define what that ministry is to be in their own lives as individuals. Throughout life in all of its various stages, it becomes crucial to maintain a relationship with God, through prayer and the daily reading of his Word, which clarifies continuity or a change in ministry. Without divine confirmation, doubts, the voice of the enemy, cultures, and other external input can create stress and uncertainty, dissuading anyone from her focus.

The goal should never be to prove one's position or to challenge a man's position, but to function comfortably and confidently in whatever role God has placed her. Instead of challenging, the critical goal is to strike an important balance. God calls both genders, but there is a more important goal than demanding equality or fighting to establish leadership rights. It has been my experience that if I listen to the voice of God's direction in my life, he will give me guidance to be where and do what he has called me to. When opposition arises, I still attempt to "live at peace with everyone" (Rom 12:18) and allow the Lord to work necessary changes. At the end of the day, I need to walk in obedience to him, doing what he has equipped me to do.

This presents a challenge as well as a focus for women who feel a call to missions and desire to minister. Husbands and mission agencies are the ones who should recognize the mutual call of men and women and support it—even encourage it. In the beginning, "they had equality. They had instructions to work as a team…that was mutuality" (Gill and Cavaness 2004). "Half of God's army is disqualified when women are silenced from ministry" (Mayo 1998, 45). The difficulty will come naturally when the woman reaches the host country. That society probably will not willingly accept a woman in leadership, so adjustments must be made on her part to accommodate the culture while heeding the call. Cultures and their internal values and/or interpretations seem to cause more difficulties for women wanting to serve than those based in theology or Scripture.

WOMEN IN TRADITIONAL ROLES

Still today there are those who contend that a woman's primary responsibility before God begins with the fact that she was created distinctly for man, based on Genesis 2:18–22 (Tuggy 1966, 13). An antiquated hierarchy exists indicating that woman was made from and solely for man. Again, this type of thinking is a result of the Fall, not divine design. But recent discoveries are now providing a paradigm shift that clarifies a biblical complementary partnership (Hestenes 1979). Denominations, incorporating opinionated interpretations of Scripture into their doctrine and polity, have historically had a negative effect on women desiring to minister. George Tavard in *Woman in Christian Tradition* (1973) cites particularly damaging aspects found in a variety of Protestant denominations, as well as Orthodox and Catholic traditions. These types of doctrine and comments have destroyed many women who wanted to minister and made life difficult for others who pursued the call despite the obstacles. Contemporary thought now shifts from "women are not leaders; therefore they should not be leaders" to "women are leaders; therefore they should be leaders" (Hestenes 1979).

Recognizing the great need for God in today's world, Cunningham pleads for releasing women along with men to obey God and to fulfill the destiny he created for them from the womb. When the focus is on whether God can use women in public ministry, people are

> actually debating which God-given gifts they will give women permission to use...Think of the implications! God's Word says we are not to touch His anointed ones or do His prophets any harm. God warns us not to quench the Spirit. Yet people routinely "touch" God's anointed women, harming their ministry and quenching the Spirit's work through them. (Cunningham and Hamilton 2000, 46)

Since two-thirds of all Bible-believing Christians are women, we cannot afford to eliminate women in ministry roles when they are responding to God's gifting and call.

Women in the Gospels gives a clear picture of Romans 12:1 when it explains that either gender submits as a servant to God's will. Both men and women must present themselves as living sacrifices to the Lord.

Then, it is as "Mary's YES," when she said "let it be to me according to your Word" (1990, 102). That gives each gender the freedom, having yielded oneself upon the altar of the Lord, to follow God's direction for service according to his purpose.

"Women lost a lot in institutionalized church," explains author Mary Kassian. "In the early church ministry was something that belonged to everybody. Everyone was a minister. Everyone was commissioned and 'called by God' to have a ministry. And so women were very involved" (Adeney et al. 1996,14). Concluding "A Complementary Perspective" on women and men in ministry, Saucy and TenElshof agree.

> Finally, men and women must recognize the need of each other so that their different contributions in church ministry are equally valued in the accomplishment of the mission of the church and its growth toward maturity in Christlikeness. Christian love that wills to understand the other and minister for his or her true good is the only power that can bring true complementarity of women and men in ministry. (2001, 341)

EARLY MISSIONARY EFFORTS

Helen Barrett Montgomery wrote a book in 1910 focusing on "the *last 50 years* in missions." That means that at least from 1860, as presented in the text, women have been traveling, often alone, to distant lands to proclaim the gospel. Many of the examples given were of women beginning orphanages and schools and even planting churches. Most were teachers of some type. Many of them went on their own rather than having an agency send them, but then established an agency.

The Small Woman (1970) tells the story of Gladys Aylward, a British parlor maid who felt the call of God into missions. She applied with China Inland Mission, which informed her that at twenty-six years of age she was too old to learn the Mandarin language and be trained to go. Determined that she had heard from God, she worked diligently, saving her earnings at a travel agency until she had a one-way passage to China. With only the coat on her back, a small satchel, and some pans, she ventured out into what became an arduous, death-defying adventure. Eventually she arrived at a way station run by a widowed missionary. Together until the older woman died, the two invited mule train drivers into the Inn of the Eighth Happiness where they told Bible stories, fed them, and gave overnight lodging. Later Gladys herself cared for orphans and took over a hundred orphans to safety during the rebellion. She also won the local magistrate to Christ. This gave her an inroad into the government, allowing her to be instrumental in the unbinding of the Chinese women's feet.

On this, the hundredth anniversary of the Lillian Trasher orphanage in Egypt, another such example looms. Twenty-five thousand documented orphans received a home, love, care, and the gospel message because Lillian left her home in the southern United States to follow the call of God and become known as "the Mother of the Nile." A married woman who also exemplified this type of obedience was Sarah Edwards. Her preacher husband, Jonathan, said of her that she hardly cared for anything aside from spending time with the Lord and meditating on his Word (Piper 2005). Jonathan wholeheartedly affirmed the spiritual drive and calling he admired in his wife. The Edwards' partnership went far beyond home as they ministered greatly together and separately.

What a great human and eternal loss there would have been if Gladys, Lillian, Sarah, and many other heroines of the faith had not been determined to follow the call of God. How many mission agencies have missed the mark by discouraging single women from fulfilling God's purpose for them? How many married women have been hidden behind their husbands' call and never felt approval to complement that by using their own gifts? These are the challenges that the body of Christ must rise to face in these last days. These obstacles present reasons for women missionaries to become overwhelmingly discouraged and lose their identity as well as their purpose. The challenge today is to assist missionary women to fit into the scheme of God's plan.

REFERENCES

Adeney, M., J. Briscoe, M. Kassian, and J.Thompson. 1996. Ministering Women. *Christianity Today,* 40(4): 14–21.

Aylward, G. 1970. *The Small Woman.* Chicago: Moody Publishers.

Baron, B. 2010. Nile Mother: Lillian Trasher and Egypt's Orphans. *Assemblies of God Heritage* 31: 30–39.

Benge, J., and G. Benge. 2004. *Lillian Trasher: The Greatest Wonder in Egypt.* Seattle, WA:YWAM Publishing.

Bicket, Z. 1998. Dealing with Questions of the Role of Women in Ministry. *Enrichment,* 2(2), 80–85.

Booze, M. 1998. God Who Calls Is Faithful. *Enrichment,* 2(2): 16–23.

Crawford, N. 2002. Missionary Women Speak. In *Enhancing Missionary Vitality: Mental Health Professions Serving Global Mission,* ed. J. B. Powell and J. M. Bowers. Palmer Lake, CO: Mission Training International.

Cunningham, L., and D. J. Hamilton. 2000. *Why Not Women? A Biblical Study of Women in Missions, Ministry, and Leadership.* Seattle, WA: YWAM Publishing.

Deen, E. 1955. *All of the Women in the Bible.* New York: Harper and Row Publishers.

DeVries, S. B. 1986. Wives: Homemakers or Mission Employees? *Evangelical Missions Quarterly,* 22(4): 402–410.

Eenigenburg, S., and R. Bliss. 2010. *Expectations and Burnout: Women Surviving the Great Commission.* Pasadena, CA: William Carey Library.

Gill, D. M. 1998. Called by God—What's a Woman to Do, and What Can We Do to Help Her? *Enrichment,* 2(2): 32–35.

Gill, D. M., and B. Cavaness. 2004. *God's Women Then and Now.* Springfield, MO: Grace and Truth.

Giltner, F. M. 1986. *Women's Issues in Religious Education.* Birmingham, AL: Religious Education Press.

Hestenes, R. 1979. Women and Men in Ministry. Collection of articles and papers compiled for course MN 578 taught by Roberta Hestenes, Fuller Theological Seminary, Pasadena, CA.

Ide, A. F. 1984. *The Teachings of Jesus on Women*. Dallas, TX: Texas Independent Press.

————. 1998. In My Opinion: Feminism in America. *Woman's Touch,* 22(1): 17.

Johnsen, G. 1998. Seven Habits of Highly Effective Ministers' Wives. *Enrichment,* 2(2): 24–31.

Joyner, R. 1998. The Greatest Teaching Ministry. *The Morning Star Journal,* 8(1): 3–9.

McGee, G. 1998. And Your Daughters Shall Prophesy. *Enrichment,* 2(2): 48–51.

Mayo, S. 1998. Who Denied the Church? *Enrichment,* 2(2): 44–47.

Montgomery, H. B. 1910. *Western Women in Eastern Lands.* New York: The MacMillan Company.

Patterson, V. 1989. Women in Missions: Facing the 21st Century. *Evangelical Missions Quarterly,* 25(1): 62–71.

Piper, N. 2005. *Faithful Women and Their Extraordinary God.* Wheaton, IL: Crossway Books.

Powell, J. B., and J. M. Bowers. 2002. *Enhancing Missionary Vitality: Mental Health Professions Serving Global Mission.* Palmer Lake, CO: Mission Training International.

Royer, G. L. 1996. *Models for Fulfilling Missions.* Waxahachie, TX: Southwestern Assemblies of God University.

Saucy, R. L. 2001. The "Order" and "Equality" of Galatians 3:28. In *Women and Men in Ministry,* ed., R. L. Saucy and J. K. TenElshof, 139–159. Chicago: Moody Press.

Saucy, R. L., and J. K. TenElshof, eds. 2001. *Women and Men in Ministry.* Chicago: Moody Press.

Tavard, G. H. 1973. *Woman in Christian Tradition.* Notre Dame, IN: University of Notre Dame Press.

Tuggy, J. T. 1966. *The Missionary Wife and Her Work.* Chicago: Moody Press.

Van Leeuwen, M. S. 1990. *Gender and Grace.* Downers Grove, IL: InterVarsity Press.

Williams, M. O. 1979. *Partnership in Missions.* Springfield, MO: Division of Foreign Missions.

Women in the Gospels. 1990. *Women in the Gospels.* Originally compiled in Milan, Italy, 1987. New York: Crossroads Publishing Company.

THREE

Making Adjustments Favorably

Marla Campbell

The adjustment period for missionaries seems to be the primary time for both genders to determine how, or if, they will successfully function in a host culture. The initial orientation sets the stage for working with a mission agency, managing within one's marriage or as a single, and ministering alongside the nationals. The largest portion of adjustment and consequent psychological considerations can be found in female missionaries. Men have far fewer issues to deal with than women. It may be surmised that this is a result of it still being a man's world and that generally they are in charge of the agencies, national churches, the family, and most decision-making bodies. Men also, as will be discussed, derive their validity from their work, more so than do women, and require less intimate relationships than do their female counterparts.

In preparation for writing this chapter, I researched and interviewed both genders as they function in missions in various locations around the world. From this and for further illustration, I have included three specific cases in the addendum at the end of the chapter. It is my purpose to recognize the psychological effects of gender roles specifically on women in order to administer preventative medicine and avoid missionary attrition, burnout or collapse, disenfranchisement or family breakup.

ACCULTURATION AND ADJUSTMENTS

Acculturation can be described as an attempt to become part of a host culture. It involves blending with a new culture in which the individual did not grow up. In many ways it is the adaptation of oneself by choice to a second culture. There are many aspects to acculturation. Most of these present some degree of difficulty as a person moves from what is familiar to what is foreign. In leaving behind much of the familiar that intrinsically holds security, a person places self in a vulnerable arena. Adding to this vulnerability, missionaries find themselves subjected to a range of concerns from personal discomfort and irritation to traumatic culture shock and even breakdown as they face a new job/ministry and interpersonal encounters at many levels.

Anxiety surfaces, beginning with the announcement to family and friends that God has called a couple or an individual to leave home for a foreign missions assignment. The response may be wrought with emotional and psychological hurts. Often those closest to the missionary question the wisdom and even the motives of making such a risky move. Some see it as irresponsible, inconsiderate of the children they're taking, lack of concern for those at home, and so forth. Whether Christian or not, loved ones may respond with anger as well as rejection at the time when those would-be missionaries need the most encouragement from their closest support group. This often begins the cross-cultural experience on a note of stress and defense toward those they love the most (Van Rheenen 1996, 50). The farewell usually is sad enough without the additional feelings of disapproval and lack of support.

Once the decision has moved to the point of embarking on the adventure, missionaries begin an emotional and psychological journey that typically occurs over several years. Gretchen Janssen (1989, 27) suggests that this process includes the following common developmental stages:

1. Entry into the host country with fascination and excitement.
2. Subtle irritations.
3. Complete frustration resulting in depression.
4. Development of coping mechanisms.
5. Belonging to the country.

Familiarity with these stages in advance of leaving one's home country helps to prepare and possibly avert unnecessary personal tragedy. Authors agree that the number one factor in acculturation involves unrealistic expectations. Mission agencies would be wise to include this information as preparatory for everyone they send. Even with prior warning, however, it is often difficult to avoid any of the stages of culture shock completely during the acculturation process.

The most widely accepted theoretical diagram on the acculturation process is found in what Kalvero Oberg called "culture shock" when he coined the term in 1960. He suggests that everyone is subject to going through the following four stages when entering a new culture: 1) honeymoon, 2) crisis, 3) recovery, 4) adjustment (Wilson 1996, 442). This may also be interpreted as: 1) glamour, 2) depression, 3) rejection, 4) identification. Oberg qualifies that those hit hardest in each of the four stages are those who are monocultural and may have never even ventured outside of their own country (Oberg 1960). Oberg explains that as culture shock takes hold it is manifested in any or all of six aspects related to the phenomenon.

Six Aspects of Culture Shock *(Oberg 1960)*

1. Strain due to the effort required to make necessary psychological adaptations.
2. A sense of loss and feelings of deprivation in regard to friends, status, profession, and possessions.
3. Being rejected by and/or rejecting members of the new culture.
4. Confusion in role, role expectations, values, feelings, and self-identity.

5. Surprise, anxiety, even disgust and indignation, after becoming aware of cultural differences.
6. Feelings of impotence due to the inability to cope with the new environment.

It can be concluded through the research as well as interviews with missionaries that these are not gender exclusive effects. Any or all of the points above may take their toll on either a man or a woman depending on the culture into which they are placed, their own personality and family makeup, and the individual assimilation of external input.

Figure 1 below identifies the options available when the anxiety sets in. It shows the progression or digression occurring inside of the individual and the eventual actions that may result. The top half of the diagram suggests a healthy, balanced approach to the probable anxiety resulting from the end of the glamour or honeymoon stage. Once reality sets in a person desiring to and able to cope will be quite self-critical. This can produce positive results if the person is realistic enough to assess oneself in light of the host culture and begin to adapt without losing his or her first culture or personality and personal identity. Identity can further be established through relationships that give interpersonal feedback, helping to develop a balanced picture of the situation thereby acculturating successfully.

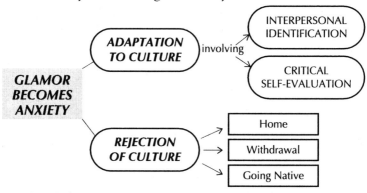

Figure 1. *Culture Shock* (Van Rheenen 1996:93)

The bottom half of the chart indicates that the anxiety factor has overtaken the person to such a degree that he or she rejects the host culture in one of three ways. Some may simply give up the task and return home. Others withdraw from the culture and relationships and become nonproductive. Lastly, there are those who completely give up their own culture and in an inappropriate, abnormal fashion "go native," seeming to become a product of the very culture they disdain. "Culture shock, though an unpleasant experience, is a potent and powerful teacher. It evokes adaptive skills that promote personal and spiritual growth and intercultural learning. It is normal, temporary and will pass" (Wilson 1996, 444).

A personal sense of well-being versus stress and anxiety can come under fire via expectations, whether perceived or real. These expectations arise from society as well as from within the individual herself. The societal expectations may exist within the host culture or the culture of origin but may also be expectations of the mission agency. Role expectation is a huge aspect of this. Drs. Elizabeth Hall and Nancy Duvall studied these contributors in an effort to address them and bring healthy perspectives to women on the mission field. They suggest ways to manage the expectations, bringing balance into a person's life (Powell and Bowers 2002, 157). Furthermore, mission organizations need to be aware in order to assist the woman, but also in order to keep all members of the organization functioning together in a productive, healthy manner.

Another difficult aspect of acculturation to briefly consider in the context of this topic takes place when missionaries return to their own country. This reentry syndrome catches people off guard far more than does culture shock. Reentry always produces an element of pain and unexpected personal reactions due to expectations of the familiar and the support groups. However, both the returning missionaries and their home, family, and friends have been changed by their experiences during the elapsed time (Van Rheenen 1996, 54). Those at home cannot relate to the country or people which have become such an integral part of the missionary's life, nor can they grasp the type and style of work done abroad. At best the most interested member of their closest sphere attempts to live vicariously and nod affirmingly, compassionately trying to understand experiences to which they have little or nothing to connect. Likewise the missionary has missed many chapters of life as she knew it in her country of origin. Again, the missionary suffers a degree of isolation. In some ways it becomes a vicious cycle of adjustment and readjustment as shown in the diagram below.

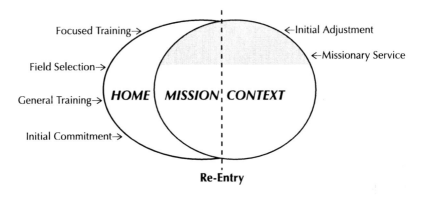

Figure 2. *The Missionary Cycle* (Van Rheenen 1996:50)

It remains crucial throughout the cycle to watch for trauma. "Trauma involves experiences that overwhelm an individual's ability to cope and hence make sense of certain life events" (Grant 1995, 73). If one ceases to cope and can no longer make sense of life events, reality has shifted to misperception. At this extreme, help is needed. But it would prove much more beneficial if preventative steps were taken all along the way to insure that this would never happen.

Two important questions are often asked at any point in this recurring cycle. "Who am I in the midst of all of these changes?" and "What does the future hold for me?" (Van Rheenen 1996, 49). These come up over and over again from the point of predeparture through the time actually on the field to the reentry period. It is therefore vital to include these obstacles in the training program so that missionaries will at least be aware prior to deputation.

With any of the concerns expressed herein, it remains fundamental to remember that "it is not what happens to us during our course of ministry, but how we react to what happens that determines our effectiveness in ministry" (Royer 1996, 159).

HOST CULTURE VARIABLES FOR GENDERS

As the dynamics for the predeparture period through acculturation are engaged, the obvious element of the host culture itself clearly plays a strong part in missionary adjustments. What is acceptable for either men or women to do in their own culture may not be the same as in their newfound home. The message that they came to convey will sorely be lost if their outward appearance and actions speak louder than their words.

Men typically have less of a problem functioning in a host culture. Their mode of dress requires little or no adaptation to be acceptable. A woman's dress usually receives much scrutiny based on modesty, fashion, religious taboos, secular connotations, and so forth. Men enter the new country with a mutual expectation that they have a job to do and will most likely be respected in that. It is assumed that the man is the leader, the teacher, or the pastor, or that he possesses credentials meriting respect. A woman traditionally follows the man as his job dictates. She is not seen as being in any of the headship or teaching roles that would unquestionably be given to a man.

A woman must not look at or talk to a man in Islamic countries. In some areas of Eastern Europe and Africa, she must not sit with a man in church. In many countries of the world any public display of affection is unacceptable even between husband and wife. Women generally accept domestic roles wherein they care for the home and children, while men do the business both in the workplace and the church. In many parts of the world it is unacceptable for women to be involved in decision-making or to speak in church unless invited to do so by the man in charge. Whether the visiting man or woman agrees with these and other cultural mores is irrelevant. These things must be learned prior to entering the country if the desire is to be effective for the kingdom of God. First Corinthians 9 becomes the guideline for gender involvement, admonishing that the only thing truly of importance is the spreading of the gospel. What we wear, eat, or drink is unimportant. Rather, as Paul, we "become all things to all people so that by all possible means [we] might save some" (verse 22). With this in mind, work can be done by preferring one another (Rom 12:10 KJV), and in this case the "one another" is the host culture as well as the indigenous church from which gender cues and clues are derived.

Accepting this biblical concept is vital, but it oftentimes does not diminish the strain on both genders for continuing to function in a framework of familiarity. Both male and female, whether married or single, must examine and reexamine their own worldviews and adapt the necessary areas to the acceptable standard, not forsaking the absolutes of Scripture. A variety of these factors will be examined based on research including interviews and surveys with missionaries.

MEN AND WOMEN ON THE MISSION FIELD

Besides the issue of fund-raising, the two largest obstacles to success in missions surround interpersonal relationships. The strength or fracturing of the family and the teamwork or divisiveness of missionaries' interaction determine the majority of longevity or attrition rates across international lines (Royer 1996, 158). Surprisingly, the location and specific cultures provide only the catalyst or backdrop for much more intimate criteria. Gender roles and communication emerge as pivotal in many emotional and psychological struggles. Although generalities can be drawn, many variables contribute to the adjustment for each man or woman. Factors contributing to mission adjustment for both include age, career length, family pressures, expectations, husband/wife relationship, singleness, interactions with nationals or church, personality type, and past profession/positions held in the home country.

An examination of attrition in missions placed six reasons above the rest for leaving the field:

Main Reasons for Leaving Field of Service *(from Allen 1986, 120)*
- Perceived lack of gifts
- Culture shock
- Unfulfilled expectations (often task or gender related)
- Morals (gender related)
- Disagreement with mission agency
- Family problems (includes parental disagreements, husband too busy or overly involved with work)

For example, using the last point of family problems for a springboard, it does seem that many times men find their validation in their work. Upon entering the new location for their work and ministry, men and women are both potentially subject to the culture shock aspects of acculturation. However, it is the man who largely gains the recognition as the one sent to do the work. He finds acceptance within the indigenous church as a leader and immediately can find projects connecting with the nationals. Both the husband and wife have a sense of calling and a responsibility to those sending from their homeland to use the funds to do mission-related work. The man locates that work early on while the woman primarily strives to establish the home and begin nesting. Women do so in order to give the family stability and make the new place livable. But the woman does not readily connect with the culture nor strictly mission-related work because she is at home so much. Guilt begins to set in as she thinks she is not doing what she was sent to do.

For both the man and the woman, coping mechanisms are being used. A man hits the ground running. He knows that he can find fulfillment in his work and therefore more easily defers uncomfortable adjustments. He throws himself into the work that is most obviously before him. The woman immerses herself in her home for security and purpose. The problem comes within the home when she hopes for validation from him but he's too busy gaining the same outside of the home where she wishes she could be trying to connect with the new culture and also wishing she had friends. An immediate catch-22 presents itself within the home.

"Although all family members experience problems and must make adjustments, it is the wife who enters this new living environment shorn almost completely of her previous roles and support systems" (Janssen 1989, 6). It is more common than not for a woman to give up her life goals or postpone her personal plans to accompany her husband. A survey of over 200 expatriate women indicated that 85 percent of business and missionary women living overseas moved because of their husband's job. The same survey concluded that these women's primary life concerns ranked personal development, family issues, and adjustment issues in the top three totaling 79 percent of all concerns (ibid., 12). Men, on the other hand, usually initiate family moves and are primarily concerned with the task.

Dr. Nancy Crawford spent many years in an African nation in a counseling capacity. She compared the women she counseled there to women in North America in ministry and/or planning to go to the mission field. Among many related conclusions, Dr. Crawford realized that "if mama ain't happy, ain't no one happy." In so saying she indicates the need for the missions team to work together to meet needs of women as well as the rest of the missions community. Working together in awareness of each one on the team will promote the health and success of the team but also of individuals. She concludes that "we need to promote a mission subculture of mutual respect, of consultative placement, and more thorough training both before and after arrival on the field of service" (Powell and Bowers 2002, 137).

Keeping the family together looms poignantly as the primary concern. It requires a concerted effort of communication in order to meet the needs of both parties and avert external invasions that could damage or destroy the marriage relationship. It is an insecure man who is unwilling to take time to listen to his wife, partner in a love that is mutually submissive, express appreciation, and follow guidelines of communication according to the need of his wife as well as himself (Royer 1996, 163–5).

In Case #2 in the addendum to this chapter, Rob presents this type of man. He makes a very conscious effort to be home and actually hear Diane's words. Together they work within the gender roles of the culture but retain their own comfort level in their roles at home. Although she is at times frustrated by the influx of people into their home as well as his long hours away from home, they talk to each other when these issues arise so that they will not explode into crisis.

Other missionary women surveyed expressed that although their husbands were aware of their difficulties adjusting, the man was also dealing with culture shock and learning how to cope with his own adjustments. In the case of "Louise" (heretofore referred to as Case #3), during a time of adjustments, her husband, "Lawrence," did stop and listen. He responded to her calmly. "If it is too much for you we will go back to the USA." Immediately she knew that he had heard her. She felt an affirming closeness taking away the feelings of being trapped. Louise described the tensions within the family.

> There seemed to always be too much to do with too little time. The demands on a person are high because the "need" on the foreign field seems so gigantic compared to the personal needs of family that seem so insignificant. To stay focused on putting your family first is a challenge and usually a source of arguments. Sometimes the nationals don't understand why you make the family such an important issue. There is also enormous pressure from the nationals for you to conform to their culture for your family needs and traditions. And very little understanding when you don't.

This quote clearly presents a plethora of pressures tugging at and stressing the woman and most likely her husband as well causing strife inside their home. She is expressing a feeling of inadequacy because there is too much to do and too little time, and the expectations of the nationals conflict with her home and her own culture. The cycle can result in bitterness and resentment between the couple and/or between them and the indigenous church members.

When asked how Lawrence related to her during this time, Louise replied, "At times he [my husband] was insensitive, harsh, and demanding, especially after he started getting involved in ministry and I was still coping with adjustments and culture shock and trying to keep the kids from knowing that I was having such a difficult time." Consequently anxiety and isolation built up inside of Louise.

None of the men responding to the questionnaire nor any mentioned in any of my research expressed any kind of frustration due to gender related tasks or pressures from the host country. Their concerns and pressures came from the basics of culture shock and adjustments as well as caring for their wives and assisting them through difficult times. Males responded to stress questions by referring to the pressures to achieve and produce.

A male missionary to Eastern Europe stated frustration over laborious interactions with government officials. To accomplish even the smallest task involves painstaking, time-consuming negotiations and renegotiations. For Western males, this takes on a time-wasting and "I-am-not-in-control" or failure sense. Men in Africa and Eurasia stated that they struggled with appropriate responses to women in their cultural context. Whereas in other cultures they might have been friendly, they could not glance at women in certain settings. They were likewise frustrated that they could not express attention or affection for their own wives until they were at home behind closed doors. One man from Asia also struggled with maintaining a strong exterior when approached by children and beggars, usually maimed. "I can't be who Christ called me to be with hardness in my eyes or heart."

All of the men appreciated their wives and the support they extended. They themselves did not overall seem as aware of gender related issues nor the effects on their wives as did the wives. One man working in Europe, though, stated, "I have witnessed extreme inequity in the treatment of females by individual mission leaders on the field. I saw situations where appointed female missionaries have been treated as secretarial workers. I've personally been treated very well, of course, because all the top people are men!" No one interviewed observed any inequality toward men. All research that comments on this concurs that we still live in a male-dominated world whose "traditional social attitudes can deliver a resounding whack to a woman's sense of worth" (Hunt 1990, 175).

Continued interviews and interactions with missionaries worldwide up to the present (2012) reveal that little has changed in the majority of mission agencies. Both men and women have expressed the inequities of salary or other compensation for missions work. In many cases, a couple gets one salary whether the woman is a stay-at-home mom, teaching in a Bible college, or working in some other mission-related capacity outside of the home. Consequently, if both spouses are working directly with the mission's tasks, the agency is in essence getting two for the salary of one. This presents its own rather shocking adjustment, especially to mid-career people who are used to getting two salaries in the USA for two professional jobs as a couple. Even the single missionary earns more than half of a couple's income, albeit usually not as much as a husband with a family gets. It is difficult to come to grips with these conditions when entering mission work and to make a positive adjustment. Throughout missionaries' careers, they have expressed the disparity in salary based on the work done and/or professional assignment (as in the States) and a salary strictly based on gender and/or marital status. Furthermore this might result in financial burden as the wife does not have the option to acquire an outside job for additional pay within the host country.

Psychologists Nancy Duvall and Elizabeth Hall (2003) explored identity and satisfaction of both single and married women on the mission field in their article "Married Women in Missions: The Effects of Role Expectations on Well-being and Self-esteem." They found additional factors in regard to the work roles, whether at home or outside the home. An abstract of their findings states that:

> The present study explored the effects of self-expectations and societal expectations of the host culture on the well-being of 37 married missionary women. The results did not support a relationship between the expectations of the host culture, and well-being. Homemakers appeared to be more relaxed and to experience life as more satisfying and interesting than women involved more actively in the mission task. The congruence of roles with self-expectations, role satisfaction, and freedom in choosing a role emerged as highly related to several indices of well-being. These findings highlight the centrality of freedom in choosing a role, and suggest that important subcultural differences in self-expectations exist in the Christian subculture which should be taken into account in research on women's issues.

In Case #1, Martha experienced such a dearth of gender equality that it finally caused extreme stress resulting in illness and leaving the field. She began her mission career as a single, very qualified missionary. Over the years following her marriage, her husband was reassigned so they moved. She no longer used her skills for missions, but had only the home and menial tasks that the mission board gave her. Despite theories to the contrary, Martha's plight is repeated over and over with both single and married females. This is quite surprising when data continues to show more females in the mission force than males (Hunt 1990, 174). In 1985 there were 1,293 single women and 13,179 married women career missionaries serving with US agencies (Patterson 1989, 64). In 1984, only 44.5 percent of the International Foreign

Mission Association workforce were male; yet 95 percent of their personnel supervision, counseling, and arbitration was done by men (DeVries 1986, 405). Unfortunately those statistics have not changed significantly in the past nearly thirty years.

In a report regarding missions in the Assemblies of God the following statistics were given:

> In spite of hardships, foreign missions in the Assemblies of God afforded women a wide opportunity for ministry. For couples, both the husband and wife were considered missionaries; this usually meant many responsibilities in ministry for the latter. Although the percentage of single women missionaries remained about the same from 1914 to 1925 (37–38%), they played notable roles and increased their number from 10 (of 27) to 95 (of 250) by 1925. The total number of women missionaries (single and married) to men increased by 9 percent (to 161) between 1914 and 1925. (McGee 1986, 91)

There was a 1 percent gain after 21 years with women numbering 329 out of a missionary force of 503. Generally, however, women were not in decision-making positions. There is one sole exception of Susan Easton, a missionary to India since 1885, who was appointed to serve on the council in 1917, but she was the last woman to serve as a full-fledged member. The irony of these statistics lies in the fact that there were and still are a higher percentage of women than men, but women did not, nor do they today, hold any decision-making positions.

The reference "many responsibilities for ministry" usually relegated women to Sunday schools, children's work, and behind-the-scenes work. Also, when a married missionary couple is introduced, it is generally said, "This is missionary X and his wife." Often the woman is known as the missionary wife but not the missionary, but the man is never referred to as the "missionary husband." "Women are an important resource in missions and are often unappreciated and underutilized" (Hunt 1990, 174).

Special Needs of Missionary Women

Women have unique needs, and one of the most important is developing an appropriate sense of worth. Single female missionaries find themselves being treated as second-class citizens socially and in task distribution or validation (Hunt 1990, 175). The Lord has equipped single and married women to meet the many tasks remaining in a world that still doesn't know him. There is freedom in realizing the gifts he's given and using them. Some women are gifted in evangelism, and some have a prophetic gift. Women pray effectively because they are often called to intercede and may be used in healing ministry or to develop prayer teams on the field (Adeney et al. 1996, 17).

In my survey women stated that they felt important and/or validated as missionaries and women when they were involved with serving in the following capacities:

31-year-old missionary, 1st term:

Speaking to Bible school students
Organizing and speaking at women's conferences
Working with children
Hosting meetings and guests

43-year-old missionary, 3rd term:

Being a mom at home when children were young
Teaching women and children
Offering help when leaders asked for input
Helping new missionaries adapt/adjust by conducting
an orientation program

48-year-old missionary, 4th term:

Giving input into a person's life and seeing spiritual change
Counseling with a wife or mother and encouraging her

60-year-old missionary, over 20 years on field:
Assisting my husband in his ministry
Teaching women
Teaching men and women in marriage, home, family seminars

32-year-old, 1st term:
Children's ministries in indigenous churches
Teaching Bible college students
Evangelism

44-year-old, 2nd term:
Pastor's wife
Women's ministry leader
Hospitality ministry both to other missionaries and to nationals

All of these involvements provide ministry, the purpose for which people go to the mission field. Most of these areas apply to both married and single women. They also give a woman a sense of purpose knowing that she truly is there because of God's call on her life. These and other areas should be encouraged by mission agencies, husbands, families, friends, and nationals. Unfortunately, most women under evangelical mission agencies are appointed regular missionaries, but wives rarely receive definite work assignments. They cannot make money through their own salary with the agency nor outside of missions work for additional income. However, these rules don't apply to pastors' wives in the States (DeVries 1986, 405). The effect of this can be seen in Case #1 where Martha felt minimized by the inability to do the work for which she had been trained and received a mission salary as a single.

The entire mission effort would be stronger, more productive, and have fewer casualties of wounded missionaries if women's giftings were sought, affirmed, and given place. "You can endure a lot of pain if you have an appreciative following" (Dixon 1990, 390). Still, task productivity does not entirely fulfill a woman as it might a man.

The woman's experience differs from the man's in six main areas, according to Linda Wilson (1996, 445):

- *Sense of Loss and Isolation:* Women have a need for intimate relationships and a need for the old and familiar. They complain, "I have no history," when in a location with new people and no connectedness.
- *Psychological Aspects:* Stress during the transitional period causes illness, egalitarian structure in Western society works toward equality/sameness between the genders with both men and women working in jobs as well as in the home. abnormalities in bodily functions, eating or sleeping disorders.
- *Cultural Inconveniences:* Men engage in work and outside activities; women bear the brunt of daily chores and life's inconveniences.
- *Marital Strain:* The absence of a husband's presence, support, and understanding or external factors affecting the marriage cause distress within the woman.
- *Identity Confusion:* Identity confusion and lack of self-confidence occurs when she doesn't know what her role is or should be. This also results from the inability to or restriction from doing what she could do well.
- *Struggling to Learn Language:* This struggle deters self-esteem and a sense of belonging to the new people group.

Of the top ten needs of women in ministry, dealing with loneliness stands boldly at the pinnacle (Briscoe 1997, 13). No matter what else seems absent or amiss, women cannot survive long without relationships. Men often find their sole fulfillment of intimacy in their relationship with their wives and their further validation on the job. A woman needs a close friend in whom she can confide. Almost every one of the women interviewed or surveyed in my research placed the lack of a close friend or friends as one of the most difficult adjustments. Many felt that if they had just one female friend with whom they could talk, share, and pray, the adaptation would be significantly easier.

Single women do have some unique giftings as well as unique needs in addition to those described for all women. It is important for both the single and the body of Christ to realize this and make allowances. For instance, the phrase "single Christian" is and should functionally be a contradiction of terms. "By definition, there are no single Christians. We belong to each other…and we continue first and foremost to be variously gifted members of "one body"—the church" (Van Leeuwen 1990, 228). A married woman does have a husband for relational intimacy and family connections on the field. She has purpose in caring for those in her home, whereas the single missionary, according to those interviewed, has her aloneness punctuated on the field more so than back home. She needs close relationships where she lives.

It is very hard because of a great divergence in backgrounds to have a national friend that becomes as close as a sister (friend) from one's own culture, although this does oftentimes help to bridge the loneliness gap. Non-mission expatriates may lend both a listening ear and an opportunity for witness, since many personnel are assigned overseas with government and business. To whom does the missionary woman talk? Just processing all that must be considered on a daily basis can become overwhelming since it comes into the woman's realm from so many differing areas, including her own personal expectations.

The conflicting or contradictory expectations for and from missionary women add much to the isolation feelings as well as the identity crisis to which they are highly susceptible. There are many sources of conflict and contradiction that produce unrealistic expectations. An identity struggle exists. The missionary woman struggles to know who she is and under whose authority she must function.

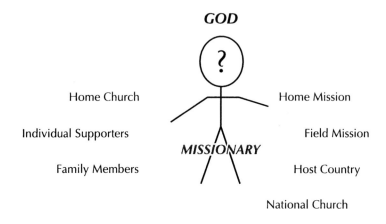

Figure 3. *Missionary's Identity Crisis* (Silzer 1994:21)

SUGGESTIONS FOR MEETING THESE NEEDS

In her book *Psychology of Missionary Adjustments* (1995), retired missionary Marge Jones emphasizes realistic expectations and mutual accommodations. By this she means that a balance must be maintained by all parties involved. The mission agency is responsible to train as best they can prior to departure for the field. She gives three guidelines for this: 1) perspective training, concentrating on developing an intercultural perspective using the cultural self-awareness approach, 2) interaction training, involvement and interaction with people from the host country, 3) context specific training, focusing specifically on the particular situation the trainee will face in the host country (1995, 22).

More and more the realization of needs and the prevention of missionary attrition have come to the attention of psychologists. Organizations such as Mission Training International in Palmer Lake, Colorado, serve outside of specific agencies or denominations. Their goal is to provide training before leaving for the field as well as during the missionary's career. The growing need for counseling has emerged, both within mission agencies and as a service offered outside of the agency.

Secondly, the missionary must continually reevaluate personal expectations, limitations, and margins of life. It is important to keep expectations realistic (especially for first-termers), and the following may be helpful for staying focused:

Keeping Expectations Realistic *(from Jones 1995, 71)*

1. Set reasonable goals.
2. Don't take your job description too seriously.
3. Be committed to you, be thankful, and be an encourager.
4. Forgive yourself and others, remembering we are all human.
5. Be flexible and don't take yourself too seriously.
6. Make all changes gradually, especially cultural ones.
7. Stay healthy and reduce stress whenever possible.

It is also helpful for women particularly to have pictures of friends and family back home and a couple of items such as wall hangings, decor, items with sentimental value, and other things that familiarize the new surroundings and make a bridge to the "old."

The third area of realistic expectation is one over which missionaries have little control and that is the nationals' view of and expectations of them. Whenever possible, needs should be expressed in an appropriate fashion. Most of the time this is idealistic, so instead one must keep personal parameters according to self and family needs, not forsaking interaction with the cultural roles and rules. Balance remains the watchword!

Oftentimes when things get out of balance or overwhelming, women withdraw and/or internalize, especially in the absence of a close friend. The lie inside of them sounds like one or a combination of several of these: "I'm weak." "I'll be letting someone [husband, children, nationals, mission agency] down if I don't keep going." "It's just something hormonal or biological." "I can get past this; I'll just press on." "I'll disappoint my supporters back home if I stop." There are many, many more such internal statements that get rehearsed until they're believed. Unfortunately these lies find support oftentimes through other missionaries, especially when distrust or conflict exists on the field. "The only army that shoots its wounded is the Christian army," said a speaker, a psychologist who had just returned from an overseas ministry trip among missionaries. He summed up the philosophy of the group with whom he worked:

- We don't have emotional problems.
- If we fail to deny the problems, never breathe a word outside the family.
- If we can't deny the problem and word leaks out, don't seek professional help! (Carlson 1998, 29)

Unfortunately this is all too true. It presents the reason why both men and women leave mission work very damaged. More and more people are realizing the necessity of preventative medicine in pre-crisis counseling or at least counseling once a red flag goes up. In order to prevent such disaster, furloughs and vacations are important. Many missionary women complain of the filthy environments. Although they deal with it and would never let on to a national, it takes a great toll on a woman used to keeping a sanitary home. A little break goes a long way towards restoration. Men who lead mission organizations and those who are married are wise to plan for such diversions.

They are also wise who make a conscious effort about their decisions and attitudes toward women. Men who encourage women and talk to them about substantive issues, issues on the field in which they are involved and decisions that affect them, do well to bring unity and utilize everyone's giftings on their field (Hunt 1990, 176). Qualified women should regularly attend and hold positions on field committees since over fifty percent of the issues directly affect the women's work in and outside of the home. Women can also serve on various advisory boards as their interests, involvements, and gifts merit (ibid.,180).

Today many, many missionary women are speaking out, articles and books are being written, and gender issues in missions finally have some platform for discussion. Many writings conclude with suggestions for mission leaders (e.g., boards, agencies) to consider all angles of women's needs and their abilities to serve as mutual partners called by God into missions.

Conference series established in various parts of the country focusing on missionary women in their roles as wives, mothers, hostesses, teachers, counselors, and church leaders realize the need to balance all of these roles to fulfillment while avoiding frustration or failure (Skeleton 1986, 411). During an interview with Dr. Stephen Sweatman, president of Mission Training International, he concurred with the concerns expressed in this chapter. He emphasized the need for retreats and conferences before going to the field as well as regularly during years of service. He and the MTI staff have seen significant differences in those who engage in retreat prior to moving into a host culture as well as profound improvements for those who go for crisis counseling. He also noted that those who "come out" from the field regularly for conferences of this nature also exhibit a greater health overall and ability to make favorable adjustments. These types of conferences, retreats, and counseling events could take place on the field as well with centralized gatherings for women ministering to a particular people group or in a specific geographic location. Women respond well to such gatherings, remarking that they have a place to vent, and can receive affirmation and the impetus to go on (ibid., 415).

Within mixed gender settings such as field fellowships, committee meetings, or even pre-field orientations, uniform educational requirements for both genders helps to provide qualified workers while validating both men and women in their abilities. Selection and placement of candidates should be based on gifts and abilities, not gender. Mission boards should avoid glaring inconsistencies like restricting ordained women or women with PhDs when less qualified men are given tasks or positions instead. Leadership development objectives should be set for both men and women. Couples and families should also have a place of reckoning in a safe, supportive environment (Patterson 1989, 69–70). Ideally organizations will begin the transformations to avoid gender exclusions and meet the needs of both genders as well as the overall purpose of evangelism and missions. Meanwhile, individuals should examine their own situations.

For the individual woman to know herself and set her own personal goals provides an element of control of the foreign scenario. Goal setting includes determining to be a friend in order to find and have friends. Once a woman can sit back, pray, and assess the situation in which she finds herself and begin to order her private, internal life, she will better be able to cope with the external. She will also be better in tune with the Lord's purpose in her as she strives to minister to others for his glory.

INTERVIEWS

Interviews were conducted both in person and via email questionnaire. The data was collected from the following respondents:
— Geographic areas: Western and Eastern Europe, Africa, Asia, and the Pacific
— Genders participating: 8 males (ages 31–60); 8 females (ages 31–60)
— Missionary terms ranged from 4–20 years on the field
— Marital Status: 12 married (not all are couples) and 1 single female

Missionary Case #1
Female missionary with non-denominational mission agency.
Served first as single missionary.
Married at age 28. Two sons.
Served 16 years in South Pacific with tribal people and 2 years in metropolitan capital city.
The name "Martha" is a pseudonym.

As a single missionary, Martha felt that she had a valid part in the work of the mission organization. She and another single woman were assigned translation work among a particular group of people. Once she was married, she and her husband worked side by side in another language group. Both had the same educational background and both were involved in translation work as well as other tasks that the organization deemed important toward the goals laid out by that mission agency.

Even after having children, Martha still had a vital role in missions as she and her husband had a translation project. There was an element of change due to the attention that her home and children now required. But the mission agency continued to need and utilize her skills. They did, however, apply pressure if she did not fulfill the task—even if it meant less time with her family—expressing that she had been sent to do this particular mission.

The greatest culture shock and gender role adjustment came for Martha when, after sixteen years with tribal people in Irian Jaya, her family was transferred to Jakarta, a metropolitan city. The two years there were tumultuous for her to the point that she experienced a great deal of cross-cultural stress. Eventually, after returning home, she became critically ill. This was brought on by extreme stress in several areas.

To begin with, the work in the capital city was an administrative position primarily for her husband, and the same type of work that she had done for so long did not find a place in this new environment. The mission agency gave her mixed messages of her importance and usefulness. They seemed upset by the fact that she was not able to do a job that contributed to mission goals.

The homemaking scenario found a twofold complication. The family inherited house help, so as Martha established a new home, she had to contend with live-in help. One nineteen-year-old young lady stayed on while others quit frequently. Martha was unaware that in this culture she was to be a mother to anyone under her roof. When the nineteen-year-old exhibited culturally unacceptable behavior (unknown to Martha), other help would be offended and leave.

Meanwhile, Martha was not only trying to establish her own bearings but constantly training new help. She felt that the time it took to keep her household functioning was taking away from work for the mission. When she finally realized what was happening, she found herself in a very distressing dilemma.

Martha's Western culture would prescribe individuality for hired help. She viewed her role as only an employer and not as a mother. As a mother she was expected to correct the young girl's behavior socially as well as her abilities to work. This one required her intrusion into the young girl's life for correction and personal, moral training. Martha's husband was involved in his own work outside the home and consequently did not participate in this conflict. Further, Martha felt guilty for 1) not being involved with mission work outside the home that she felt pressure to do, and 2) not being aware that there was a mission field right there in her own home with the house help.

The two-year tumult gained further complications because of a crisis the mission agency faced which deeply affected Martha's husband. This caused the two of them to be so entrenched in their own stresses, and often debilitated by them, that they had no time nor little compassionate energy left for one another. Also, Martha had gained inroads to the expatriate community to which she believed God had opened doors. Excited about this opportunity to minister, she received speaking invitations. This certainly helped her feelings of frustration and uselessness. However, the mission organization suggested that she curb her activities with expatriates as the mission goal was Bible translation for unreached indigenous groups, rather than ministry to one's own culture. They stated that these were not the specified reasons for their being in that country and the opportunities did not meet the agency's goals and purpose statement. Consequently, the only valid outside evangelical ministry available to Martha was restricted, but there was nothing to do within the organization either.

All of this brought up another point in Martha's thinking. "What about those trusting people in the States who are supporting us, expecting that I'm using God's money to further the Kingdom?" Finally the composite of unresolved conflicts and impasses resulted in critical illness after they had returned to the States.

Missionary Case #2
Couple—Missionaries with denominational mission agency
Married at age 28 (f) and 40 (m).
Two children (boy and girl).
Served four years in Eastern Europe, two years furlough, and are
    now returning for four more years.
Names "Diane" and "Rob" are pseudonyms.

Rob and Diane have a strong, healthy marriage. They came to a saving knowledge of Jesus Christ together after they were married a short time. Having served as laity in their home church for some time, they felt called to be missionaries in a specific country and to a particular people group in Eastern Europe.

On most issues of missions and ministry they seem to agree. On gender issues they functionally understand the roles in America as well as in their host country. Though the stresses of serving in a third world, quite impoverished country have taken their toll, both Rob and Diane strive to talk about issues affecting each and both of them. They have agreed upon their own handling of gender related issues within their home, despite the culture, and concluded that they need to conform to the culture outwardly but will make necessary adjustments between them.

Diane expressed several examples of this. "Women are not viewed as equal to men. They do not participate freely in conversation with men or where men are present; men make the important decisions. My husband did realize and try to help. In public he tried to, without demeaning me, respect their ways. In private he remained an American husband." She went on to say that he considered and valued her opinions and comments.

Another example of acculturating was expressed by Rob. "Water shortages force women to find water and haul it (literally) home during dry summer months. Men never do housework. So I waited for Diane to get the water to the first floor of the apartment building, then I secretly hauled it up to the fourth floor. Also I would often get up at 3:00 a.m. to draw water during shortages, and no one knew I did that."

The difficulties and stresses for both came in a fairly natural fashion. Both passed through the honeymoon stage of mission, in Rob's words, "to disassociation to acceptance of [host country] as they are." Both concurred that they dealt with issues as they arose and that Diane, especially, kept a normal and balanced home for Rob and the children, which provided a sanctuary for them all. Rob also considers it a crucial part of his ministry to maintain their own cultural norms without stepping on the host culture's norm and to focus on Diane as his primary ministry. "Our relationship will last long after this time of our life, and it is imperative to keep all of our personal building blocks and expectations of the relationship in place."

They also concurred that the biggest strain is on Diane. "Demands on the physical body, emotions, and time are great on the field." Overload, as she explains, in one or more of these areas caused the most friction and exhaustion. They had difficulty finding time alone as a family, even though this is for them a priority. In that culture, no one knocks and people drop by constantly. She was most in need of furlough and many times thought she would not make it.

Throughout their first term, Diane prayed and prayed for a best friend. Although she was surrounded by women, there was never a strong affinity with someone who could be a confidante. She had one very special, close missionary friend whose work took her throughout Eastern Europe. Although they shared deeply, they were not often in the same geographic location. This absence of intimate friendships with women proved to be the single most difficult factor for Diane because she needed that type of support and team structure.

Early on she realized that her position would be based on her husband's and her home. She has made it an act of her will to focus on God's calling. "I count it a privilege to be on the field and don't really have major complaints about treatment as a woman. God put us there, and whatever happens, I trust we'll be there as long as he wills. Men and women are different and I can deal with how I get treated, probably more easily than most, because I know my husband respects me and protects me and promotes me (even in my own eyes) and he encourages me." This seems to be the stabilizing factor of their successful marriage and work on the field. Rob, of course, has outside work with the nationals, the church, and government when necessary. Along with this, as previously mentioned, is Rob's focus on Diane. Diane's ministry largely involves her home, hospitality (one of her primary gifts), and women's ministries in the church as an outreach. She views these as vital parts of the entire picture of their denomination's ministry in this host country.

As they prepare to return, Diane prays again for a good friendship to develop there in the country. "I am home preparing to return this summer. No major changes over the first term are anticipated. As I pack up enough stuff to last four years, I am packing more household furnishings, as much of my ministry centers around the home and there is nowhere to go but home. So I plan to make it somewhat nicer. How do you do that when you might lose it all in an evacuation? But there will be no more camping out if this is truly home!"

Missionary Case #3
Female missionary with denominational mission agency.
Married. Three children.
Served twelve years in Africa.
"Louise" and husband "Lawrence" are pseudonyms.

In the case of Louise, during a time of adjustments it was expressed that although her husband was aware of their difficulties adjusting, he was also dealing with culture shock and learning how to cope with his own adjustments. Finally, at one point her husband, Lawrence, did stop and listen. He responded to her calmly. "If it is too much for you, we will go back to the USA." Immediately she knew that he had heard her. She felt an affirming closeness taking away the feelings of being trapped.

Louise described the tensions within the family prior to that moment. "There seemed to always be too much to do with too little time. The demands on a person are high because the need on the foreign field seems so gigantic compared to the personal needs of family that seem so insignificant. To stay focused on putting your family first is a challenge and usually a source of arguments. Sometimes the nationals don't understand why you make the family such an important issue. There is also enormous pressure from the nationals for you to conform to their culture, even to adjust your family needs and traditions. And very little understanding when you don't."

This quote clearly presents a plethora of pressures which had been tugging at and stressing Louise. Most likely this was happening to her husband as well, causing strife inside their home. She expressed a feeling of inadequacy because 1) there is too much to do and too little time, and 2) the expectations of the nationals conflict with her home and her own culture. The cycle can result in bitterness and resentment between the couple and/or between them and the indigenous church members.

When asked how Lawrence related to her during this later time Louise replied, "At times my husband was insensitive, harsh, and demanding, especially after he started getting involved in ministry and I was still coping with adjustments and culture shock and trying to keep the kids from knowing that I was having such a difficult time." Consequently anxiety and isolation built up inside of Louise.

REFERENCES

Adeney, M., J. Briscoe, M. Kassian, and J. Thompson. 1996. Ministering Women. *Christianity Today,* 40(4): 14–21.

Allen, F. 1986. "Why Do They Leave? Reflections on Attrition." *Evangelical Missions Quarterly,* 22(2): 118–122.

Briscoe, J. 1997. How to Be Friends with Jesus' Friends. *Enrichment,* 2(2): 12–15.

Carlson, D. L. 1998. Exposing the Myth that Christians Should Not Have Emotional Problems. *Christianity Today,* 42(2): 29–35.

Cummings, D. 1987. Programmed for Failure—Mission Candidates at Risk. *Evangelical Missions Quarterly,* 23(3): 240–246.

DeVries, S. B. 1986. Wives: Homemakers or Mission Employees? *Evangelical Missions Quarterly,* 22(4): 402–410.

Dixon, J. 1990. Unrealistic Expectations: The Downfall of Many Missionaries. *Evangelical Missions Quarterly,* 26(4): 388–393.

Duvall, N. S., and M. E. Hall. 2002. Married Women in Missions: The Effects of Role Expectations on Well-being and Self-esteem. In *Enhancing Missionary Vitality: Mental Health Profession Serving Global Mission,* ed. J. R. Powell and J. M. Bowers, 153–158. Palmer Lake, CO: Mission Training International.

———. 2003. Married Women in Missions: The Effects of Role Expectations on Well-being and Self-esteem. *Journal of Psychology & Theology,* 31(4): 303–314. La Mirada, CA: Biola University.

Grant, R. 1995. Trauma in Missionary Life. *Missiology,* 23(1): 71–83.

Hunt, C. F. 1990. How to Meet the Needs of Women on Your Team. *Evangelical Missions Quarterly,* 26(2): 174–180.

Janssen, G. 1989. *Women Overseas: A Christian Perspective on Cross-Cultural Adaptation.* Yarmouth, ME: Intercultural Press.

Jones, M. 1995. *Psychology of Missionary Adjustment.* Springfield, MO: Gospel Publishing House.

McGee, G. 1986. *This Gospel Shall Be Preached.* Springfield, MO: Gospel Publishing House.

Oberg, K. 1960. Culture Shock: Adjustment to New Cultural Environments. *Practical Anthropology,* 7(4): 77–82.

Patterson, V. 1989. Women in Missions: Facing the 21st Century. *Evangelical Missions Quarterly,* 25(1): 62–71.

Powell, J. R., and J. M. Bowers, eds. 2002. *Enhancing Missionary Vitality: Mental Health Professions Serving Global Missions.* Palmer Lake, CO: Mission Training International.

Royer, G. L. 1996. *Models for Fulfilling Missions.* Waxahachie, TX: Southwestern Assemblies of God University.

Skeleton, M. 1986. Gap in Women's Needs Addressed. *Evangelical Missions Quarterly,* 22(4): 411–415.

Sweatman, S. 2011. Interview at Biola University.

Tuggy, J. T. 1966. *The Missionary Wife and Her Work.* Chicago: Moody Press.

Van Rheenen, G. 1996. *Missions: Biblical Foundations and Contemporary Strategies.* Grand Rapids, MI: Zondervan Publishing House.

Williams, M. O. 1979. *Partnership in Missions.* Springfield, MO: Division of Foreign Missions.

Wilson, L. 1996. Women and Culture Shock. *Evangelical Missions Quarterly,* 32(4): 442–449.

FOUR

Constraints and Opportunities
Laurel A. (Cocks) McAllister

For the feast, whom do you sit with?

Quite a dilemma for a single woman missionary working on an unwritten language project in a rural area! The constraints that she and her single missionary colleague on the committee encountered in ministry were many. The members of the committee were working in a second language most of the time, some of them in their third language. Life was physically hard, living in a village where everyone had to get water from a source some distance away or hire somebody to get it. This missionary's own cultural values, a strong work ethic learned from her childhood, became a constraint that often pushed her to work beyond a healthy limit.

Also, she and her colleague were always third category persons, being single. They were accepted—they were educated and they owned a vehicle. However, they were the only women on the language committee—all other members were men. And, for social occasions and feasts, there was always that awkward question, whom do you sit with?

The issue was more being a woman than it was being single: anyone who didn't know them very well had questions (often unspoken), like, "Why aren't you married?" and "Where is your husband?" It was hard for the local people to understand them, but their being single didn't seem to be a constraint. That gave them more freedom to do the work, but facing the interaction effect of these constraints was extremely challenging.

If constraints are part of life, and they are—for both men and women missionaries—how do women missionaries use their God-given gifts and strengths in the face of sometimes overwhelming constraints? In evangelical Protestant missions today, women make up approximately two-thirds of the personnel. God is surely glorified and the gospel of Jesus Christ is proclaimed more effectively when these women are encouraged to use their gifts and to fulfill their calling. Today's world is needier than ever before, with the concerns of women and girl children to be addressed, and many culturally restricted areas open only to the ministry of women.

Mission organizations sometimes utilize research and ideas from the corporate world. An important development of the 1990s has been the affirmation and encouragement of women's leadership styles (Helgesen 1990). Well into the twenty-first century, women are now serving on mission boards, in member care and staff development departments, and on leadership teams. However, few evangelical missions have women in top leadership positions. One possible reason may be that women are perceived to be less visionary than men and therefore overlooked for top positions. This interesting finding came to light in a recent study of over 2,000 male and female executives from 149 countries (Ibarra and Obodaru 2009). Forward-looking mission organizations would do well to review such studies in order to find out how women, as well as men, can take advantage of opportunities to learn the skills that enhance envisioning, a key component in strategic leadership roles.

Even a cursory look at the history of modern missions points to the important role women have played. Many identities and contributions, however, have been omitted or given a mere passing reference in many mission histories. Samuel Escobar has described this as "the strange loss of memory about the massive involvement of women in missions" (1996, 18). Recent historical and biographical research into the roles and contributions of women missionaries has begun to prove helpful in righting this imbalance (Robert 1996). My research provides further perspective, going beyond exemplary women in missions from the past to address the daily struggles of women missionaries today—through identifying the constraints that they encounter as they minister inter-culturally—and allowing their voices to be heard with clarity.

My concern for the issues of women missionaries grew out of my personal and professional experience: ten years as a single missionary teacher, sixteen years engaged in training women and men for inter-cultural ministry around the world and coordinating annual workshops for women missionaries in particular. During this time, I listened to the heartbeat of hundreds of women, members of a wide variety of evangelical mission organizations and churches. I sensed their deep commitment to carry out the call of God on their lives. Their accounts of disappointments and stumbling blocks, as well as their joys and open doors to ministry, gave me a broad perspective in the foundational thinking of my doctoral dissertation, *Constraints Encountered in Ministry Activity: Single and Married Women Missionaries* (Cocks 1997).

My research addresses the constraints women missionaries en-counter as they carry out ministry activity. I also address the personal impact of the constraints on women, and the forms and effectiveness of their coping strategies. Through careful articulation and broader understanding of the issues facing women missionaries, my hope is that we can better equip both women and men in missions so that they can work together for more effective service in the kingdom of God.

The findings reported here are based on the face-to-face struc-tured interviews I conducted with twenty-six members of evangelical Protestant missions, both single and married women. They had all lived and ministered interculturally for at least six years and for at least two terms of service. The women spoke freely and illustrated their answers liberally with stories about experiences throughout their lives. They told these special stories with deep emotion and humor. Many expressed appreciation to me for the opportunity to recount these experiences of God's grace in times of sadness, stress, and also great enjoyment. Interacting with these women was a privilege as I entered with them into these deeply personal stories.

Analyzing their experiences also proved interesting. An important part of this analysis was a comparison between the responses of the single and married women missionaries.

CONSTRAINTS ENCOUNTERED IN MINISTRY ACTIVITY

The term *constraints* refers to things that held the women back or limited or hindered them in any way in their ministries. The women did not find this term negative. Rather, constraints were simply part of the reality of intercultural ministry in a fallen world where life does not always run smoothly, and where one has to cope with certain issues and situations. The constraints can be grouped any of a number of ways. Here I address constraints associated with culture and language, marital status and role, gender, children, interpersonal relationships, and organization.

Culture and Language

The culture and language of the host country was the constraint mentioned most often. The strength of its impact depended somewhat on the host culture itself and its attitudes toward women. The effect of the culture and language constraint on life and ministry was somewhat different for the married women than for the singles.

For married women, facing cultural differences meant relating to the country's medical and educational systems and to the national church, as well as setting up and managing a household. They faced role ambiguity and conflict as missionaries, and as wives and mothers. Most were expected to carry out ministry as missionaries, and they had the desire to do so, but often lacked time and energy because of their responsibility for managing the household.

Ministry for one woman and her husband meant having an "open door" for people with whom they were building relationships. This was especially difficult when their children were small. Visitors tended to come between 4 and 7 p.m., the worst time of day for small children! The solution was to have their helper stay longer hours to help care for the children, serve tea, and cook food the visitors liked. When guests came, the hosts always had to feed them and never be too busy for them, or else they would never come back—they had to feel welcome.

The local orientation toward children, that they are to be seen and not heard and never ever disturb guests, represented a big cultural barrier to overcome. However, for this couple and for the other married women in the study, coping required being willing to put down roots, to live life for the long haul, and to be realistic in the cultural context where they ministered. They accepted the good and the bad; they determined to learn, listen, and laugh; they organized their homes to meet family needs and also ministry demands; and they built relationships with a variety of people in their communities.

One woman commented, "When I was weary or feeling down, I went to the market. I got a new perspective on what life was really all about. They [the local people] built me up; they always made me feel good about myself. It [a visit to the market] kept forcing me to get next to the real person in the street."

For single women, the constraints of culture and language included divergent values, different ways of thinking and living, and the stress of working within the complexities of an unfamiliar cultural system. Although aspects of the local culture could be a source of frustration, anger, and confusion, single women also observed that they increasingly found elements to appreciate and enjoy in the culture and people. They wore national dress, learned local cooking, and adapted their homes to better suit their ministry needs. As they experimented with behaviors and ministry initiatives, they found that they had to change their ways and sometimes apologize to those they had offended. Like the married women, the singles built relationships with a variety of people.

"I realize now that it was because of personal relationships and friendships and getting acquainted with their families, living on their standard and not mine, that I think bridged the gaps," reflected a single missionary who had navigated through cultural and language differences for twenty-three years.

Marital Status and Role

Marital status was a constraint specifically identified by the single women. Even though the married women did not identify this constraint, their roles were affected by the fact that they were married. In most cultures, being married brings acceptability and status. The personal impact of being single, however, did vary with the geographical and cultural location.

When being single was viewed as a constraint to be coped with in their host or home culture, they tended to find creative ways, acceptable in the culture, to carry out life and ministry. For example, in a culture where a moral single woman does not live alone, one missionary coped by building a relationship with a key family who then introduced her to the community. Several found living with another single missionary helpful. Undergirding their coping activities was the knowledge and acceptance of God's control and grace in every aspect of their lives.

The married women mentioned the constraint of having to develop their own ministry role(s) within the context of, or in a manner that was aligned with, their husbands' role. For some, this was expected and normal, even helpful in a difficult situation. Much depended on the ministry situation and the couple's relationship, as the following story illustrates.

In the early days when their ministry was developing and the children were small, one couple lived in a large city. The husband traveled by motorcycle up into the surrounding mountains to get acquainted with the people they were interested in ministering to. When he returned, they talked for hours about ministry and people, brainstorming ideas. This was a truly mutual relationship in which the wife felt very much a part of the ministry. She later developed a relationship with a young woman student who became a key person in the ministry there. Through her, the missionary couple learned how the people think and how to help them. The wife's relationship with this young woman made all of this possible.

Other married women talked of constraints that were a source of stress, like being expected only to make her husband's vision succeed, dealing with changes in her own position resulting from changes in her husband's role (e.g., when he became field leader or they changed organizations or fields), and coping when her husband's stress in ministry increased. In some organizations, the role of a leader's wife is not highly valued, or even discussed adequately by everyone involved before the transition takes place. This ambiguity and uncertainty causes the wife personal distress and unexpected difficulties in fulfilling her ministry. It is an unnecessary, damaging constraint, and great loss for the kingdom of God!

The types of impact the married women reported were fear and lowered self-confidence, uncertainty, loss of relationships, and isolation. They usually coped by getting involved where they saw needs in the community. This required refocusing the ministry activities to meet the expectations for their marital status and gender, such as evangelizing and discipling women and children, volunteering in a home for orphans, or holding seminars for missionary and national women.

At times, when they knew they had reached their limit, some women withdrew for a short time within themselves in order to find renewal in God, or they took advantage of Bible studies in English. As one woman described her action during a stressful time, "Up until that point I had tried not to get involved with Americans and things in English. But I just felt like I needed that Bible study." This support gave her the strength and encouragement to go on.

Gender

Gender constraints interacted with both culture and marital status constraints. Single women identified the gender constraint much more often than did married women.

Being single, and a foreign woman, was especially difficult—and abusive—in certain traditional societies. No coping strategy seemed to work very well for many. These poignant words sum up the problem: "I tried to disguise myself: it didn't help. It must be the way I walk. I'd cover, I'd dress, but they knew I was a foreigner. A constant stress was always there."

In less closed traditional societies, the single women still found ambiguity in the roles that society gave them. In the work setting, they were included with the men, but they were social anomalies and, therefore, not well understood. In her ministry running mobile medical clinics to rural villages, one woman saw herself walking a fine line between being seen as a neutral person (neither man nor woman) or as a macho woman. Neither categorization appeared desirable from her viewpoint!

All coped by working as hard as they could in their ministries, and functioning as men when necessary (in such ways as caring for vehicles and maintaining buildings). They also managed the ensuing stress by getting away, exercising, listening to music, and fellowshipping with other single women, as well as enjoying time with missionary couples and their children and with national friends.

Less commonly reported in this study, but evident in many mission fields, is the difficulty that single women face as they serve as leaders in ministry. One experienced woman heard this challenge on several occasions from younger male team members who had recently arrived in the country. "You're a woman. You can't teach a man. God won't bless."

In truth, she had been leading a neighborhood Bible study (for men and women) for several years, God had been blessing, and the church was growing. It wasn't a problem to the team leader or others on the team. And, as she wryly commented, "It wasn't like some man had fallen because I had taught him!"

Such a challenge to a gifted, godly woman felt like "an emotional blow." Challenges similar to this caused others to wonder about their gifts and callings. They coped by going to the Lord about it all, and by trying to sort out the issues with team members. The pain was remembered as they recounted the experiences, however, even though as one put it, "We all settled into different levels of comfort and areas of service...Yeah, the dust settled, and life and ministry went on."

One wonders about the mission's selection procedure, the importance of posting new missionaries to fields and teams where there is a good fit, and the importance of guiding men and women on expectations for women's roles before they are sent to the field. Many missions now have good policies and practices in place for missionary member care so that damaging conflict in this area can be avoided. In this regard, the *Code of Best Practice for Member Care* developed by the Evangelical Fellowship of Canada (2002) is a resource that some missions are finding helpful.

Children

A constraint for women with more than one child was the children. These mothers faced great role overload as they coped with challenging situations such as difficulty in attending or completing language school, managing and/or directing homeschooling, maintaining the children's schedule, or caring for them while the husband traveled, all within a different cultural context.

How heavy this constraint became seemed to depend on the woman's personality and gifts, the degree of support from her husband, and the cultural setting. When these factors became too many and too negative, the impacts expressed were difficulty, frustration, guilt, and tension. However, for a more easygoing person with linguistic ability and both a supportive husband and a supportive mission, the response regarding meeting children's needs was, "At different times in your life, your family itself and homeschool itself become a priority in terms of having a mission."

Those feeling greater constraint did cope by taking the children with them to meetings, to the market, to church, or to visit in the community. Some organized their homes and learned to work with house help so that they could minister through hospitality and yet keep the children's schedule as much as possible. Some shared with other mothers in the care of the children, although they wished for more of this than they had.

A small minority homeschooled their children, but then only after some experience with national schools and when it seemed the best option. The mothers kept clear communication with the children and tried to maintain a good balance between structure and flexibility.

All the mothers implied, and several mentioned, that their children loved the country where they lived and thought of it as home. One mother told why: "I would take my kids to the market. That's where they learned to love _____. All my kids would die to go back!"

Interpersonal Relationships

Conflicts and differences of opinion with other missionaries represented unique challenges and became a source of stress for many. Although neither the single nor the married women cited this as a major constraint, conflict among missionaries was evident. All who did identify this as a constraint felt very deeply the impact of breakdowns in interpersonal relationships.

The most common issue for the single women had to do with the functioning of the teams on which they served. Varying expectations for effective teams contributed to constraints in ministry. Lack of ministry focus caused frustration, and a related constraint—independence among team members—left a single woman feeling lonely and unconnected. Another felt isolated when she had to handle heavy leadership responsibilities alone. Yet another wondered if a needed break in the United States for rest and counseling might have been averted if she had not been so alone. Members of one team slid into an unhealthy conforming relational pattern in the face of many behavioral expectations, such as pressure to tell everyone everything they were doing. This kind of artificial community became emotionally confining, rather than the safe environment that single women appreciate.

Some teams functioned with strict accountability patterns. How much this was a constraint depended on the personality of the single woman. It was not much of an issue if she easily rolled with the punches and kept lines of communication open. It also depended on what the issue was. If it involved a difference in theological understanding of women's roles, it was harder to handle.

Most of the single women had experienced a variety of living situations. Options included living alone, with national women, with other missionary women, or, very occasionally, with a missionary family. About half felt they had a degree of control over their housing situation, and this increased their satisfaction and sense of well-being as they faced various constraints in ministry. Most of them did not say that living with other single missionary women was a major problem to them.

Good coping strategies for singles with these interpersonal constraints include interaction with nationals, missionaries from other organizations, families with children, and colleagues. It is also good to take regular breaks from the situation in order to stay healthy and have the ability to cope with difficulties.

Field-wide conflicts created a great deal of stress for several of the married women involved, especially when their husbands held leadership positions. One field had a long history under a leader who made all the decisions for the field. This strong, one-man style led to unhealthy communication patterns throughout the field and created an atmosphere of secrecy, unspoken demands, and power struggles among the missionaries. After he left office, a married man who had served on the field council was appointed. The style of the new leader was more participative and open, but the field remained stuck in the past. The leader's wife was unprepared for the change in her position and the pressure on her from other missionaries who thought she might now have access to information and power. She felt caught in the middle, and they both found that their relationships with other missionary couples changed. The mission sent out a counselor to help everyone cope with the situation, but the emotional trauma took some time to heal. In another situation of field conflict, the missionary couple tried to bring the difficult situation into the open on the field and then talked to leadership in the United States.

Interaction with missionaries from other organizations was sometimes experienced as a constraint. Some sat in judgment on one couple's ministry, bringing an initial response of frustration and anger before the woman decided to laugh and keep her reactions between herself and her husband. When an organization accused another couple of "sheep stealing," the only way to cope was to let go of the new relationships they had been building and begin to develop another ministry.

The interpersonal relationship constraints of the single women seemed to occur most often on their ministry teams, while most of the married women did not refer to team conflicts. Possible explanations for this difference include the following factors. Some couples did not work closely in ministry with other missionary couples. Those who did work on a team or institutional staff may have had realistic expectations regarding interpersonal conflict. When ministry is one's major role, as it was for the single women, team relationships are of prime importance. Team conflicts may then cause more pain for single women than they would for married women who have to put much of their energy into other important roles, such as wife and mother.

Organization

When questioned specifically about how their missions functioned, the women described various policies and practices. Both single and married women said that in the candidate process, men and women were treated equally—each expected to meet certain standards, and each appointed as a missionary. Women occupied leadership positions in some organizations (though not at the top) and also were board members. Several said that mission policy regarding women's roles had broadened in recent years, and that women's roles were currently under discussion.

I found considerable variance across mission organizations in the roles accorded to married women. Most missions seemed to give families the freedom to decide how much the wife and mother would minister. The majority of the women in such organizations said they were happy with this arrangement, usually participating actively with their husbands in ministry. For some women, however, this role ambiguity and lack of direction left them feeling devalued. This was especially the case for one woman, formerly a single missionary who had been affirmed in her ministry. She found that her contributions as a married missionary were valued only insofar as they helped her husband's ministry to succeed.

Several others said they felt pressure—from more energetic women or even from their own husbands—to do more than they thought they were able to. Possible explanations for this pressure may include a history of strong, active women in the mission and/or an organizational ethos that valued women working hard alongside their husbands.

Several said that women had freedom to do whatever ministries were available within the constraints of culture. Interestingly, the constraining aspect of culture was rooted more in the culture that the missionaries brought with them than the culture to which they had gone. Attitudes toward women's roles varied somewhat across mission organizations, depending on the mind-set of specific field directors and/or the men on the field. Discrepancies between women's roles in the United States and abroad were also identified, with most women perceiving substantially greater freedom in ministry abroad than at home. One woman summed up this contradiction: "We've had many instances where we've had our single women do everything that can be done."

Several single women with important ministry responsibilities experienced frustration in their interactions with mission leadership. God gave one woman the vision for a language and orientation program for new missionaries and also the ability to develop and lead it for over twenty years. Recognizing her limitations in administration, she asked the mission for someone to help. Instead, she was affirmed that she was doing a good job, which sometimes felt like only a pat on the shoulder. When she was encouraged to take a degree in intercultural studies in preparation for increasing the scope of the program, she was delighted. However, she was shocked to find, on her return to the field, that the mission had appointed a younger man with little intercultural training as supervisor of the whole program, and herself as linguistic advisor. Didn't the mission know what she had just been studying and preparing for?

However, the mission (and God, she says!) gave the two of them six months to get to know each other and learn to work together. Not easy for either of them, but a wise decision, as she noted in retrospect. To their surprise, they found that their vision did go in the same direction, and they became good friends as well as respected colleagues. She also became sure of the importance of his leadership. The final miracle, in this saga of miracles, came when she convinced the top mission leadership that he was the leader to make the program better! They continued to work together, in their areas of giftedness and experience, so that the program became a model for other fields.

Many times over the years, this woman found that she desperately needed to depend on God's call on her life. She said, with deep emotion, of one such experience, "I was never tempted to quit as a missionary, but once I wanted to leave my mission. I fasted and prayed for three days, and the Lord showed me it was right to stay—it would have been well to do that more often."

All the women attributed their long-term missionary commitment to a calling from God. However, many were also able to outline ways they would have appreciated help from their missions, and ways in which they could have helped their missions more.

HOW MISSIONS COULD HAVE BEEN MORE HELPFUL AND WOMEN IN TURN COULD HAVE HELPED THEIR MISSIONS

A number of the women said they had seen improvements in their missions so that what they would have found helpful is now current practice. Some examples are pre-field training, ongoing training for missionaries and field leaders, reentry help, and debriefing after a term of service. Other women still saw the need for more help in these areas. Some expressed a desire for more visits from headquarters staff, for encouragement and improved understanding of missionaries' lives and concerns, including the particular needs of wives. Helpful visitors would probably include women, but any visitors would need to listen well and inquire effectively for greater understanding. These qualities and skills would be more important than the gender of the visitor, provided there was an atmosphere of mutual trust.

A memory from my own field experience surfaced as I heard the women's voices and their stories. One year when our international director visited us at the annual field conference, he listened carefully to me and encouraged me to take a needed change of direction. His wife accompanied him on that trip, and her gracious sharing of her own life journey brought a new level of openness and sharing among the missionaries.

The kind of help the women mentioned would be useful for all missionaries, men included! In fact, one woman said that having some-one from their organization "personally caring and keeping up with us might have helped prevent my husband's burnout." Although they were not part of this research, single men very likely face many of the constraints that single women do. These would include lack of under-standing in the host culture about their not being married and, in the missionary culture, dealing with the false assumption that they should carry extra ministry responsibility because they do not have family demands on their time and finances. Single missionaries also have to keep up with specific tasks such as communicating with their mission and raising financial support, all without the help of a spouse.

When asked how they could have helped their missions more, several of the women found the question difficult to answer. Others mentioned that they wished they had spent more time in prayer and been more of an encouragement to leadership. However, half of both single and married women said they wished they had been more open in sharing and giving input on the particular issues they were involved in, through letters or face-to-face, in appropriate ways, to those responsible.

Several thought they could have better communicated their needs but did not think of expressing them at the time, or did not believe that their concerns would have been seriously addressed. Others wished they had taken more responsibility to bring about change. One expressed it this way: "I could have tried to help the men on the team see that women need to be part of the team—in on decisions."

All expressed the need for more and clearer communication, both with home and field leadership. "I lost opportunities for ministry by not communicating enough, by leaving things to assumption," said one woman, thoughtfully but regretfully.

These comments show the women shifting the responsibility from the organization, with its predominantly male leadership, to themselves as members of the organization—a heavy load of responsibility indeed. They also tried to put the best interpretation on the situation and make the most of it. While expressing regret about lack of communication, lost opportunities, and the difficulties they experienced, the majority of the women said they thought they had been able to use their gifts well, some even very well. "As much as I was willing to put into it," commented one. And from another, "I used just about every gift I had." Still others found that their missionary experience provided "opportunity to learn skills and develop in a more well-rounded way, if the task doesn't match exactly."

Some, however, qualified their statements, "no opportunity to use leadership gifts as a married woman." With a second thought, one admitted, "I never felt squelched—this depended on the men I worked with."

Today, many women continue to be reluctant to speak up even though they are thoughtfully engaged in the missionary task and believe that their perceptions and ideas would be valuable in bringing needed change to their organizations. One does not have to talk very long with missionary women, whether they have retired, resigned, or are still active, to hear similar stories of women who have suffered silently or have tried to communicate but been unable to make their voices heard.

This is not just a phenomenon in mission organizations and churches. Women also choose not to speak up in the business world. Management scholars refer to speaking up as "Issue Selling" and recognize that it is important for women to choose selectively which issues to try to "sell." Under what conditions will women speak up? Research shows that it is important that women trust that management cares and is open to taking action. No trust and women remain silent (Ashford et al. 1998).

CONTRIBUTIONS, COMMITMENTS, AND INFLUENCES

History affirms with clarity that women have had considerable impact for the cause of Christ on world mission and evangelism, and I have no doubt that they will continue to do so in the years to come. The fact that they persevere in ministry, in spite of the constraints and stress that they experience on a daily basis, should not be interpreted either as evidence that all is well or as an endorsement of the status quo. Further action needs to be taken so that all women can be encouraged, empowered, and released for the ministries to which God is calling them.

Before recommending action, it is important to summarize the following themes that recurred throughout the Constraints study.

1. Women evidence great loyalty and commitment to their missions. Most of the women in the study were long-term members and had served with the same organizations throughout their missionary careers.

Surprisingly, only a few identified these organizations as a constraint in carrying out ministry, in spite of the hindrances that seemed clear from the stories they told. Instead, many noted ways in which their organizations had recently improved the care of their members, and thus the missionaries' ability to minister effectively. Though this is true, more effort is needed to lessen organizational constraints and increase the probability of attracting and keeping gifted, qualified women.

2. Women missionaries do not always become involved in organizational matters. For a variety of reasons, many have not been active in championing organizational change to address their concerns. They may feel that they are in a minority position, they may feel that taking on the traditional structure could be too great a risk, or they may not trust that those in leadership will act on their behalf. The practical result is that some women don't rock the organizational boat but leave matters to leadership, to their husbands, or to other women who are gifted in administration. Instead, they use their energy to deal with the organizational constraints as best they can in the course of their busy lives. Women's valuable insights and gifts are thus lost to the Kingdom, and the voices of the women themselves are not heard.

3. Women's commitment to God and to his call on their lives is extremely strong. About half of both single and married women recalled times when they had seriously considered quitting—giving up missionary life and ministry—but they did not. This group of women missionaries persevered through the various constraints that they faced. However, we must be careful not to equate God's call to missionary service with commitment to one specific organization for many years. This could lead only to long-term missionary careers without effective life and service. Organizations should aim for the best practice in missionary retention (Hay et al. 2007). These practices would encourage members to follow their Lord in obedience throughout their lives, wherever this may lead.

4. Devastating effects result from the cumulative stress of isolating factors in women's lives. Both married and single women in the research study felt a strong sense of isolation when they were deprived of important, supportive relationships. Usually a combination of circumstances contributed to such situations.

Several single women related that at times they felt cut off from meaningful, mutual relationships with colleagues. They also felt physical isolation—from team members and/or from mission leadership and thus from needed help and resources—as did the married women. Sometimes the isolation was psychological—from a partner, a spouse who was under a great deal of pressure, or from colleagues in ministry. Cultural isolation caused stress for most of the women, particularly at the beginning of their missionary careers when language and cultural barriers were greatest. However, cultural isolation existed for some women later, too, when desires for deeper, intimate relationships with nationals seemed impossible, or when expectations for ministry were not realized.

No one factor would probably have caused an inordinate amount of stress. However, when several piled up over a period of time—sometimes combined with unexpected personal or family stress—the result was overwhelming. The critical issue of isolation, whether physical, psychological, relational, or cultural, surely demands attention throughout the lives of women missionaries.

5. Male influence is strong within evangelical missions. This influence was felt in several ways. As has already been mentioned, the married women tended to develop their ministry roles within the setting of their husbands. (This, of course, depended on the practice of their mission and worked well for many.) The husband's values regarding the place of women in ministry, in the church, and in the home and family were important in shaping how the wife managed the family and took on ministry responsibilities. The expectations of the man for his wife, and for other women, also had an effect on the direction the ministry

team moved. Increased awareness of the strength of male influence is called for. Unless steps are taken to lessen the negative effects when this dominating influence is misused, women may leave the field or continue to be prevented from using their gifts. We long for God's glory to shine more brightly as men and women minister effectively together.

These themes emerged as I interviewed the women missionaries, listened to their moving stories, and attended to what the data said. Throughout the process, I gained an ever-deeper appreciation for women missionaries and a stronger desire that their voices be heard.

In 2000, my own life took a major change when I married for the first time and moved to British Columbia, Canada. For several years I taught on the cross-cultural ministry faculty at the ACTS Seminary of Trinity Western University in Langley, British Columbia, Canada, and directed the ACTS Intercultural Ministry Centre. I also facilitated workshops in missionary member care and interpersonal skills for missionaries. Now in active retirement, I continue to interact with mission personnel and also with missionaries—from those new to intercultural ministry to veterans with many years of experience. The issues I discovered several years ago continue to be present realities for all, both men and women. In God's grace, however, we still have the opportunity to make a difference.

A POSITIVE RESPONSE TO PRESENT REALITIES

God is calling his people to love and follow him into intercultural ministry. Approximately two-thirds of these "called-out" ones are women. Women missionary candidates, appointees, and missionaries are well educated and experienced in their professions and ministries. They are gifts of God to his church around the world, equipped by him with gifts for service. They must not be reduced, intentionally or by default, to functioning as second-class citizens. Rather, they need to be affirmed in using their God-given gifts and abilities. Married women especially need to see evidence that their own ministry careers, not just those of the men and the single women, are significant.

Women look carefully at mission organizations before they make application to join. They investigate a number of issues, such as how member care is carried out, if women are in leadership and in what roles, and also what policies are in place to ensure that women and men are encouraged to develop throughout their lives.

Women missionaries are eager to serve their God within the context of their organizations. They will try to find the ways and means to minister in spite of the hindrances and constraints they encounter. The reality of living in a fallen world means that various constraints are sure to come. Missions cannot be responsible to save or preserve their members from what is inevitable in intercultural life and service. In fact, biblical theology recognizes that God uses suffering to shape his servants, conform them to the image of Christ, and make them more effective. However, organizations should take all possible steps to nurture and develop each of their members. This means helping to remove or diminish constraints wherever possible, rather than causing constraints. With this in mind, the following suggestions are made to missions, their leaders, and members.

Suggestions to Mission Organizations

- Respect and take advantage of the unique contributions that women make to the world mission enterprise. For example, they tend to bring a relational, nurturing balance to men's factual, rational focus. Women may also pick up cultural nuances more than men do and so help men understand subtleties of the culture in order to minister more effectively.

- Regard women as full missionaries and give recognition for their service. Be sure to mention them by name in listings of staff roles and responsibilities, and in reports, not only in connection with a husband's or male colleague's achievements. Husbands also need to affirm their wives by making appreciative mention of their roles in ministry.

- Provide an organizational environment that values growth and provides for the development of all its members—women and men, married and single. New missionaries expect staff development and lifelong learning opportunities to be part of the organizational culture. The timing for specific learning is critical and needs to be individualized. For example, since constraints to ministry are inherent in certain stages of family life, many missionary mothers will be encouraged when mission leaders communicate their awareness that caring for children and home is an acceptable and important role in which they expect husbands will share the responsibilities. Mothers often need assurance that they are not useless until the children are grown and they are able to make greater contributions to the ministry.

- Encourage all women to take advantage of training opportunities in order to further develop and use their God-given gifts. Experienced women and men colleagues can empower and be advocates for women who hesitate to take a risk and move beyond their comfort level.

- Make clear to candidates when they are joining the mission what the mission's policy and practice is regarding women's role in ministry. Sometimes differences exist between the mission's stated policy and the field or national church policy and practice. If so, let both men and women know so that no unnecessary surprises meet them when they arrive. Also, make candidates aware of the freedom that international professional women may have, as physicians or educators, for example.

- Ensure that all mission appointees receive the best possible preparation for their transitions to a different language and culture. Such training should be realistic regarding the difficulties inherent in the process of learning new ways and integrating into new cultural systems. It should also be positive regarding the advantages and necessity of both wives and husbands learning the language and culture.

- Make ministry assignments carefully, not just on the basis of the husband's role. Encourage field leaders to deal sensitively with gender issues should they arise.
- In ministry transitions, make sure that the wife has a voice in the changes, rather than making decisions only for the husband's ministry role and career. When the family returns to the home country, encourage husbands, wives, and children to continue to talk together about their new vision, and the place, ministry, and life which God has for them all.
- Take intentional steps to bring women into leadership positions. Many missions have sophisticated leadership development initiatives and programs to overcome the lack of emerging leaders. Gifted women, as well as men, need to be included. How can this be accomplished? Men who are concerned about the lack of women leaders in their organizations—and a number are—can feel alone and helpless to bring about change. Meyerson (2001) offers a broad spectrum of incremental approaches for introducing organizational change. She calls this *the quiet way* to introduce *radical change*. Thoughtfully and prayerfully applied, this could become a very effective means to bring about necessary change in mission organizations.
- Coach and mentor women to enter the predominantly male world of mission leadership. A minority position can be a lonely place for women unless they are well prepared. Learning from the experiences of both female and male mentors can increase women's confidence and hope. They will then be encouraged to speak so that their voices are heard and respected, and the door of opportunity is open to other gifted, skilled women as well.

Women and men missionaries are called to treat each other with respect and to build relationships of trust as they encourage and learn from each other. They will then serve effectively together and bring people around the world to love and follow our Sovereign Lord.

Dr. Lyle Schrag,[2] my colleague and friend, offers a wise response to the important issues raised in this chapter on women missionaries and speaks to the broader implications of the mission to which God calls his people:

> As I read this chapter, the challenges or "constraints" of a cross-cultural ministry are evident. What is striking is the fact that women must burrow through extra, and seemingly unfair, layers of challenge in order to unburden themselves of the calling God has clearly given. If Hercules was given 12 tasks to perform, it appears that women have been given 13. Given the added dimensions of challenge, it's not hard to generate a great sense of respect and admiration for the courage and strength evidenced through their graceful persistence.
>
> While the chapter does provide valuable advice that would empower women to serve with greater freedom, I have to believe that the greatest obligation upon any mission agency would be to find a robust voice to honor and respect the presence and service of women. Such a voice should go far beyond the level of appreciation and heartfelt gratitude that, by applauding their heroic service, blesses women who are missionaries. It would reveal core theological values and communicate to a culture what it means to be men and women of God by the way they live, act, and serve together. The issue is not simply a parochial matter of the treatment of women missionaries—it needs to be seen as a cosmic validation of the Gospel, communicating to everyone reached through mission that women, equally with men, are invested with love, honor, and value in the eyes of God.

---

2   Dr. Lyle Schrag is an Associate Professor in Church Leadership at Northwest Baptist Seminary in Langley, BC, Canada.

The Lausanne 2004 Forum for World Evangelization offers a challenging call in this summary affirmation: "We call on the church around the world to work towards full partnership of men and women in the work of world evangelization by maximizing the gifts of all."

REFERENCES

Ashford, S. J., N. P. Rothbard, S. K. Piderit, and J. E. Dutton.1998.Out on a Limb: Role of Context and Impression Management in Selling Gender-Equity Issues. *Administrative Science Quarterly,* 43: 23–57.

Beach, N. 2008. *Gifted to Lead:The Art of Leading as a Woman in the Church.* Grand Rapids, MI: Zondervan Publishing House.

Cocks, L. A. 1997. Constraints Encountered in Ministry Activity: Single and Married Women Missionaries. PhD diss., Trinity International University.

Crawford, N. A. 1999. Perceived Ministry Roles and Measures of Well-being Among Missionary Women. PsyD diss., Wheaton College.

Dzubinski, L. 2011. *Women on the Cutting Edge of Missions:Yesterday and Today.* Retrieved from http://lausanneworldpulse.com/archives.php.

Escobar, S. J. 1996. Mission Studies Past, Present, and Future. *Missiology,* 24(1): 3–29.

Evangelical Fellowship of Canada. 2002. Code of Best Practice in Member Care. In *Doing Member Care Well,* ed. K. O'Donnell, 272–276. Pasadena, CA: William Carey Library.

Hay, R., V. Lim, D. Blocher, J. Ketelaar, and S. Hay, eds. 2007. *Worth Keeping: Global Perspectives on Best Practice in Missionary Retention.* Pasadena, CA: William Carey Library.

Helgesen, S. 1990. *The Female Advantage: Women's Ways of Leadership.* New York: Doubleday/Currency.

Ibarra, H., and O. Obadaru. 2009. Women and the Vision Thing. *Harvard Business Review,* January 2009: 62–70.

Meyerson, D. E. 2001. Radical Change, the Quiet Way. *Harvard Business Review,* October 2001: 92–100.

Lutz, L. 1997. *Women as Risk-Takers for God.* Grand Rapids, MI: Baker Book House.

O'Donnell, K., ed. 2001. *Doing Member Care Well: Perspectives and Practices From Around the World.* Pasadena, CA: William Carey Library.

Robert, D. L. 1996. *American Women in Mission: A Social History of Their Thought and Practice.* Macon, GA: Mercer University Press.

Roembke, L. 2000. *Building Credible Multicultural Teams.* Pasadena, CA: William Carey Library.

Schrag, L. 2012. Personal Correspondence. March 9, 2012.

Spencer, A. B. 1985. *Beyond the Curse: Women Called to Ministry.* Peabody, MA: Hendrickson Publishers.

FIVE

Dealing with Loss
Dianne B. Collard

TEARS! tears! tears!
In the night, in solitude, tears;
On the white shore dripping, dripping, suck'd in by the sand;
Tears—not a star shining—all dark and desolate;
Moist tears from the eyes of a muffled head;—
O who is that ghost?—that form in the dark, with tears?
What shapeless lump is that, bent, crouch'd there on the sand?
...away, at night, as you fly, none looking—
O then the unloosen'd ocean,
Of tears! tears! tears!

—Walt Whitman (1900)

The doors of the airplane closed; the "fasten seat belt" sign was brightly lit. I sat in the crowded row of the economy section between my husband and twelve-year-old son, my face wet with tears. Just a few steps away, left standing in the terminal, were our two eldest children. Our family dream of leaving for the mission field was coming true, but four years later than hoped and now it was tarnished by the reality of the separation from our two college-age children. I wondered how I could feel two diametrically opposing emotions simultaneously…both joy and debilitating sadness assailed me at the same time. Life on the mission field became a cycle of this conflicting reality. Bittersweet became my existence.

What was I experiencing? The emotions I felt were the normal reaction to loss, an all-too-familiar experience in the life of a woman on the mission field. Yet so many women feel guilty for such grief and do not know how to handle it.

THE REALITY OF LOSS

Research and personal experience reveal that loss is an integral part of the missionary experience. The causes and responses are varied, but the pain is an all-too-common theme. According to one writer, "Grief is the pain and suffering experienced after loss…mourning is a period of time during which signs of grief are shown…and bereavement is the reaction to the loss of a close relationship" (Raphael quoted in Humphrey and Zimpher 1996, 1). This phenomenon called grief is a common reaction to any significant loss in our life. Such *loss* is defined as "the state of being deprived of or being without something one has had, or a detriment or disadvantage from failure to keep, have or get" (ibid.).

Loss in the area of relationships is part of the warp and woof of missionary life. The leaving of family, friends, and colleagues is painful, and it only begins with the initial separation at the beginning of the first term. Over the life cycle of any missionary are numerous tearful good-byes. One woman remarked, "The only constant in this life is the constant cycle of farewells—both on the field and at home!"

But there are many other contributing factors to such loss for the missionary woman. Loss is recognized as one of the significant elements in what is called culture shock or transition stress. One of the first writers in this field of study, Dr. Oberg, listed "a sense of loss and feelings of deprivation…in regard to friends, status, profession, and possessions" as one of the six aspects of culture shock (Furnham 1988, 44). Such "loss, grief, and bereavement violate personal boundaries and remove a sense of security and control" (Humphrey and Zimpher 1996, 1). Grieving as a result of a sense of loss is a normal, real reaction to the realities of missionary life.

Arrival in a new culture often strips new missionaries of their feelings of being in control of their circumstances. All the normal cues that affirm they are acting in a socially appropriate manner may disappear. Feelings of incompetence may produce a vague feeling of loss for who they were before. Initial forays into language learning reduce a well-educated and productive adult woman to a child status, or even worse. One missionary in Romania exclaimed the humbling recognition that even the neighbor's dog understood more language than he! This loss of competency often results in a grief response.

Too often the role of a missionary wife is undefined, and therefore success is not measurable either. Again, the loss of feeling of self-esteem may be experienced. Her husband may be defined as the missionary—whether church planter, educator, or another definable role, while often the wife has no defined role. The missionary wife may face a reduction in the occupational status formerly achieved in her home country. Such a life-change produces feelings of loss.

Loss and the accompanying grief reaction may also result from the loss of treasured objects. The missionary journey may demand the surrender of furnishings, jewelry, favorite foods, adequate medical care, or housing—all objects that have great meaning to a person and may even define them in their own culture. It is normal to grieve even these things for a time. While we, as Christians, desire to hold these things with open hands, we still experience the emotional results of their loss.

THE RESPONSE OF GRIEF

The emotional response to loss, whatever the source, is a form of grief. The intensity, length, and recovery will differ depending on the nature of the loss, history of loss in a woman's past experience, and the maturity of the person suffering the loss. But it remains a form of grief.

The reality and work of grief became real to me when nineteen months after arriving on the field we faced the ultimate experience of loss when we received the traumatic news that our eldest son had been murdered in California. Deep grief overwhelmed us, and we began the long journey to rebuild our lives—to create a "new normal"—by incorporating the loss into our lives. The experience of grief over the death of a child overshadowed, yet definitely resonated, with the memories of past losses in my life. I was deeply aware that early experiences of loss as a missionary woman had been a form of grief reaction also. It was similar but obviously not as devastating.

The Reaction of Bereavement

Individual experiences of loss are deeply affected by previous losses and can be either magnified or managed, depending on a person's history of coping with loss. A missionary woman needs to intentionally assess her past reactions and coping skills in preparing for the losses attributed to missionary life. Humphrey and Zimpfer affirm this, writing, "Each loss is influenced by past losses, and each loss will be affected by additional secondary losses...Our belief is that there is never just one loss event...even more significant are the past repressed losses that emerge to compound and complicate the present experience" (1996, 2,8).

While coping mechanisms for such loss appear to be extremely individualized, there are recognized gender differences in response to loss as well. Jim Head gave a helpful chart in a pre-field training session at the Center for Intercultural Training (Head 2010), in regard to gender distinctions in grief response:

Women's Responses	Impact on Husband	Men's Responses	Impact on Wife
Talking and showing emotions	Feeling overwhelmed Responsible to relieve, fix	Keep to self, internalize grief, not burden wife	Feels alone, emotionally disconnected
Lose sexual desire	Feels unloved by lack of interest & intimacy	Seek sexual intimacy for comfort	Feels used
		Overwork or sleep	Feels alone or ignored

My experience with all grief over the losses of missionary life and the loss of my son would affirm many of these distinctions. My grieving husband found strength in burying himself in his work. Traveling to meetings, forming strategies, meeting goals—all became his means of coping with the losses in his life. My response was significantly different. I was easily overwhelmed with the mundane issues of life and desired to retreat. Normal responses of emotional distress, negative physical symptoms, and a preoccupation with personal health, loneliness, anger, and memories of things of the past became very much my focus (as described by Staudacher 1987, 29–38).

One result of the individual nature of response to loss produces the perception of alienation and deep loneliness, even in the midst of a family or team. The need for someone to listen to your story and understand your pain may be intense. Blessed are those women who have team members who understand this need and become the "sounding board" for verbally and emotionally processing grief.

The Resolution Required

The outlook isn't hopeless for someone in such grief. Every missionary woman will experience loss at some level of her life and may have a variety of grief reactions. But God does not leave us in such a miserable state. Loss can be experienced, faced, and positively incorporated into the richness of our lives, if we desire it. According to Karen Kaiser Clark, "Life is change; growth is optional; choose wisely" (Caplan and Lang 1993, 17).

Ultimately each woman will determine whether the loss and accompanying grief will be debilitating or enriching. This was one of the hardest and most significant lessons I learned through the cycles of grief during my life as a missionary. "Resolution is a choice…It demands active response," according to one expert (Humphrey and Zimpfer 1996, 2,61). Recovery from loss is a process that *begins* with the willingness and desire to recover. Thomas Attig wisely states, "We can choose our own responses…we can choose how we reshape our daily lives" (1996, 19).

Recovery Is Possible

Broadly stated, the stages of recovery (categories adapted from James and Cherry 1988, 10) include:

- *Develop awareness.* Recognize the signs of a grief reaction to the losses in your life. Identify your responses and what is prompting them. Often the emotional responses may seem exaggerated, which indicates a deeper source or a compilation of unresolved grieving experiences.
- *Accept responsibility.* It is essential that each woman accept that she is responsible for her attitudes, responses, and actions. While support is needed, it ultimately isn't the responsibility of the mission agency, coworkers, or family to make things better for her; she alone can choose how she will respond.

- *Seek coping strategies.* Be creative in seeking means of maintaining relationships, or building new ones. Communicate appropriately your needs and surrender the unfulfilled areas of your life to our compassionate, loving heavenly Father.
- *Do it.* Be proactive, not merely reactionary. This alone contributes to a sense of personal control and a hope for the future. Ask a colleague or mission leader to help you define your "job description" or role, and be accountable to someone for the fulfillment of this role—whether you are a mother with young children or actively involved in the missionary task outside the home. Surround yourself with something familiar that brings comfort, such as pictures of your family or a painting of home. Keep a journal faithfully, expressing both your pain and plan for recovery. The prophet Jeremiah said, "This I recall…the daily renewed faithfulness of God…therefore, I have hope" (author's paraphrase of Lam 3:21, 22). Review regularly the faithfulness of God in your life—and act in hope. I required each missionary arriving on the field to immediately write out the details of their "missionary call" and to list all God did to enable them to get to the field. They kept one copy and gave me one that we reviewed whenever the challenges, frustrations, and grief became overwhelming.
- *Move beyond loss.* This does not mean that you forget the people or things that you are grieving over. You likely will continue to experience pain over such losses. But loss can be incorporated into one's life, and one can learn to live triumphantly with it. Thriving is the goal. Mere survival is not enough. We cannot allow our pain to close us off from risking building new relationships and being effective in our missionary calling. As Thomas Aquinas sagely commented, "A ship is safe in harbor, but that is not what a ship is for" (Attig 1996, 25).

The experience of loss is real. The grief is painful and hard work. The recovery may be difficult. But the future is bathed in hope. One anonymous writer expresses it clearly:

To hope is as human as to love. We were made to face the future just as we were made to face each other…Unlike optimism, Christian hope doesn't opt out when faced with harsh realities. The reason for the realism of Christian hope is the fact that it is cast in the mold of the crucifixion and resurrection of Christ. Christian hope can face any situation because it is not based on changeable circumstances, but a settled conviction that nothing can overtake us that Christ hasn't taken care of. It is willing to risk all on the reality of the resurrection. We welcome the future, because it bears the face of Jesus.

Response to loss will require an honest evaluation of what is being experienced and why. Then there must be a decision to take responsibility for my responses and recovery. In these difficult times of loss, it is helpful if the mission home office and team leaders acknowledge the reality of the grief response and provide both preparation and support for the individual missionary. Some measure of compassionate, pastoral care from either peers or leadership would greatly facilitate healthy recovery.

Loss and the accompanying grief for missionary women cannot be avoided or ignored. But such grief does not have to debilitate or render women ineffective. May we, as missionary women, live in this reality of our hope, enfolding into our lives both the painful and joyous experiences inherent in living out the missionary calling, to the glory of God.

REFERENCES

Attig, T. 1996. *How We Grieve: Relearning the World.* New York: Oxford University Press.

Caplan, S., and G. Lang. 1993. *Grief: The Courageous Journey: Step-by-Step Process for Surviving the Death of a Loved One.* London, Ontario: Courage Books.

Furnham, A. 1988. The Adjustment of Sojourners. In *Cross-Cultural Adaptation: Current Approaches,* ed. Y. Y. Kim and W. B. Gudykunst. Newbury Park, CA: Sage.

Head, J. 2010. Lecture on Gender and Marriage at the Center for Intercultural Training. Union Mills, NC.

Humphrey, G. M., and D. G. Zimpfer. 1996. *Counseling for Grief and Bereavement.* London: Sage.

James, J. W., and F. Cherry. 1988. *The Grief Recovery Handbook.* New York: Harper and Row.

Staudacher, C. 1987. *Beyond Grief: A Guide to Recovering from the Death of a Loved One.* Oakland, CA: New Harbinger Publications.

Whitman, Walt. 1900. Tears. *In Leaves of Grass,* Vol. 19. Sea Shore Memories (publisher unknown).

SIX

Negotiating Reality Single
Sharon E. Soper

I believe the freedom exercised by a single missionary is a great privilege requiring the highest degree of personal responsibility and individual authority since she is naturally obliged by circumstances to make important personal and ministerial choices alone. Indeed it is a divine mystery how she thrives in the conflictive surroundings that threaten her identity and relationships and how she discerns ways to display her unique creativity while engaged in effective and meaningful ministry.

A single woman missionary is a chameleon of changing colors. She adapts to unpredictable circumstances, diverse social environments, and leadership authorities, forming a natural camouflage to ensure her survival and success on the mission field. While following a divine calling and submitting to the local church and mission, an individual develops relationships and responsibilities under the canopy of collectively established guidelines. These authority structures provide a spiritual and material shade of protection in a reality of new structures within the culture, even amidst emerging leadership that is negotiated and/or competes for frontline positions.

The opportunities for single missionaries have dramatically improved since the early nineteenth century when aspiring women were "forced to marry or stay home" (Tucker 1992, 178). The stigma of gender and marital status branded them "misfits" for mission work.

The first American unmarried single to serve as a foreign missionary was Betsy Stockton, an African-American, sent to Hawaii in 1823. In order to go, she had to accept working as a maid under the supervision of a married missionary couple.[3] Social changes at the time of the industrial revolution and revival in the churches fueled mission outreach so that by 1860, women had emerged independently and successfully organized into a mission society force that provided the necessary infrastructure that authoritatively backed so many eager single women volunteers (ibid., 179). Numerous American church groups matured so that by 1909, an amazing 4,710 unmarried women were on the mission field. This explosive growth is very impressive compared to fifty years earlier when records show only one single missionary serving in 1861 (Montgomery 1910, 243–244)!

These unprecedented Western historical advances of one-and-a-half centuries ago are encouraging. And today, we see many more single women being sent from non-Western countries who are just as determined to significantly advance the mission cause. Single women should be affirmed as they willingly embrace the ambiguities and dilemmas that are related to status, gender identity, and authority. In this chapter I reflect on the ups and downs of my personal journey, and in doing so, this should help us understand and appreciate the dynamic process and unique issues that inevitably challenge all single women on the frontlines of ministry.

MY MISSIONARY JOURNEY

I was accepted by my mission during my last semester of Spanish language school. They needed a nurse immediately, so after graduation, I flew back to California and had two weeks to pack and say good-bye to my family before hopping the plane to Bolivia. My mind was full

---

3 Betsy Stockton, a former slave, "applied to the American Board, and the directors agreed to send her abroad—but only as a domestic servant for another missionary couple" (Tucker 1983, 231–232).

of nursing, Bible, and Spanish phrases. But there was one phrase that kept rehearsing in my head. It was the wisdom of my grandmother's voice saying, "Don't criticize anyone for a whole year!" She knew from her own short missionary experience that hasty judgments and initial reactions could jeopardize long-term ministry.

First-Term Survival Rites of Passage

The first two years[4] in Bolivia were a rigorous survival rite of passage as I tried to belong and adjust to so many unexpected circumstances. Of course I was eager to fit in and anxious to be an active player in my new divinely appointed setting. The first disappointment that burst my bubble was that strong biases had already formed before my plane ever touched down on foreign territory. It was only natural that my co-workers would question why an American English-speaking missionary with virtually no Mennonite background who was still learning Spanish would be a very good fit. Some of the clinic staff and clients only spoke the Low German dialect, and these differences in nationality and culture were accentuated with other unspoken concerns of propriety related to gender, age, and marital status.

Mealtime was another eye-opener for the task facing me. Though clinic staff attempted to include everyone by conversing in Spanish, inadvertently some reverted back to Low German. When we spoke

---

4   Unmarried pioneers like Lottie Moon, Amy Carmichael, and Gladys Aylward refer to similar types of struggles, especially starting their missionary terms, and they all mention how they suffered loneliness and depression. At some point, they seriously wrestled with the issue of not marrying. They would not be deterred by gender constraints and confronted situations of sex discrimination even before going to the field. They specifically mention their disillusionment with field missionary acceptance and relationships. Lottie Moon did not find the society "agreeable or edifying" (Tucker 1983, 235), and Amy Carmichael when first starting her career in Japan discovered that "the missionary community was not the picture of harmony she had envisioned" (ibid., 240). Gladys Aylward's "independent spirit clashed, and finally after one heated eruption (less than a year after her arrival), Gladys was ordered to leave" by the veteran missionary who was very set in her ways (ibid., 252).

in English, someone always was left out. The food was also different. Eating bread at every meal was never a custom in my home, and while everyone else loved the traditional Mennonite staples of cabbage soup and beets, I was secretly craving a crisp green dinner salad.

Numerous adjustments to this diverse group were more than any of us had bargained for—three nationalities, different Mennonite backgrounds with contrasting degrees of legalistic tradition, and communication problems. Trying to relate to the Spanish-speaking nationals living a couple of miles from the compound, by comparison, looked like paradise.

I was fairly confident that common professional interests would surely facilitate bonding. After all, the clinic desperately needed a qualified registered nurse with labor and delivery experience. Never did I dream that the hard-earned bachelor's degree would pose a threat to my coworker because she had graduated from a hospital program. My innovations and zeal to do community health development outside the compound also met with lukewarm enthusiasm. Less time in the clinic meant they would need to work more hours in order to keep the 24/7 operation running.

Ministry roles for single women followed traditional fundamental stereotypes. It was okay to teach Bible classes with women and children at the nearby church, and we could share gospel tracts and recordings in the clinic consulting room. Basically, the men were the top leaders doing the decision-making, church planting, and preaching. Wives played supportive roles with their focus on caring for the family.

Unmarried women, nurses, and staff had separate living quarters, and they shared the daily chores and clinic duty. Families lived in their own homes geographically distant from the single dormitory so everyone's reputation was safeguarded—so I thought. As a novice missionary, I was not allowed to attend the monthly field council meetings. At one of these meetings one of the wives requested that a rule be made prohibiting single women from going out alone with married men. Yours truly was the culprit for this "ceremonious sanction"! That week one of the husbands had kindly offered me a lesson on how to ride the mission motorcycle. We did a test run so I could learn to safely maneuver the heavily sanded roads without wiping out.[5] When my field directors informed me about the council meeting, it really hurt. I protested to myself: "After all, we were riding separate motorcycles!" But what worried me most was that my reputation was at stake. Eyebrows had been raised about my behavior before I was even given a chance. Now, it was too late. The discussion and new rule were officially recorded in the council minutes and mailed off to the mission board.

Paranoia began to set in about this time. I noticed myself slipping in and out of rooms in order to avoid being left alone with one of the men. It had never occurred to me that such accusations and misunderstandings would occur with my fellow missionaries. My hope of belonging and being accepted on the team deteriorated, and a feeling of isolation and loneliness formed a cloud of despair. At the time, I was fully convinced that some people wanted me to fail and disappear altogether.

Resignation and Acceptance as the Turning Point

Long-term goals seemed impossible to actualize, and my normal sense of identity and psychological equilibrium were starting to erode. For years, I had worked so hard to jump through the hoops, and I had seen God miraculously open doors. Quitting was not an option my mind would easily entertain. Since we usually got three days a month off from work, I used my precious time to escape to be with friends in the city. On one occasion the harsh winds dried my tears while I made the reluctant and ritual motorcycle ride back for another month. I forced myself to return to what seemed to be a huge mistake, but I wanted to make the best of a "bad" situation and at least finish out the four-year commitment. When I decided to stick it out and do what was right, this was a turning point that also gave me a glimmer of hope.

---

5   This was a practical precaution. On one occasion, when driving a dirt bike to town with a friend on back, I started to fishtail in some deep sand and she fell off and broke a rib.

Positive adjustments were made by finding purposeful activities to engage in during the long clinic evenings and slow night shifts. Time was turned into a tutor. I listened to shortwave radio, taught myself to play accordion by ear, and practiced the Inca rhythms on my newly purchased Bolivian *charango*. That year I read over a hundred leftover books from the compound library and memorized one hundred verses in Spanish. The extra down time allowed me to become friends with the one and only national couple working on the compound. They were the highlight of my week because I could spend a lot of extra time to prepare weekly Bible studies for this couple, and together we memorized the entire Evangelism Explosion course.

My adjustment came after wrestling with the dissonance and cultural clashes that were at war inside me. But unbeknownst to me at the time, I was banking credibility in these initial relationships that would later become instrumental for developing future ministries. For example, after the national couple left to attend Bible school, his evangelistic gifts developed, and he later became pastor of the second largest church in our denomination. I was later able to support this new church plant by organizing soybean cooking classes and by discipling new believers. Years later, this particular pastor was on the national ministerial, and his influence was crucial to rally needed support for my efforts to organize and expand the Theological Education by Extension (TEE) program.

New Ministry Opportunities

My mission then followed a new vision to reach the outlying national population, which was a switch from the exclusive focus on the Low

---

6   All names being used in this chapter are pseudonyms.

7   Before I went to the mission field, the debate in Hardesty and Scanzoni's book, *All We're Meant to Be: A Biblical Approach to Women's Liberation* (1974), intrigued me. A hunger to find answers motivated me to take a semester of New Testament Greek and read other books on the subject. Finally, I realized that this controversial debate was not easily resolved and certainly bound to continue; however, at least I had made an honest effort to find the definitive answer for myself. This subsequently influenced me to take a

German population of Mennonite colony farmers. After two years of fulfilling clinic duties, everyone agreed I could switch over to community development and work with a Bolivian pastoral couple to pioneer a church plant amongst squatters outside the peripheral city limits.

Javier,[6] the Bolivian pastor, apprenticed me to community life and ministry. He encouraged me to participate in numerous activities such as serenades, all-night wakes, and personal visitation. Through all this, relationships were deepened. His male leadership did not generate friction between us, and we pooled our resources to reach the people with the gospel and meet the needs of the community. The current field director, who created this new church planting team, took time to come from the city and help us start a school, grades 1–5. God blessed our collective efforts, and this fast-growing outreach soon became our largest church.

Bickering over gender roles would have slowed down the progress, and we did not feel plagued with an unhealthy competition that can typically develop when men are *machismo*. The field director couple, national pastoral couple, and I were all strong leaders in our own right, but we worked harmoniously as a team with very little conflict. This was also creating a new comfort zone that increased my ability to work with Bolivian men in general.[7] We formed music groups, and I taught married couples in the in-depth discipleship classes. Our relationship was strengthened because I was willing to comply with pastor Javier's requests to lead, teach, and, in his absence, preach. I was affirmed and at liberty to use my spiritual gifts. Following the pastor's lead and doing whatever was asked of me seemed to be a wise and appropriate strategy as I finished out my first term. Though I still exercised cau-

more pragmatic approach. By adapting to situations, as led by the Holy Spirit, I was able to avoid falling into a static, permanent interpretation of the role of women in ministry. While biblical interpretations could be used to strictly define women's ministry roles, in my mind, biblical illustrations of godly women also challenged such restrictions. My father had encouraged my egalitarianism, and his parental authority deeply influenced my identity as a woman. In addition, my mission conference tended to be egalitarian, as evidenced by their silence when I crossed some gender lines.

tion when relating to the opposite sex, the prior paralysis disappeared. Now there was confidence to take calculated risks, and while still conservatively testing the boundaries, I did find many practical ways to legitimately relate and minister.

Symbiotic Ministry Relationships

One day, pastor Javier noticed I was at my wit's end trying to keep some semblance of cleanliness. There was no running water, and dust kept filtering in through the windows. It was frustrating to try to clean all the time just to see everything completely dusty only two hours later. Javier thought I should ask Maria to work part-time, and this could simultaneously facilitate a discipleship relationship. Maria had inadvertently gotten baptized by Mormons, though she had become a believer at an evangelical campaign. This discipleship relationship changed to a long-term partnership that was significant to my life and ministry.

As a child, Maria had been beaten unconscious by her drunken father, and this incident forced her migration to the city where she worked and forged out a life of her own at age fourteen. At first, it took four weeks for her to correctly memorize two Bible verses. I assumed she had a learning disability of some kind, probably related to her childhood trauma.

After working one day, Maria decided to stay overnight. Two nights went by and she still was there. By now, I was perplexed by this strange behavior. My two small rooms were cramped, and the small clothes closet was doubling as a garage to park the motorcycle. On the third day, I directly confronted Maria and asked when she was planning to return home. She replied confidently, "No, I've decided to stay!" The initial shock silenced my verbal objections, but through this new permanent living arrangement, we became great friends and ministry partners in the coming years.

Discipleship was an ongoing process, and we also did church planting together. In the community, we experimented with soybeans and created a cooking course. With my help, Maria established her own business producing soy-based products because we wanted to combat the protein-deficient malnutrition that was prevalent in children. She learned everything informally. For example, her lack of basic math was circumvented by learning to use a calculator to run the business. This skill was helpful when she got elected treasurer of the church Ladies' Society.

Studying in the Theological Education by Extension (TEE) program reinforced her theology, and eventually she was chosen to be a tutor for a group of first-level TEE students. Our initial patron-client relationship transitioned into a partnership. She gained knowledge and advanced economically, spiritually, and socially. At first the relationship appeared one-sided, but in reality it was mutually beneficial. Maria was a loyal sounding board on questions of culture, an emotional cheerleader, and a very good friend who was a blessing from God.

Ambiguous Leadership Expectations

At times, long-term plans were affected because the styles and expectations of those in authority could be unpredictable. The Canadian mission conference changed board members every two years. During my seventeen-year career, changes in the top leadership led to my working under three home mission directors and three different field directors—some of whom were quite the opposite in terms of personality, leadership style, and ministry philosophy. I worked hard to conscientiously figure out my views, and it felt comfortable to find my place and role in ministry. Then a new set of field directors would arrive. They had their own set of beliefs and ideas that inevitably would influence my participation and ministry plans. Great credit goes to one couple of field directors who affirmed my work. When they saw my potential, they encouraged me to grow and expand more. But when the next set of field directors came on the scene things changed.

The well-defined hierarchical beliefs about male authority and traditional views about the leadership roles of women in the home and church posed a new challenge to me and the national women already doing evangelistic outreach and public ministry. It was subtle at first, and I wanted to keep the team harmony. I tried to reduce some of the tension by accepting ministry role changes, and this was when we adopted an indirect approach to ministry by focusing on community development. This eventually led to creating a holistic soybean cooking course that gained great popularity and momentum (Soper 1994).

It caught me totally off guard when my Canadian mission agency asked me to develop the new TEE program. Church leadership and theology have not always been legitimate arenas for women to be so directly involved in, so this raised some red flags in my mind. It was not by chance that some timely encouragement came from men outside my mission circle—one Anglican missionary and a Mennonite TEE director from Paraguay, and then even my field director and the national pastors unanimously voted for me to take over. While I was shaking my head "no," this confirmation afforded me enough freedom to authoritatively forge ahead and create a program that grew to an interdenominational level. To do this, my plans to expand the popular holistic soybean courses had to be sidetracked. But, with God's guidance and amidst favorable circumstances, the TEE ministry became a thrilling challenge with tangible results.

Contacts were directly made with the TEE curriculum producers and the accrediting faculty from a TEE organization in Argentina. A two-day bus ride to Buenos Aires for a "spontaneous" visit to the Latin biannual meeting of TEE directors was a calculated risk that proved profitable. I intended to glean information and solidify the relationship. But the men cordially invited me to a formal meeting, and after they reviewed our academic paperwork, they decided to grant our program accreditation. This "technical support" boosted the TEE program and gave it more credibility. The graciousness and acceptance of these TEE leaders who represented different Latin American countries was so affirming to me, especially at a time when I was experiencing internal struggles and tensions with a director whose biblical interpretations meant a woman's role in leadership should be restricted.

After expanding the TEE Bible school to reach beyond our own denomination, a national pastor finishing high school was apprenticed to be director. He proved to be a motivated experiential learner. We did everything together, like traveling to Buenos Aires to have the proper introductions with the TEE directors from other countries. The program practically doubled each year. Two years after I left the mission field, there were 600 students studying in TEE under the leadership of this national director.

AFFIRMING AND EMBRACING SINGLENESS

This brief synopsis of my journey is illustrative. Hopefully, this will allow us to explore ideas on how to affirm and embrace different challenges knowing that status, gender, and authority are integral to the relational process that comes to bear on a single woman's ministry and identity. When she is secure and well-balanced in these areas, her ability for cross-cultural adaptation, ministry effectiveness, and longevity is enhanced.

"A single woman has no business being a missionary in South America." A fellow master's degree classmate was asking me if I thought this statement was true. My experience seemed to go against such a perplexing generalization. Certainly unmarried women face obstacles related to status and gender, no matter where they end up serving. Probably statements similar to this have deterred some single women from working in hard-to-reach populations or areas deemed dangerous. But Scripture also reminds us that it is not unusual for God's providence to supersede human wisdom in order that his power may be manifested. "Let him who boasts, boast in the Lord" (1 Cor 1:31 NASB).

My mind was again wrestling with the issue, because implied in the graduate student's statement above, being married seemed better. I had no marriage plans in the making and in a few months I was supposed to be back in Bolivia again. Married women may find personal satisfaction in being a missionary wife and mother. They naturally enjoy the benefits of intimacy, companionship, and security. In addition, marital status and the maternal role are positive identities highly respected in other societies—common ground that facilitates ministry relationships with other women and social credibility. While she is rightly occupied by her responsibilities and relationships to children and husband, a sense of purpose comes by successfully accomplishing these roles. Her husband shares the responsibility of family, and a measure of comfort, security, and protection are afforded when under his authority.

The Bolivian ideals of marriage and motherhood were observed in the way the nationals avoided calling attention to my lower unmarried status by calling me "sister," (hermana) instead of the technically correct term, "miss" (Senorita). Only my closest friends knew the truth that age was closing the biological door to motherhood. Occasionally, close friends would lovingly refer to me as "mother," a title of honor and esteem that had naturally been denied.

Accepting Marginality

A single missionary may feel vulnerable due to her marginal position even when she has purposefully chosen to circumvent the norms of society.[8] Even one who must make the best of her lot in life is probably more vulnerable to feelings of fatalism or victimization. For this reason, she must wisely prepare herself for and expect certain kinds of rejection and losses due to the lack of status and not having the relationships that result from marriage and motherhood.

Unfortunately, society reinforces an "old maid" stereotype as a way to pressure women to conform to a status of higher prestige. And

---

8 See Marvin Mayers (1987) for further discussion on the norm of the person in society. "By maintaining one's norm, one maintains identity and the authenticity of one's identity" (Mayers 1987, 80). A single missionary is able to be culturally adaptable while still retaining her own norm. For example, she need not fear that she is less honoring or useful to God when not conforming to the special norm of marriage or motherhood. Her self-acceptance is based on the norm of God's calling or place for her, and this may go against the mainstream of societal ideals.

perhaps the spiritual gains and advantages of marginality have been overlooked and underestimated as a result. The single missionary is not to find comfort in pity even when emotionally overwhelmed during times of crisis. There can be no regrets. The eunuch in Isaiah 56:2–6 is comforted by God in his choice, and he is exhorted not to complain:

> Blessed is the man who does this…And let not any eunuch *complain,* "I am only a dry tree." For this is what the Lord says: "To the eunuchs who keep my Sabbaths, who *choose* what pleases me and hold fast to my covenant—to them I will give within my temple and its walls a memorial and a name better than sons and daughters." (emphasis mine)

The privileged relationship of being God's daughter and choosing to be an instrument for his master plan are all the honor she affords, and denying earthly power and prestige as a spiritual calling or discipline fosters spirituality.

An unmarried woman will benefit by deciding early on what priority marriage and motherhood have in her life and by taking time to weigh the benefits and risks involved as she prays for direction. Protestant single missionaries are not inclined toward formal vows of celibacy, but if forced to choose between remaining single and childless the rest of her life versus being a wife and mother, what will it be? She could still leave the door cracked open in the event that God leads differently, but being led to choose a life of ministry as a single can help protect her from distractions or regrets. The choice of service over society helps her focus better on her ministry rather than marriage. Her identity is related to the way she envisions herself in the future. She decides and allows God to control her identity and destiny, and Christ is her source of strength and stability.

Handling Identity Crisis and Transitions

All this tends to backfire during an identity crisis. For example, if involvement in missions abruptly ends, even for good reasons, the career single missionary feels this very acutely. When her sense of purpose is attached to her vocation and mission calling, a sudden vacuum is created that deeply disturbs her sense of well-being. The situation worsens if major ministry changes coincide with natural transitions occurring during midlife crisis. During reentry into her home culture, she may have no clue where or how she fits in, and this creates an emotional war zone where attacks from unanswered questions and doubts emerge as she tries to cope with another new reality. Nothing seems clear except that culture shock adjustment is a painful process with no escape.

These are some of the inherent dangers and difficulties of being marginal to start with—and there are certain points of no return. The eunuch cannot undo the operation that symbolizes his chastity vow. This permanent state not only changes his reproductive capacity but, in turn, affects his identity. The enemy tries to attack the identity of an unmarried female missionary with accusations surrounding her reproductive capacity. Since it is impossible to detach the biological and societal drives that give a woman meaning in life, he uses this dirty tactic in an attempt to try and destroy her spirituality.

Some have chosen to remain single, and others accept their single state. Others hope and pray for a miracle. We love second chances and fairy-tale endings like the story of Ruth and Naomi who recuperate the losses caused by premature widowhood. We know God blesses and works miraculously to resolve the negative circumstances in order to change or improve a marginal situation dramatically.

Something similar to Ruth happened with my Bolivian copartner, Maria, after my resignation from the mission. At age thirty-nine, she felt abandoned and lonely, and she was experiencing the powerlessness of a childless unmarried woman. Her marginal status and identity were attached more to not having children. She wasted no time getting married, and soon after she was blessed to bear a daughter. This was a relief to me, knowing that later in life she would have family to care for her—a very important consideration in an area where retirement benefits are almost nonexistent. Maria's status improved, and the crisis surrounding her identity and reproductive ability passed.

Certainly, God's blessing comes differently to different people. And, by bearing the same hardship of the husbandless and childless of Isaiah 54:1–6, a single missionary is also in a position to receive a unique blessing that God wishes to bestow upon her.

> "Sing, O barren woman, you who never bore a child; burst into song, shout for joy, you who were never in labor; because more are the children of the desolate woman than of her who has a husband," says the Lord. "Enlarge the place of your tent, stretch your tent curtains wide, and do not hold back; lengthen your cords, strengthen your stakes…Do not be afraid; you will not suffer shame. Do not fear disgrace; you will not be humiliated. You will forget the shame of your youth and remember no more the reproach of your widowhood. For your Maker is your husband—the Lord Almighty is his name—the Holy One of Israel is your Redeemer; he is called the God of all the earth. The Lord will call you back as if you were a wife deserted and distressed in spirit—a wife who married young, only to be rejected," says your God.

The apostle Paul could personally advertise the benefits for not marrying. "An unmarried woman or virgin is concerned about the Lord's affairs: Her aim is to be devoted to the Lord in both body and spirit" (1 Cor 7:34). In Christ's public life, he is an unmarried single actively engaged in ministry and willing to risk being accused of impropriety with the opposite sex when relating to women on several occasions. The Samaritan woman is an example (John 4:27) where gender lines are crossed.

Following Christ's example, however, means maintaining integrity without always being confined by gender and cultural barriers.

This supports the basis for single women becoming effective missionaries. And there are times when the rules of society cannot be followed in terms of gender. Obviously, gender and sexuality both have significant influences on the identity and relationships of the single female missionary, and deserve more attention in this discussion.

Dealing with One's Sexuality

Biological sex is determined by birth; however, gender roles and relations are learned by the socialization process varying from culture to culture. The unmarried missionary is strongly influenced by the gender and sexual experiences of her own background, and by cultural osmosis, her thinking processes attempt to redefine themselves according to each new social environment.

Gender relations require moral sensitivity in any culture, and only purposeful efforts to discern and learn discreet behaviors can prevent a missionary from becoming a liability. One single missionary acquaintance of mine with a friendly personality didn't realize how attractive she was to the opposite sex. Her Western behaviors were inappropriate, resulting in her being asked to change assignments after being spotted hugging and kissing one of the Bible school students.

God has created female missionaries as sexual beings who have sexual desires that are expressed or satisfied in different ways. In our fallen condition, sexual temptation is also a reality. For example, to a lesser degree, missionary women may feed themselves on a steady diet of unwholesome romance novels or find pleasure viewing inappropriate videos or media on the Internet. Others may struggle privately with impure fantasies or actions. Sexual fantasy can be a tempting way of escape during times of loneliness or rejection and is something we all must battle.

Appropriate expressions of sexuality and accepting sexual feelings are necessary for women to maintain holiness and purity, recognizing that some are more vulnerable than others in this area. Victory over sexual impurity comes through confession and forgiveness, not self-condemnation. Those continuing to struggle may need to maintain accountability in this area, if possible, finding an understanding fellow missionary who can hear her confession and provide healing prayer (James 5:13–16). Embarrassment alone is a strong deterrent for married Christians to openly admit their struggles in sexual matters. And perhaps it is even harder for the unmarried missionary to admit and seek help due to ambiguous ideas or unrealistic expectations that have been placed on her by others or by herself.

Dealing with Celibacy and Asexuality

Certainly, sexual feelings must be guarded when relating with men, not only to avoid raising unwanted suspicions but also to avoid arousing undue temptation. In my particular case, an egalitarian disposition had influenced my ideas and behaviors concerning gender relations and sexuality. Working effectively with male leaders meant automatically relating on an equal level, believing that being a woman makes no difference in terms of value or power. My childhood also reinforced "masculine behaviors" such as being athletic, competitive, articulate, and authoritative while some of the outward feminine behaviors of revealing dress and movements were suppressed. In my opinion, it was more practical to avoid the annoying problems related to sexual attraction, and this behavior seemed to function well for me when working as a leader with both genders.

Inadvertently, I was slipping into the societal role and behavior of the "asexual" nun and enjoyed the due respect of a "religiosa." The traditional role of a foreign missionary woman in South America is the Catholic nun. In parallel fashion, some assumed that single evangelical missionary women must also be virgins even though no formal vows of celibacy have ever been made. One national pastor explained this perplexing phenomenon, saying all the single nurses in our clinic used medication in order to have no sex drive. Over time, different contradictory spiritual, medical, or historical perceptions do affect one's sense of sexuality and identity, and in subtle ways, these do influence how ministry relationships and roles evolve.

Personally, after years of establishing a degree of credibility in the area of gender relations, there was a lot of freedom to do ministry. Even the married women trusted me to work alone with their husbands. For example, when apprenticing the TEE director, he and I traveled several days by bus on a business trip to Argentina. By this time, those who knew me were convinced that romantic or sexual interests were not on my agenda. Celebrating my femininity or expressing my sexuality in mixed company was secondary to maintaining my integrity and good reputation as a missionary. Displaying romantic interests for single men during my first or second mission term would have jeopardized or affected my reputation in the long run.

I am the first to admit that this is not exactly healthy for one's identity, and in some societies extremes of denial may not be necessary. But one is faced with the evasive task of retaining the norm of one's identity and natural sexuality in balance with the context of conflicting ideas concerning the same. This is such an intimate area hitting at the very core of femaleness affecting both emotional and spiritual well-being. A large measure of God's grace and supernatural touch to accept and forgive when faced with unfair situations are essential to the adaptation process of change that affects sexuality. This is the only way to maintain a healthy sense of self.

Mission agencies and missionaries must avoid sweeping these issues under the rug. Secrecy and denial are incubators for temptation and sin. But all too often, the norm is to react by silence or condemnation. By boldly discussing these issues openly, missionary health and longevity can be promoted through prevention, diagnosis, and treatment. When serious difficulties arise, single missionaries can be treated with compassion and dignity that bring restoration and healing.

In the pressure cooker of cross-cultural circumstances the effects of past sexual abuse or other related dysfunction could be a trigger causing some problem areas to surface faster. Even though finding candidates with healthy backgrounds may be the ideal in missionary selection, the reality is that too many single missionary women live with troubled pasts. God specializes in changing liabilities to assets. And the crucible of suffering victimization or even personal failure may be the most effective way to develop coping skills and a godly character—both positive attributes needed for reacting and adjusting to the injustices, sexual oppression, and abuse found throughout the world.

Recognizing Authority Relationships

The last area to be explored affecting the relationships and effectiveness of the single missionary is authority. The same power and authority given to Christ by the Father has been granted to us. Christ said to the seventy-two who returned successfully from their mission, "I have given you authority" (Luke 10:17–19).[9] Intimacy with the Father and submitting to his authority is not independent from submitting to the different human authorities we are under, but occasionally, submitting to God's authority takes precedence over obeying earthly authorities. Jesus reminds his parents of this reality through the question, "Didn't you know I had to be in my Father's house?" His parents felt he had behaved on his own by staying three days in the temple while they could not find him. Yet, Scripture clearly states that he was obedient to them (Luke 2:49–51).

Submitting to God and submitting to a variety of human authorities is ultimately what is important in decision-making. There are no simple answers, however, and the single missionary must study the situation and pray to hear the "voice of authority" in her own life. When she submits to God's authority or exercises his authority, she can avoid excesses or sin by submitting and being accountable to others.

For some, being in God's will means an unmarried missionary always needs to have a godly male authority over her, but this is not always possible or practical. I believe most single missionary women

---

9   Defining authority (legitimate use of power) and understanding how we function in Christ's authority has different biblical interpretations. Proper exercise of the authority given to believers by the Holy Spirit is detailed in *I Give You Authority* (Kraft 2012). Human authority is integrally related to the divine use of authority.

have a naturally strong desire and need to work under authority, provided that their sense of identity and loyalty to God's calling are not destroyed. And, in the absence of a man, perhaps they are not as deficient or independent of male authority as one may think.[10]

For example, the values and teaching of my father, who is no longer living, often pop into my mind. God uses memories and past experiences to direct me when human authorities are absent or weak. This collective voice of authority is active when submitting to the past instruction of parents, pastors, or professors and even through the authors of spiritual books. The Holy Spirit guides by bringing to mind these memories at the appropriate moment. This is a legitimate system of accountability that some would call a conscience. And when striving to understand and submit to the different authorities of a new culture, the conscience goes on a new exercise program and is strengthened and refined as it attempts to harmonize or transform culture in accordance with the authority of Scripture.

Authority issues for unmarried women are a different knot to untangle than for married women. Egalitarian societies and missions may find it easier to trust unmarried missionaries to work independently, releasing them to greater ministry. This is a humbling and encouraging experience. In spite of the authoritarianism or legalism felt throughout my ministry, there was much affirmation coming from my mission. Mutual trust led to starting new ministries. By embracing authority and having a strong support group, my autonomy was affirmed and this kept me motivated and encouraged.

For unmarried female missionaries not coming from an egalitarian or Western culture, the dynamics may differ significantly. According

---

10 Regardless of gender we submit to the authority of both father and mother where male and female authorities are different and complementary. Applying hierarchical views has inadvertently led some to make unhealthy distinctions that can lead to the conclusion that one gender is of more value or more powerful than the other. Men are strongly influenced by their mothers, and adulthood does not detach them from nor destroy female authority in their conscience.

to a study done by Steve Sang-Cheol Moon, the attrition rate for all returned Korean single missionaries was 46 percent, but what is more significant is that more than twice as many single female missionaries returned home than single males (Sang-Cheol Moon 1997, 135). The author suggests parental pressure for Korean women to marry as the reason (ibid., 136).

Another related possibility is that the higher attrition rate for single Korean female missionaries is due to hierarchical male authority. Not only are Korean women strongly influenced by the strong group values of family, but perhaps submission to male authority is also a factor. This might explain the reason why single men have a much lower attrition rate by comparison. Then it would stand to reason that single Korean female missionaries might find it more stressful adjusting to independence and individualism on the mission field. The price tag of marginality may be higher depending on race, gender, or class. Regardless, single female missionaries of any nationality will share one thing in common in that they will have to cope with identity crisis related to wrestling with conflicts in status, gender, and authority.

Newer sending countries are making significant contributions for the rapidly growing missionary expansion that is taking place today. Sending churches, agencies, and field teams need to seriously consider that single women from newer sending countries will have strong feelings of isolation and unique struggles to overcome. It will take time and resolve to learn an additional language and culture if they are assigned to live or work with a culturally different partner or field team. Water seeks its own level, and different people groups and newer sending countries will learn to find effective ways to accomplish the task. In many ways single female missionaries from new sending countries are pioneers in the twenty-first century. They too will use their unique chameleon abilities to discover ways to adapt to the unique configuration of variables in a changing world.

CONCLUSION

This discussion has revolved around the identity of the single female missionary as she negotiates relationships and ministry roles in a changing context, especially looking at issues of status, gender, and authority. The testimonies and experiences of past missionaries along with illustrations from Scripture provide guidance for the single female missionary who must continually process how to practically exercise her spiritual gifts as she follows God's call on her life.

Survival and success of the female single missionary will depend partly on her finding stable and supportive national relationships for her own person and ministry, and a lot will depend on her ability to submit to the authority of various individuals and groups even when she may not completely agree. Organizational changes, cross-cultural clashes, and working under different leadership personalities will produce tensions that threaten to upset her personal identity and spirituality.

By listening to God's Word, the Holy Spirit, and a community of believers, she can wisely discern when to submit or how to accommodate her ministry while still maintaining the courage to follow her heart and step out in faith. The female single missionary is a "chameleon." She is uniquely gifted with a transforming beauty that allows her to maintain her integrity during difficult periods in her life or when facing the extreme situations encountered in cross-cultural ministry. Ultimately, God's creative power and glory are miraculously displayed in the process of successfully living out her life according to his purpose.

REFERENCES

Kraft, C. H. 2012. *I Give You Authority,* rev. ed. Grand Rapids, MI: Chosen Books.

Hardesty, N., and L. Scanzoni. 1974. *All We're Meant to Be: A Biblical Approach to Women's Liberation.* Waco, TX: Word.

Mayers, M. 1987. *Christianity Confronts Culture.* Grand Rapids, MI: Academie Books.

Montgomery, H. B. 1910. *Western Women in Eastern Lands.* New York: Macmillan.

Sang-Cheol Moon, S. 1997. Missionary Attrition in Korea: Opinions of Agency Executives. In *Too Valuable to Lose: Exploring the Causes and Cures of Missionary Attrition,* ed. W. D. Taylor, 129–142. Pasadena, CA: William Carey Library.

Soper, S. 1994. *Soybeans and the Kingdom of God.* Winnipeg, Manitoba, Canada: Evangelical Mennonite Mission Conference.

Thompson, F. C., ed. 1990. The Thompson Chain-Reference Bible: New International Version. Indianapolis, IN: B.B. Kirkbride Bible.

Tucker, R. A. 1983. *From Jerusalem to Irian Jaya.* Grand Rapids, MI: Zondervan.

————. 1992. *Women in the Maze.* Downers Grove, IL: InterVarsity Press.

SEVEN

Negotiating Female Missionary
Roles Cross-culturally
Donna Downes

WHEN GENDER INTERFERES WITH OUR MINISTRY: TWO TRUE STORIES

Two key incidents immediately come to mind when I think about my own experiences as a woman ministering in missions on two continents. They are remarkable for two reasons: first, because they shocked me into realizing the depth of strongly rooted values about women's roles in my host culture and forced me to evaluate how I should respond to those values in a way that honored God; and second, because they produced in me unforgettable feelings of uncertainty, shame, and resentment that I had been unprepared to deal with in all my pre-field training.

True Story #1

Macmillan (my African colleague) and I had just finished co-teaching a two-week seminar on communications and public relations to some thirty-five Christian workers in Nairobi, Kenya, and were in the process of eliciting verbal and written evaluations from our students when a remarkable incident occurred.

Most of our students had something to say about the course—what they had learned and how they were going to apply it—and the hour we had allotted to this evaluation session soon stretched well into overtime. Macmillan and I were thrilled with the discussion and had heard from almost all the students in the course when our oldest participant (a church leader in his seventies) rose slowly from his chair, cleared his throat, and asked for everyone's attention while he made a few comments. The room was quiet as this gentleman began.

"Brothers and sisters," he said, "I would like to thank God for this seminar, especially for Bwana [Macmillan] who has opened my eyes to so many new ideas that I can put to use in my ministry. I am an old man, and I didn't expect to learn many new things here, but I certainly learned much in this course. However, the biggest surprise to me was that I could learn something from a woman. Imagine—at my age, learning from a woman! But with God anything is possible!"

The room was filled with quiet whispering as the old man sat down, and then, all eyes were on me! As the lead teacher, I was expected to respond to this backhanded compliment! I could feel my face burning with embarrassment: my mouth was dry—I just wanted to run! Should I say something humorous? Should I just ignore the comment? I remember trying to be enthusiastic and to appear nonplused as I said my "thank- yous" to everyone, but inside I was churning. My colleague, Macmillan, and many of our students individually came to me during the tea time that followed, expressing their embarrassment and regret about the man's comments and saying that such comments could only be expected from the older, "unenlightened" generation. But despite their words of encouragement, I couldn't help wondering how many times my gender had interfered with my message, and I had been totally unaware of the problem. I wondered if, indeed, my teaching short-term courses for Christian leaders was an effective ministry at all and if I should refuse to teach in that setting again because of the danger of trespassing accepted cultural boundaries.

Much prayer, learning from others, perseverance, patience, experimentation, and a sense of humor helped me to overcome some of the cultural barriers in Africa, and I spent the next decade there in some of the most fulfilling ministries I've ever experienced. Several years later, however, when my husband and I were asked to begin a new OC International field in Romania, I had little or no idea that I would face even greater challenges with gender issues in Eastern Europe than I had faced in Kenya. I should have had some clue, however, from the following incident which took place in America as my husband and I met with a prominent Romanian church leader just prior to leaving for our new assignment.

True Story #2

My husband and I were seated in a large office across the desk from a well-known Romanian leader who had been living in the United States for many years. The man began with a question: "So, what do you understand to be the religious and social situation in Romania that you are going, there to address?" My husband mentioned several ideas and then looked at me to comment since I had been reading and writing recently on the social, educational, and moral challenges facing the country. For the next minute I waxed eloquent about all the things I had been learning about Romania and how I felt our mission's strategy was particularly appropriate for the Romanian situation. I noticed about halfway through my minute that the man had ceased his eye contact with me and begun to fiddle with various papers on his desk, but I continued on, perhaps unwisely on my part. When I came to the end of my few thoughts, hoping to regain his attention, I said, "Of course, this is all secondhand information, and we are here to learn from your experience and suggestions." His response absolutely floored me. "Well," he said, "my wife shall want to meet you. She will find you most interesting." He then directed all of his attention to my husband for the next hour, discussing our organization's strategy for Romania. All my husband's efforts to include me in the conversation were in vain. Even when I interrupted occasionally with what I thought were relevant questions or comments, the man's response was always directed to my husband, not to me. Yet when we got up to leave, his gracious good-bye included me (a kiss on my hand and a renewed invitation to get together WITH HIS WIFE whenever it was possible). I felt that I had been politely but summarily dismissed. Even my husband commented on this man's odd behavior toward me almost as soon as we left the building.

Little did I know then that this experience was a harbinger of things to come, as we excitedly and somewhat idealistically entered into our new ministries in Eastern Europe. Mistakenly secure in the knowledge that I was now a seasoned missionary with experience in dealing with culture stresses, including gender issues, I hadn't been more than a week in my new country when similar experiences to the one above chipped away at my confidence in our calling to Eastern Europe. Whether it was handling mundane issues like resolving a plumbing problem, handling our missionary shipment, locating housing, shopping for furniture, or ministry-oriented questions about legal registration, strategic denominational partnerships, mission vision, etc., whenever we were in conversation with Romanians, all final decisions (unless they were related to food or children) were routinely deferred to my husband. My contributions or opinions were politely accepted but ignored. Real estate agents would not enter into any negotiations for an apartment unless my husband was present. Contractors would do building improvements only if my husband signed for the work to be done. Even the plumber wouldn't take my initial list of needed repairs. He told me: "It is nice that you take an interest in these things, but you need not worry. Your husband and I shall discuss and resolve the problems." Being rather independent and accustomed to making such decisions on my own, I found myself more than slightly miffed.

Over the next several months, I learned that the church culture was similarly restrictive about women's roles, and even more so. I was told by my Romanian culture and language specialist that women generally sit separately from their husbands in church, "so as not to tempt the men to be distracted from the Lord." The married women cover their heads "to show they are under the authority of God and man" and wear little or no makeup or jewelry so as not "to attract attention to themselves."

Women, she said, never ascend to the pulpit to speak, and they are permitted to pray aloud only after the men have finished praying. Restrictions about women teaching men are strictly followed both inside and outside the church in Christian society, except for what my Christian sisters called "acceptable" realms like "teaching English as a second language" or "the teaching of women and children," or participating publicly in music. One article reproduced in a prominent Romanian Christian magazine even went so far as to say that for Christian women to seek secular management roles where they have authority over man is against God's natural order for things and produces problems in the workplace (Bauman 1998).

As I repeatedly slammed into the barrier of cultural role expectations versus my own ministry role expectations, I wondered if I would find a way to get beyond the barrier and once again enter a productive teaching and discipling ministry in a Christian university or seminary, or if I needed to adjust my ministry expectations so that I would focus primarily on women and children. And then I wondered how many other women were as unprepared as I was to deal with the cultural restrictions on their roles, their identity, their giftedness—especially when their ministries took them outside the boundaries of their homes and into contact with male leaders in their host culture. How do missionary women respond to the cross-cultural challenges of role expectations in their host culture? Do mission agencies provide help to ease the challenge? If part of our ministry as good missionaries is to adapt to cultural expectations and norms for the sake of the gospel, was I wrong in feeling so resentful about the cultural restrictions I saw as so unfair?

These questions and others gnawed at me, and as I soon discovered in conversations with other women, the questions were gnawing at them as well—especially those who were trained for and expected to have ministries in mission that were outside of or in addition to the traditional role of homemaker. Stories of role frustration, depression, identity crises, and self-doubt began to surface. For example, one single missionary working in relief and development said, "I've just about given up trying to have an impact in the church. I think I could do better and be less restricted if I just took a secular job here and abandoned the idea of trying to work in Christian circles. The normal cultural bias against women in combination with the Christian bias saps any initiative I might have." Another woman told me, "I had expectations of teaching on spiritual development, prayer, and missions when I came here; however, I find myself teaching English because teaching anything else at the seminary seems to be a man's job. But I make the best out of what God has given me and try to understand the cultural and biblical reasons for these restrictions."

Lest I leave the impression that the majority of missionary women struggle with their roles in interacting with the local culture in the workplace, such is not the case. Many women missionaries have chosen ministries, for example, that revolve around the home, children, and neighborhood women. While these women do, in fact, encounter several types of cultural shock (Wilson 1996), facing gender bias in the workplace in ministering with nationals is not usually a major problem for them. In fact, as Bowers points out for married women,

> Concerns about role, recognition, etc. do not occupy the missionary wife's daily attention. Much more immediate and pressing problems demand her attention—coping with primitive living conditions, adapting to a different culture, child rearing, etc. Issues [related to their roles] are often ignored because they are less obvious and relate to underlying assumptions and tensions. (1985, 486)

However, the fact remains that women encounter fairly significant role challenges when they venture outside the culturally acceptable boundaries of their home environments, and their responses to such challenges can affect their ministry effectiveness and satisfaction as well as their emotional well-being. In an article on generational reasons for missionary attrition, authors Kath Donovan and Ruth Myors (1997) mention that men and women from the boomer and buster generations, which make up most of the American missionary force today, have high expectations for fulfillment in ministry. They note that role deprivation, lack of professional development, and unsatisfactory role for wives, among other issues, figure prominently in reasons commonly given for premature departure from missionary service (1997, 49). Laura English, in her dissertation, *Life Dream Development of Married Missionary Women* (1995, 158–159), adds another perspective. Her study showed that rather than departing from their mission fields, the married women she studied often temporarily shelved their dreams while faced with the reality of their restricted roles in the mission setting, and they hoped for a time when they would be able to pursue their dreams. She also points out that women consistently struggled with God about the reality of their restricted ministries and sometimes were forced to unhealthy rationalizations for the social reality around them. She writes:

> Unfortunately, the ways in which the women tended to resolve such incongruence and tension tended not to support the well-being of the women. Instead, they often internalized blame for the resistance experienced and adjusted their thoughts and feelings of disappointment and anger in order to live in peace with their external realities. And since the anger often stemmed from a sense of spiritual injustice, the adjustments made often took the form of spiritualized rationalizations. (1995, 150)

English also mentions that the women she studied really felt they had nowhere to go with their frustrations. Their mission agencies and local church leaders provided little help (1995, 159–160), and often the agencies actually caused more problems because of their own restrictive philosophies of women's roles and/or their subtle suggestions that to be frustrated or depressed about lack of personal role fulfillment was unspiritual (ibid., 27–29). A more recent study by Susan Barclay (2006) regarding women in missions in British organizations confirms English's findings. Barclay writes that a combination of organizational culture, theological issues, leadership structure, and leadership development policies have led to a form of "institutional sexism" that offers little support for women who are frustrated in their mission field experiences. Furthermore, although the literature on women in missions is growing, the vast majority of it is historical in its perspective.

The available literature on cross-cultural adjustment, language learning, and missionary anthropology written in the last two decades does not address the specific difficulties and barriers women face, which are quite different from those faced by men (Wilson 1996, 443). Women can, of course, learn from and be inspired by the several biographies that are available on various heroines in missions, pulling principles out of the stories that they can apply in their own lives from the boldness of a Lottie Moon (Allen 1993), the formidable productivity of an Ann Judson or a Sarah Boardman (Robert 1996), the admirable self-sacrifice of an Amy Carmichael, or the dogged perseverance of a Helen Roseveare (Tucker 1983). But the fact is that modern missionary women, the boomers, the busters, and the millennials, are products of their own generational idiosyncrasies and norms, and they need more specific guidance to help them understand and cope with the particular cross-cultural adjustment issues and problems they currently are facing or will face on the field (Donovan and Myors 1987). For example, three books commonly used to train and prepare people for missionary work (Pocock, Van Rheenen and McConnell 2005; Moreau, McGee, and Corwin 2003; and Winter and Hawthorne, eds. 2009) devote very little space to women's contributions to or unique place in missions. Yet Moreau, McGee, and Corwin (2003) acknowledge that the subject of women in missions remains a major controversy that must first be addressed through "repentance and forgiveness between the sexes." They write: "So much hurt and moral disquiet festers just below the surface that dispassionate and honest theological reflection is nearly impossible right now" (229).

All that said, when women enter the missionary force with ministry dreams and relevant training and experience, and they expect to have a ministry role outside the home working with nationals, they need to be prepared for the sometimes adversarial and certainly always complex field contexts in which they will be working. The remainder of this chapter is dedicated to them and to identifying some of the coping mechanisms and skills for transcending the gender biases women face as they heed God's call to missions.

COPING WITH AND TRANSCENDING GENDER BIASES IN THE MISSIONARY WORKPLACE: TOWARD A TAXONOMY OF ROLE CHOICES FOR MISSIONARY WOMEN

Grunlan and Mayers, in their text on *Cultural Anthropology: A Christian Perspective* (1988, 127–141), have a helpful discussion on status and role that is pertinent to missionaries of both sexes. They note that "status" is "a position or place in a social system and its attendant rights and duties" whereas "role" is the behavior, attitudes, and values associated with a particular status (ibid., 127–128). They identify two main options for missionaries facing role conflict: "1) changing one or more of the statuses with which whole roles are in conflict and 2) changing the role behavior that goes with one or more of the statuses" (ibid., 134). In the case of women missionaries, these approaches would require that they either spend time trying to change the status of women in the ministry context in which they work, or that they change their behaviors to come into conformance with the status expected of them. Neither option seems very attractive to missionary women who want to have relevant and culturally contextualized ministries yet do not desire to constantly battle profound social issues. The authors also mention three coping mechanisms for handling (but not really resolving) role conflict (ibid., 134–135). I have summarized these methods here and attempt to apply each of the three to women's experiences.

One "coping method," according to Grunlan and Mayers, is "rationalization" where the "individual recasts a difficult situation into one that is acceptable." An example of this might apply to a woman who, in experiencing rejection in her attempts to transcend cultural role restrictions, may retreat to a role only within her household and the expatriate community, rationalizing that God seems to have closed other ministry doors.

A second coping mechanism is "compartmentalization" where a person "boxes off" various roles "accepting the obligations and responsibilities of each role separately" but rarely integrating those roles. So, for example, a woman might act very much in accord with cultural expectations when she is on the field, perhaps resenting the cultural restrictions, and then revel in her freedom when she returns to her own cultural milieu. A second more positive view of "compartmentalization" would be to participate to the fullest way possible in circles where women's roles (especially leadership roles) are less of a controversy while leaving the more debated roles (teaching both male and female adults in a church setting, for example) to male colleagues. For example, I personally participated on various leadership levels in both African and Romanian university teaching roles where female leadership was less controversial and related mainly to the education degrees I had earned. I did not, however, aspire to similar leadership or teaching roles in my local church where such participation would have been difficult.

The third coping mechanism is "adjudication" or delegating to others the activities that bring the woman into conflict with cultural role expectations. So, for example, a woman might decide to contribute her ideas through her husband and let him handle the interface with nationals while she remains safely within acceptable role boundaries.

In Mayers' book *Christianity Confronts Culture,* another helpful model is introduced for resolution of conflict between the "real person and the ideal....Discrepancies between the real and culturally defined ideals produce emotional unrest, a state of living in tension" (1987, 185). Mayers identifies four ways of dealing with the tension between the ideal and the real: 1) escape or withdrawal from the tension-filled situation; 2) conformance to role expectations (either forced or desired on the part of the missionary in conflict); 3) seeking a scapegoat for the conflict and thereby escaping resolution; and 4) forming a new group of people who are in agreement with the missionary's desired role.

These discussions of handling role conflict are extremely pertinent to this chapter because they encapsulate many of the responses to role conflict that I've encountered in my own experiences and in my interviews with other women. But because Grunlan and Mayers (and other anthropological texts for that matter) do not apply these ideas specifically to women in missions, in this chapter, I am attempting to do so, albeit adding to, changing, and synthesizing the categories to develop a new taxonomy of coping methods. Furthermore, rather than just creating a new taxonomy of coping, I attempt to suggest methods that not only allow for healthy role negotiation and learning, but also help women adapt to and appreciate local cultural norms. It would be nice, in other words, for women to be able to celebrate their ministries rather than merely cope with them.

From reading various literature on women in missions and from observations and interviews with women missionaries, I think three coping mechanisms are readily identifiable as ways in which women attempt to work through gender problems when they encounter them in working with nationals on the field: role insistence, role abdication, and role adaptation and integration. Each of the three has merit, and each has its problems. Missiologists will likely critique methods one and two as either missiologically unsound or psychologically unhealthy, but nevertheless these methods exist, and they may very well be the norm for some women in missions. Method three may seem more attractive missiologically, but women must be aware that this method, too, can have its drawbacks.

COPING METHOD 1: ROLE INSISTENCE

"I'm not going to change my ways of doing things simply because they don't accept women as leaders or managers. They're going to have to learn that this is the twentieth century and women are just as capable as men in management positions." Angela, an American missionary woman was explaining to me her missionary strategy in teaching Romanian Christians what she called "principles of Christian management." She told me, "I ignore the male chauvinism here and just go on with what the Lord has called me to do. Of course, I probably get away with it because I'm an American, but maybe I'm helping change things for Romanian women, too. I hope so!" She encourages other young Romanian women to ignore the social biases against them and to follow God's calling in their lives. "If they do what God's telling them to do, despite the prejudices against them, little by little, society will change, and the church will come limping along afterwards." She continues, "I don't worry about what Romanian men think of me. I only worry about what God thinks of me. And so far, my method has worked."

Angela exemplifies one of the coping methods that some women resort to on the mission field: they ignore the cultural biases to the degree they can and insist on the role they feel called to fulfill, even if it means clashing with local cultural norms to some degree. While the missiological wisdom of Angela's coping method may be questionable, her short-term results seem impressive on the surface: within a few years she has started two income-generating projects which she co-manages with Romanians and is working on a third. Angela is just one of several women missionaries I've interviewed who feel that their "calling" by God overrides the necessity to cater to or placate cultural biases. One missionary woman who runs an orphanage in Romania said, "I do what God has called me to do, regardless of what the men around me think. Sure, they probably think I'm crazy sometimes, but then I answer to God, not to them."

Obviously, in some parts of the modern world (the Arab Muslim world for example), role insistence would be ludicrous and perhaps dangerous and could result in disaster for the woman herself and, if she is married, for her family. But the fact remains that role insistence is one of the common coping mechanisms for women. Pamela George (1995), writing on cross-cultural educational concerns, stresses that such role insistence can also be a platform for proactive reform— similar to the kinds of reform Angela was trying to foster in Romania. She quotes one American teaching overseas about her goal in cultural reform through role modeling and discussion in the classroom:

> I am very aware of the gender dynamics in the classroom and among those that will become teachers themselves. My presence has the impact of opening [the] perceptions they've held of teachers. I want to help them see that definitions of who they are were socially constructed, which means they can be changed, if they are not happy with them! They can stop being an object, a goose that is being stuffed with education and everything else, and become persons who take some charge of their own lives. (1995, 111)

Grunlan and Mayers would likely categorize this coping method as "changing one or more of the statuses with which whole roles are in conflict" (1988, 134), even though the missionary may not intentionally set out to be a social reformer. The pitfalls of this coping method, however, are numerous. Women risk the possibility of being seen by nationals as a negative influence by bringing "decadent Western social ideas" about women's roles to destroy what they consider to be cohesive cultural structures. Indian political scientist Kumari Jayawardena writes:

> The concept of feminism has...been the cause of much confusion in the Third World countries. It has variously been alleged...that

feminism is a product of "decadent" Western capitalism; that it is based on a foreign culture of no relevance to women in the Third World; that it is the ideology of women of the local bourgeoisie; and that it alienates or diverts women from their culture, religion and family responsibilities on the one hand, and from the revolutionary struggles for national liberation and socialism on the other. (Jayawardena 1986, 2)

Furthermore, the people you desire to reach, especially the men, may reject the Christian faith because of the social changes they envision will be required of them as converts. Also, when missionary women transfer their positions of authority to women in the local culture, those women will not have the special status of foreigner that sometimes insulates missionary women from rejection in their host culture. I have often heard national women say to me, "That's fine when you do it, Donna, but we could never get away with that. People judge us according to our own cultural standards." The new local leadership may experience rejection and failure because their own society refuses to acknowledge the women's designated status.

One Romanian man, in criticizing some of the new missionary-led churches in Romania that were established after the fall of communism in 1989, told me that one of the elements he resented about the missionary-led churches was their blatantly Western liberality with regard to women's behavior and roles in the church:

Missionaries here are planting churches that steal our young people—especially the young girls. They attract them with rock music, and they give them freedom to wear makeup, to dishonor God by wearing trousers to church, and to shamefully display their heads and bodies in front of men. Women are even given responsibilities to teach and lead in ways that are totally foreign to us. This kind of behavior by women and youth would never be acceptable to our local churches. Don't the missionaries see that their methods are eroding our Christian faith and families by giving women freedoms that God never meant them to have?

While both young men and women were attracted to these new Christian fellowships, women especially enjoyed them because, as one Romanian woman put it, "I feel free to worship God without feeling confined to some prescribed female role." Women in these churches usually need not cover their heads. They can wear a little jewelry and makeup, and can even wear trousers to church. The pastor of one such congregation told me that he and his wife do have social reform as part of their agenda in church planting, discipleship, and evangelism, and they want to provide a place of fellowship for those men and women who feel disenfranchised from traditional churches:

> We're providing a model, not only of new social patterns of Christian behavior, but also a model of what it means to worship freely in Christ. We trust God that our existence, however troublesome it is to the traditional churches, will eventually lead them to change. Even if we don't change the older generation, we're certainly influencing the younger generation.

It is true that many of these missionary-led congregations have coped with conflict in expected Christian social roles by doing what Mayers refers to as "forming a new group." Some of these new groups have been highly successful because they attract younger generations who desire change from tradition. Obviously, while this coping method for role conflict has its attractions, one must also consider whether this approach is merely an excuse for judging the social structure of the host culture and asserting that Western cultural practices, especially with regard to women, are somehow superior and more Christian. Whatever the case may be, role insistence often leads to formation of a new group within which the insisted roles can be practiced without fear of rejection—whether that be a new church, a new Christian organization, a new club, or a new school. Is it a sustainable pattern that leads to mutual respect among congregations and cultures, or is it divisive and destructive? Could it lead to Christianity being identified with Western culture instead of a faith God intended to be multicultural? These are questions that need to be discussed among all missionaries as they evaluate the pros and cons of various church planting approaches.

COPING METHOD 2: ROLE ABDICATION

"I don't play any role here except that of wife and mother," said Joann, a mother of three school-aged children, a skilled musician, and a gifted administrator with organizational experience in the States. "I'm not thrilled with that restriction, but I think a visible role for me in the church or mission would compete with my husband's ministry and might even embarrass him in front of the church leaders with whom he is working. If we ever return to the States again, maybe I'll pursue my career, but given the cultural situation here, my career is one of the things I gave up to come to the mission field." This particular woman busies herself with homemaking, hospitality, and activities with expatriates and in general sees her career as a major sacrifice "for the Lord's work."

Although this particular statement was made by a missionary wife in Africa, I have heard it repeated in a variety of forms in the Eastern European setting as well, as missionary women decide to abdicate active ministry roles because of cultural (and sometimes organizational) restrictions (Barclay 2006). One educated missionary mother of two in Romania told me, "I came here with all sorts of great ideas about what [my husband] and I could do in our discipleship ministry together, especially with couples in the church. What I've found is that men don't want to learn together with their wives, and they certainly are not open to me as a co-teacher. I have never envisioned myself as being involved strictly in women's ministries. So here I am—still exploring what God would want me to do in this country. Perhaps I simply need to be a good example as a wife and mother." This woman and her husband eventually withdrew their involvement in attending a Romanian church and are now attending an international expatriate congregation where, the woman says, "I can feel more at home and appreciated, and I can have a ministry that uses my gifts and talents."

I must make it clear at this point that this coping method does not apply to those women who have chosen deliberately to minister within their home environments and/or within the expatriate community. Rather, these cases refer to women who have "withdrawn" as Mayers (1987) puts it. They attempt to escape the role conflict around them by withdrawing to an acceptable role, even if that role leads to inner conflict with their own ideals, desires, and dreams. Laura English (1995) writes that missionary women "often found themselves in environments that did not support" their dreams for ministry. She says that missionary women, especially married women, are greatly impacted by their ministry environments that "gave them few opportunities" to pursue their dreams and/or "communicated messages disapproving of their having certain dreams." She writes,

> The women tended not to fight their environments in order to pursue their Dreams; rather, they either abandoned the restricted Dream or held onto it, in secret, until they found themselves able to pursue the Dream in freedom and safety. (1995, 149)

Some women may rationalize their role abdication as role modification because they wish to meet the expectations of the nationals around them and thereby to be more culturally acceptable. The main difference, however, that I see between the two concepts is that role abdication is a negative, forced reaction to conflict whereas role modification is a proactive choice to conform to accepted social behaviors and standards. Role abdication can bring some rather unhealthy results, says English, especially if the missionary woman internalizes her anger "in order to live in peace" with her external realities (1995, 150). Wilson offers two examples of wives expressing such anger and resentment. One was her own story as she struggled with culture shock and identity confusion. She especially resented being seen only as "Gene's wife." "I was the popular one in the States," she writes. "And I had a fulfilling career at a National Exemplary school" (1996, 447). Wilson then tells of a neighbor who "had a similar experience when she took a two-year leave of absence from her lucrative counseling career to join her [husband] working in the Philippines." Although her neighbor enjoyed not working to some extent, reports Wilson, she resented her identity in the Philippines. Wilson quotes her frustration: "I've become Richard's wife or Hugh's mother! I had a name and a business in Montreal!" (ibid., 447).

Women who abdicate their roles unwillingly may find themselves withdrawing from and resenting the national culture altogether, becoming critical of the culture around them, and representing gloom and doom rather than salt and light. They may also face physical consequences of their psychological stress. Wilson mentions that such cultural stress can result in "headaches, ulcers, lower back pain, fatigue, skin eruptions, mental inefficiency, compulsive eating, excessive sleeping," and a host of other problems (1996, 446). Wilson, like many other authors on cross-cultural adjustment, recommends that the only solution to these stresses is "a purposeful pushing on," adaptation and adjustment, or proactive change (ibid., 449). This solution will be discussed under Coping Method 3 described below.

It is important to note here that single women missionaries usually do not have the option of withdrawal or abdication from their roles with the exception of leaving the field altogether. Some, however, may withdraw from ministries directly with nationals and decide to concentrate their attention on the expatriate community where their gifts are more appreciated and contextually acceptable and where needs for evangelism, discipleship, and church planting also exist. For the most part, however, single women will likely resort to employing Coping Method 3 to cope with the role conflicts they are likely to encounter.

One additional method of role abdication is for the missionary woman to seek a position in the secular environment in her host culture where she might have the opportunity to use her gifts in ways that would not be available to her in the Christian environment. While many women see this type of opportunity as a strategic way of influencing the secular business environment with the gospel, some women opt for this possibility because they are frustrated with the limitations on their roles in the mission environment. They see secular or government jobs as a way of escape from the tedium of their limited roles. For example, one missionary woman who is a specialist in Christian education said to me recently in Romania,

> It seems that being a missionary wife has so little status or influence here in Eastern Europe—even among women. Add to that the fact that I am a woman trying to work within a male church hierarchy and you can imagine how frustrated I feel. Working for a government NGO[11] or for a private education organization is awfully attractive to me. I'd get paid for my contributions, I'd have a role identity separate from my husband's, and I'd feel like I at least have something to answer when people ask, "What do you do here in Romania?"

Women must realize, though, that this type of role abdication can bring with it some fairly significant problems. First, women may find that they lose their partnership with their husband and mission teammates because they are no longer working toward the same goals. They may begin to feel isolated from their missionary teams and perhaps even from their husbands. Furthermore, some of the same role difficulties that occur in ministry settings will occur in the secular business or government setting as women work with national colleagues who may not accept a woman's professional status easily.

One additional aspect of role abdication has to do with the policies, practices, and structures of mission agencies themselves. In a

---

11 Non-governmental Organization

frank article entitled "Are Mission Agencies 'institutionally sexist'?" one theologian writes that according to research conducted among UK mission agencies in 2003, very few women hold senior leadership roles in mission agencies, nor do they apply for such roles. Her research showed that theological issues, psychological pressures, and organizational culture and structure often discourage women from seeking after leadership positions in the mission (Barclay 2005). She writes:

> Institutional sexism is not the whole picture for mission agencies. Here, as in other parts of the Christian world, a theological matrix of beliefs and assumptions about men and women is imposed on top of the unconscious attitudes and becomes part of the organizational culture. (ibid., iv)

When such attitudes permeate an agency, to whom can a female missionary turn to explore her concerns, frustrations, and/or potential?

COPING METHOD 3: ROLE ADAPTATION AND INTEGRATION

Glory Dharmaraj, writing in *Missiology* (1998), presents the theory that throughout history, women in mission more or less deliberately *negotiated* their roles from the margins of society in relation to the center or patriarchal power structure. She observes that women, from their margins, variously submitted to the center, circumvented it, confronted and challenged it, and in many cases transformed it. This purposeful strategy of repositioning oneself in relationship to cultural gender norms is the central theme of Coping Method 3.

The number of choices available by using this coping method, however, is large and ranges from accepting and working within cultural norms for gender roles, to strategically planning ministries to include those norms, to learning how to negotiate and integrate roles so that norms are transformed rather than threatened.

A few case examples help to illustrate this range of responses to encountering cultural gender biases in working with nationals.

Case #1: Accepting and Working Within Cultural Norms

When Shelly and Joan were posted to Romania, they envisioned themselves as part of a team of evangelists and church planters, helping to start churches, disciple the people, and encouraging others to do the same. However, as they began their work, they repeatedly encountered male Christian and non-Christian biases against their leadership both from within their mission organization as well as from the community around them, and they became discouraged. As they prayed for God's guidance, God began to bring into their lives many Christian women who needed help. Some were suffering from emotional or physical abuse and needed healing and help in restoring their spiritual vitality. Others were Christian women who desired to dedicate their lives to God in missions and ministry, but who were encountering much resistance from parents who felt that a female call to ministry was odd, counterproductive, countercultural, and probably unbiblical. Shelly and Joan felt God was redirecting them to stop "kicking against the goads" and work productively within gender norms by helping women "discover and celebrate their identity in Christ." "We feel we are effecting change in traditional churches and in society by empowering women to be all they can be in Christ." For several years, Shelly and Joan ran a restoration, prayer, and teaching center for women in Romania and were quite thrilled with the results God gave them.

Case #2: Ministry Strategies to Accommodate and/or to Transform Cultural Norms

Frontiers mission, in developing part of its strategy for reaching Muslims, includes the following purposeful vision statement for the women in its mission: "Frontiers will help serve and equip its women to be women of virtuous character who are actively encouraging and mentoring one another and who are effectively ministering to and for Muslim women. Frontiers sees women missionaries as key in church planting efforts among Muslims because they can penetrate a part of Muslim culture that would never be open to men. Women work as part of a team of church planters and they specifically target building relationships with women as part of the team strategy for church planting in Muslim societies." (Love 1999, 26–29)

The above is a great model statement for enabling women to see their missionary calling as strategic and critical to the evangelization of Muslims, even when conducted without pressing for change in cultural norms.

Confirming this high calling, but going a step further, Melanie McNeil (2010), who leads with InterServe and works in a Muslim context, suggests that women's ministry to women can also lead to transformational change—especially when those changes are already in process from within the culture itself:

The world of Muslim women in Arab countries is undergoing significant and rapid social change. Global pressures, failed dreams of nations in the post-colonial world and initiatives in areas like health and education are some of the pressures that create a potential for change…I believe there is a need for those of us who engage in mission to Muslim women to engage with this dynamic of change. (2010, 793–794)

Measures that change the structural position of women in society, thus providing them with true security, must be engaged in, both in the gospel that transforms lives and communities, and in allowing the truth to challenge structures that perpetuate marginalization, discrimination and deprivation. The gospel changes more than our status with God; it challenges and transforms every area of our lives. (ibid., 795)

The idea that missionary women can assist other women in responding to change that is already taking place is an exciting and strategic way of viewing what some might call a "more traditional" missionary role. Yet the actual result may be transformed tradition.

Case #3: Learning How to Negotiate and Integrate Roles

Pamela came to Kenya with a rich education and experience in her field, hoping to bring new insights into the Christian university environment in which she worked. She wanted to create a new major for the university as well as to augment the program already offered in the university's non-formal training program. But, as she put it, "I was a woman in a man's world." Although academically and experientially qualified to run a department, she was overlooked for that leadership role, she told me, "because they needed a man in that position." "But," she said, "I soon realized that I could help him be successful by offering my ideas and working through him. That method has worked wonderfully, and I'm seeing many of the things accomplished that I dream of doing here. I may not have the title, but I certainly have influence!" As Pamela gained the trust and partnership of the man she was helping, he in turn trusted her with more and more responsibility and she often ran the department in his absence.

The cases cited here could be augmented by hundreds of others. For example, Dana Robert's book, *American Women in Mission* (1996), is filled with stories of women who worked within the cultural norms and achieved great results—including, in some cases, what Dharmaraj (1998) calls "transformation of the center" of power. Whether it was combating the binding of feet in Chinese culture, protecting lower-caste women from prostitution in India, providing education for women, or training women in family hygiene and community health, missionary women worked within accepted norms from the "margins" to effect changes in the status and role of women in their host societies. They did not preach feminism, but by the nature of their ministries to women, they were transforming the culture of women and, therefore, eventually the broader social structure. Such transformation can take place when women are willing to place on hold their own desires for recognition and encouragement, choosing instead to celebrate the results of their influence, rather than their role or status in effecting change.

NEGOTIATING AND INTRODUCING NEW ROLES

While cases are few where mission agencies have deliberately formed policies encouraging an inclusive role for women in their ministries, those numbers are increasing. For example, the AD2000 Track for Women has as its goal "to help women around the world break barriers, and use their gifts to help fulfill the Great Commission" (Lutz 1999, 34). And Youth With A Mission (YWAM) made a specific appeal to women in its October 1998 *New Digest* to consider serving as missionaries among Muslims. Dana Robert (2002) has lauded World Vision for its positive and practical encouragement of women in ministry. While these organizations evidence great strides in recognizing and encouraging women's ministry roles in mission, there is much more to be done.

For example, while many women in missions successfully minister to other women through "evangelistic coffees," Bible studies, and various types of informal and formal training, it is seldom that these ministries are recognized or encouraged as contributing to the overall goal and strategy of the mission. Volunteer ministries in orphanages, in schools, and in community work are also often overlooked as strategic missionary work. Because of this oversight, according to English (1995), women—especially married women—can feel worthless and isolated, even though they consider their call to missions (or their missionary dream) as valid as their husband's. Leanne Dzubinski confirms English's conclusions:

> At a time of unprecedented movement toward the full inclusion of women at all levels of church and society in North America, many

mission agencies and structures continue to promote a strictly gender-based division of labor as the model of life and work on the mission field…In this scheme, the husband is the missionary and the wife is, well, a "missionary's wife." (2010, 151)

Even though she may have many neighborhood-based ministries, organizations rarely consider them part of the formal goals and objectives of the local team. Mission organizations definitely need to reconsider how they view and recognize the contribution of their female missionaries, how they define "ministry," how they integrate women's contributions into the strategic work of the organization, and how they might leverage women's leadership abilities for the success and growth of the mission.

Despite organizational biases and cultural challenges, many women find that they are able to negotiate and integrate their roles into their host cultures and therefore eventually transform cultural values about women. In fact, if more case studies could be gathered and documented about women who are using this type of coping method, the potential is great for developing missiological theory and strategies for women in missions. A few examples of such cases include the following.

An article by Kraft and Crossman (1999) tells of one woman who is working in a nomadic sub-Saharan African tribe, training Muslim male teachers (imams) in the gospel. The authors describe her ministry: "Building on a foundation of interpersonal relationship and Bible knowledge, she does not give them answers herself, but directs them to the Word." As a result, the imams see her as non-threatening, and she is accepted as "a loving, caring, elder sister" (Kraft and Crossman 1999, 16).

Another example of negotiation and integration comes from my colleague in Africa who loved her "informal chats" with her African supervisor, for when she suggested helpful improvements or new programs, weeks later she would find her ideas written up in papers and presented as the "recommendations of the department." "I didn't care who got the credit for the idea. The important thing was that the idea was adopted and put to work," she told me. Her willingness to serve in this role earned her much respect from her African supervisor, and she was generally seen as a trusted "expert advisor."

Another approach is being used by my missionary colleague in Romania. "Whenever I have a new idea for a program in the church, I talk it over with my husband and if he likes it, he presents it to the church Leadership Committee as an idea that was 'recently suggested to him.' That way, I can present some creative ideas for change without threatening anyone."

My own experiences in Africa suggested that when women have the covering of a formal institution (in my case, being part of the teaching staff of a university), it is easier for them to fulfill their own role expectations and for men to accept their teaching as authoritative. Although this was not always true, as the case study at the beginning of this article shows, for the most part, the women associated with the university where I taught enjoyed a certain status that gave them acceptability and influence among male Christian leaders.

In the same vein, new efforts at using business as mission or the idea of tentmaker missions can open doors for many qualified women who can function as business or NGO leaders and experts without threatening the position of male church or mission leaders. They can influence transformational social and spiritual change partnering with local churches while still upholding the authority of pastors in those churches.

It is good to mention here, however, that the status of a professor, a business leader, or a medical expert did not always guarantee acceptance of such status outside of the organizational environment. For example, despite the status I enjoyed at the university in Africa, that status did not carry over into the home when we entertained African male guests or when we visited the homes of pastors. Other women who are able to negotiate and integrate their roles in one setting may find that their roles must change in other settings within the same culture.

I found myself compartmentalizing my roles depending on the situation, justifying my compartmentalization with the explanation that it was my way of assisting my husband in his leadership role with pastors. When African church leaders were in our home, or we visited their homes, I found myself playing a more traditional role of serving, cooking, and not inserting myself into male conversation unless asked. Although this type of compartmentalization seemed dishonest at times, it was a practical and reasonable way for me to avoid role conflicts as long as I had a suitable outlet for ministry beyond the confines of the traditional role models.

CONCLUSION

It should be rather obvious as we come to the conclusion of this chapter that women experience a type of culture shock and adjustment on the mission field that is unique to them. While men also struggle with role issues on the mission field, rarely, if ever, are these issues related to a gender bias that restricts their activity greatly or requires them to considerably modify their leadership or ministry strategies with nationals in their host cultures.

As Fiona Bowie points out in *Women and Missions: Past and Present,* "Women and men live in different cultural worlds and this will inevitably manifest itself in missionary life and attitudes" (1993, 18). Because their experiences are different from men's, women need to be aware of the options for coping with the gender biases they are likely to face in their ministries with nationals.

Several options have been outlined in this article. Whether this awareness comes through pre-field reading and training or on-field counseling and consultation, such awareness is essential for the well-being and spiritual and professional development of women in cross-cultural ministry. With female missionaries comprising about two-thirds of today's missionary force, it is critical that mission agencies, churches, and academic institutions address the roles of women in cross-cultural missions in their various training venues. As one mission executive writes in reference to her own organization's ministry:

by increasing awareness and understanding of these issues, our hope is that proactive steps will be initiated to meet the unique needs of female workers so that they can thrive individually and strengthen the health of the [missionary] ministry team. (Lindgren 2012, 109).

REFERENCES

Allen, C. 1993. The Legacy of Lottie Moon. *International Bulletin of Missionary Research*, 17(4): 146–152.

Barclay, S. 2006. Are Mission Agencies "Institutionally Sexist"? *Global Connections Occasional Paper* No. 22 (Spring), i–iv.

Bauman, L. 1998. Femeia Crestina: Locul Ei in Ordinea Stabilita de Dumnezeu (Christian Women: Their Place in the Order Established by God). *Semanta Adevarulu,* May.

Bowie, F., D. Kirkwood, and S. Ardener, eds. 1993. *Women and Missions: Past and Present: Anthropological and Historical Perceptions.* Providence, RI: Berg Press.

Bowers, J. 1985. Women's Roles in Missions: Where Are We Now? *Evangelical Missions Quarterly,* 21(4): 352–362.

Corwin, G. 1997. A Second Look: Women in Mission. *Evangelical Missions Quarterly,* 33(4): 400–401.

Dharmaraj, G. E. 1998. Women as Border-Crossing Agents: Transforming the Center from the Margins. *Missiology,* 26(l): 55–66.

Donovan, K., and R. Myors. 1997. Reflections on Attrition in Career Missionaries: A Generational Perspective into the Future. In *Too Valuable to Lose: Exploring the Causes and Cures of Missionary Attrition,* ed. W. D. Taylor, 41–73. Pasadena, CA: William Carey Library.

Dzubinski, L. 2010. Innovation in Mission: Women Workers in the Harvest Force. *Evangelical Missions Quarterly,* 46, 2 (April): 150–156.

English, L. L. 1995. Life Dream Development of Married Missionary Women. PhD diss., Fuller Theological Seminary, Graduate School of Psychology.

Franzen, R. 1997. The Legacy of Ruth Rouse. *International Bulletin of Missionary Research,* 17(4): 154–157.

George, P. 1995. *College Teaching Abroad: A Handbook of Strategies for Successful Cross-Cultural Exchanges.* Boston: Allyn and Bacon.

Grunlan, S. A., and M. K. Mayers. 1988. *Cultural Anthropology: A Christian Perspective,* 2nd ed. Grand Rapids, MI: Academie Books.

Hall, M., E. Lewis, and N. S. Duvall. 2003. Married Women in Missions: The Effects of Cross-Cultural and Self Gender-Role Expectations on Well-Being, Stress, and Self-Esteem. *Journal of Psychology and Theology,* 31(4): 303–314.

Jayawardena, K. 1986. *Feminism and Nationalism in the Third World.* London: Zed Books.

Kraft, M., and M. Crossman. 1999. Women in Mission. *Mission Frontiers,* 21(5–8): 13–17.

Lindgren, L. 2012. Helping Women Thrive: A Key Component of a Healthy Team Approach. *Evangelical Missions Quarterly,* 48, 1 (Winter): 109–113.

Love, F. 1999. Blessing Women in Missions. *Missions Frontiers,* 21(13–17): 26–29.

Lutz, L. 1999. The AD 2000 Women's Track. *Missions Frontiers,* 21 (5–8): 34–35.

Mayers, M. K. 1987. *Christianity Confronts Culture.* Grand Rapids, MI: Academie Books.

Moreau, A. S., R. McGee, and G. Corwin. 2003. *Introducing World Missions: A Biblical, Historical and Practical Survey.* Grand Rapids, MI: Baker.

Pocock, M., G. Van Rheenen, and D. McConnell. 2005. *The Changing Face of World Missions.* Grand Rapids: Baker.

Robert, D. 1993. Evangelist or Homemaker? Mission Strategies of Early Nineteenth-Century Missionary Wives in Burma and Hawaii. *International Bulletin of Missionary Research,* 17(1): 4–12.

———. 1996. *American Women in Mission: A Social History of Their Thought and Practice.* Macon, GA: Mercer University Press.

Robert, D., ed. 2002. *Gospel Bearers, Gender Barriers: Missionary Women in the Twentieth Century.* Maryknoll, NY: Orbis Books.

Tucker, R. 1983. *From Jerusalem to Irian Jaya.* Grand Rapids: Academie Books.

————. 1988. *Guardians of the Great Commission.* Grand Rapids: Academie Books.

Wilson, L. 1996. Women and Culture Shock. *Evangelical Missions Quarterly,* 32(4): 442–449.

Winter, R., and S. Hawthorne, eds. 2009. *Perspectives on the World Christian Movement,* 4th ed. Pasadena, CA: William Carey Library.

EIGHT

Emotional Straight Talk
Ruth Ann Graybill

Thank you, thank you, thank you from the bottom of my heart for giving me the freedom to talk about my emotional needs as a missionary. I can't begin to tell you how utterly therapeutic this has been for me. Somehow there always seems to be the unspoken idea that missionaries aren't supposed to have emotional needs, BUT I DO!! Or somehow we're supposed to live above our needs, as if we weren't quite human. But the truth is I have more needs than what I typically care to acknowledge, and often I just downright don't know what to do with them!

This particular response is similar to many that I have received as a result of surveying one hundred women on the subject of their emotional needs on the mission field. The responses to these surveys, along with gleanings from counseling missionaries for over thirty years and my own experience as a missionary associate for three years, have provided the basis for this chapter. I would like to address here the needs most frequently identified, ways to address them, the consequences of unmet needs, and several practical applications that can be made.

How are the emotional needs of missionary women different from other women? Frankly, there is probably very little difference, but trying to meet emotional needs on the mission field can be much more challenging. Women are typically more isolated in mission settings, thus limiting opportunities for developing friendships. The challenges of missionary living are greater and more demanding as women contend daily with a multitude of cross-cultural stresses and demands. Simple conveniences of life are often missing.

Many basic supports that most of us take for granted are frequently not available on the mission field, such as reliable postal and telephone systems, dependable transportation, or even hot water and electricity. Furthermore, there is no ready access to the many helpful resources, such as family members and friends living close by, a supportive and sound church with quality teaching and worship, Christian bookstores and television and radio programs, professional counseling, or support groups. The absence of familiar resources and support systems tends to quickly heighten one's sense of vulnerability…and how readily sin natures can manifest themselves in the midst of neediness!

Because missionary women are involved in fulfilling the Great Commission in some of the darkest places in the world, they tend to be on the front lines of spiritual battle and are often subject to heightened resistance from Satan. As a result, these women are especially vulnerable to his attacks, some subtle and some anything but subtle. One tactic of the enemy commonly used against missionaries is attacking them through their emotional needs. When these needs are not being recognized and addressed in healthy ways, the door is inadvertently opened for discouragement and despair that ultimately could lead to devastation in any number of ways. Unfortunately, too many of our missionary women become casualties in battle, and the whole world suffers for it. Their loss becomes our loss.

At heart, most women seem to thrive on roots, security, and safety—elements hardly characteristic of the typical missionary woman's experience. If anything, missionary life seems to be marked more by the antithesis of roots, security, and safety. A woman's emotional makeup does not suddenly change just because God may call her to the far ends of the earth. To the extent that she can identify her needs and address them appropriately, her effectiveness on the mission field will be significantly increased. And to the extent that we as the non-missionary population can better understand our missionary women, our effectiveness in supporting them will undoubtedly be increased as well.

One particular missionary woman articulates clearly her thoughts on dealing with the issue of emotional needs. She states:

> I was stunned—no, shocked—to realize I'd have to grapple so much with emotional needs on the mission field. I think I just naively assumed that because I'm a committed Christian called into full-time ministry overseas, I would never have to worry about this area of my life. I guess I just expected these needs to get taken care of automatically or that God would somehow miraculously remove them from me. I had never realized how much energy would later go into trying to meet my needs or how much pain I'd experience trying to live with needs that I had no clue how to meet. If only I had been encouraged to think about this area of my life in advance.

EMOTIONAL NEEDS OF MISSIONARY WOMEN

The following were ranked as the most commonly identified emotional needs for both single and married missionary women:
- Intimacy and close friendship
- Validation and affirmation
- Healthy relationships in the missionary community
- Spiritual nourishment and support
- Time alone
- Maintaining close contact with family members living elsewhere
- Being understood by people back home

Intimacy and Close Friendship

Hands down, the number one need most often expressed is the need for an intimate, close friend. This type of longed-for friend is described in a number of ways:

> A friend with whom I can share my very soul and know that everything will be kept confidential; someone with whom I can be completely transparent, sharing even my secrets, and still be fully accepted and loved; someone who will allow me to process issues with her and just be willing to listen to me without trying to fix things; someone who will provide support, encouragement, and honest feedback; a kindred spirit; someone who will remain a trusted friend through the years.

One particular woman sums up her need this way: "How I long for a consistent and long-term soul mate, someone I can be myself with…and know I'm accepted even at my worst emotional and least spiritual times."

This longing for intimacy and close friendship on the mission field characterizes both single and married women, older and younger women, veteran missionaries as well as newer ones. Even if happily married, missionary wives still need close female friendships, realizing that there is something special in the friendships of other women. States one missionary wife with a twinkle in her eye:

> Face it, men just don't often listen and respond to us the way we need. Much as I deeply love my husband, often we're just on different wavelengths and I desperately need close female friends with whom to connect. Besides, he's often so busy and simply doesn't have time to just sit down and talk. And when we do talk, he wants me to get right down to the bottom line, but I need to think and process out loud. That often drives him right up a wall! My women friends give me the space to do this.

Indeed, married women blessed with close female friendships comment that their marriages are inevitably stronger because of these friendships. These fortunate women state that having good female friendships in place considerably lessens the pressure they might otherwise place on spouses to meet their emotional needs. Sadly, though, many missionary wives do not have any such close relationships, and their marriages suffer for it. They struggle with the unending demands placed on their husbands' time and energy, restricting their time together as a couple, and with no close female friends to help fill in the emotional gap. Frequently missionary women express intense loneliness in their marriages as they try to grapple with their husbands' preoccupation with work and hectic travel schedules.

Not surprisingly, this longing for intimacy and close friendship is especially the cry of many single women. In contrast to married women, a single woman does not arrive on the mission field with a built-in companion or an already established support system. Rather, she goes as a unit of one. She has no guaranteed intimate partner, no primary committed person with whom to share her joys and sorrows, with whom to build a future. She enters the mission field alone, likely with no one there knowing or sharing her history. Over time, this sense of going it alone can lead to a real feeling of isolation and loneliness if good, solid relationships are not eventually established. As one single woman says who has long struggled with this area, "I came into this experience alone and I'm in it alone." In fact, loneliness is by far the biggest struggle single missionaries seem to face.

If the need for intimacy and close friendship is so important, what prevents it from getting met? For many missionary women, the blockage is partially the result of isolation and geographical distance from other missionaries or from other Christians with a common language and culture. Though some missionaries live close together in their communities, many live in isolated settings, in remote places far removed from their coworkers. In some cases, a missionary woman may be the only person in a city or village who speaks her mother tongue! Comments one woman living far from others, "The isolation is at times unbearable. In my first term, I was so isolated and life was pure survival. I would have given *anything* for some kind of emotional support. Communication was almost nonexistent during that time of isolation." And even when women are able to get together, the opportunities may seem too infrequent to make it worthwhile attempting to build any meaningful relationships.

The missionary lifestyle tends to be constantly mobile—full of many moves, transitions, hellos, and good-byes. This degree of mobility makes it difficult to develop ongoing, consistent, and deepening relationships. One woman tearfully comments, "I find it hard to establish relationships that are long-term and stable because of people coming and going all the time. Somehow I seem to live with a sense of uprootedness." Notes another woman, "The friend you make today will be gone a year from now, or else you will have moved on." Yet another reflects, "This kind of living leads one to shut down, rather than risk the hurt of continual change." In a similar vein, one woman questions, "Why bother trying to develop a close friendship when the other person will invariably either be moved to another site before long or going home on furlough, or else I'll be the one leaving? What's the point to it? It's just too painful! I don't have the energy to keep starting over and over again."

Lack of a safe environment for sharing and lack of confidentiality are two other reasons why women may not experience intimacy on the mission field. Some missionaries have had unfortunate experiences of sharing confidential information with a coworker, only to have that information later leak out and be used against them. As a result of feeling hurt, betrayed, and violated, they no longer feel safe to share. Understandably, anonymity tends to be limited for those missionaries who live and work closely together, making it more difficult to feel safe in disclosing their thoughts and feelings. Some missionaries find the pain of loneliness at times easier to live with than the pain of further misunderstanding among their coworkers.

Limited ability to relate deeply with each other is another reason women may have difficulty in finding close friends. The mission field tends to attract highly committed people, some who may be inclined to invest considerably more energy into their work than into relationships. The very nature of mission work historically has called for hardy, pioneer-spirited individuals who are fully capable of "going it on their own" in the toughest of circumstances. This type of person, however well suited to isolated settings, harsh elements, or sparse accommodations, may have a much harder time dealing closely with people and all the intricacies of relational dynamics. For these missionaries, the thought of opening themselves up to others can be quite intimidating. One spunky, veteran missionary freely admits she feels immeasurably more confident contending with poisonous snakes that on occasion show up on her mission compound than with relational conflict among her coworkers!

The busyness of life can likewise hinder close friendships from developing. Many missionary women comment that there is simply too much to do by too few people. Frequently, they speak of the unending, pervasive needs that continually confront their community. They often struggle with feeling overly committed, but are uncertain how to reduce the demands placed on their time. They are surrounded by the needs of nationals, regularly having a steady stream of needy people coming to their front door. Many women feel stretched beyond measure, resulting in their own needs simply getting lost in the process. They often wish their mission could somehow allocate more time for relationship building between missionaries. One woman describes the challenge this way: "Everyone here at our missionary center is so overworked and tired and often struggling themselves. No one has anything left to give anybody." One missionary woman I counseled several years ago asked, with tears streaming down her cheeks,

> Why, oh why, can't our mission recognize that unless we cease from our super busyness long enough to look at the needs among

our own people, we won't be very effective in ministering to others? Many of us are so lonely, but no one seems to notice. Can't they see we're heading for burnout? Why can't our own needs be validated? Mine are screaming to be heard, and I can't seem to stuff them down any longer, no matter how hard I try.

Another barrier to meeting friendship and intimacy needs comes in the form of "emotional baggage" carried onto the mission field. This baggage is essentially unresolved emotional issues, such as unhealed emotional injuries from the past, family secrets or "ghosts," or those destructive habits that hold one hostage. Examples include childhood physical or sexual abuse, parental divorce, addictions, sexual sins, perfectionism, or chronic low self-esteem, to name just a few. This type of "baggage" taken to the mission field invariably has a negative impact on ministry relationships and effectiveness.

A number of women who are in leadership positions in the mission community cite the scarcity of other female leaders as an additional contributing factor to their unmet relational needs. These women often experience isolation and loneliness as the rare women in leadership, working primarily in the company of men. They state how they long to connect with other women in leadership, to process things out loud, and to have a safe place to share confidential information with other women.

Validation and Affirmation

Ranking almost as high as the need for intimacy and close friendship is the need for validation and affirmation of both their personhood and ministry. Missionary women long to have their gifts and abilities respected and utilized, their God-given potential fully developed. They want to be accepted as full members of their team, seen as equals by their male counterparts, with their ideas and contributions given equal weight. Writes one missionary, "I want to be able to serve nationals and coworkers with my gifts and abilities and not be seen as a threat to male egos." The opportunities for women on the mission field are numerous, and women can thrive when given the freedom to tap into them without reservation.

This need for validation and affirmation is similar for both single and married women, though expressed somewhat differently. Single women do not want to be assigned a lesser role because of their marital status or gender. They want equal recognition given to their skills and leadership abilities as is offered to men and to married women. Some single women find that their mission organizations grant a greater status of adulthood and maturity to married couples than to singles. One particular single shares how she was placed under the authority of a couple in ministry situations even though she was older and considerably more experienced than the couple. Another single woman comments:

> I sometimes feel like an appendage to a larger ministry team with most of the decision-making and general direction being handled by the men. Many times the single woman in a larger ministry comprised of couples feels that she is just a helper even though she may carry a heavy responsibility in the work.

In contrast to feeling underutilized, other singles mention just the opposite. In some mission settings, there seems to be the unspoken assumption that because singles have no marital or family obligations, they naturally have much more free time and should thus be expected to work longer hours, take fewer vacations, or even to be on call around the clock.

Because the single missionary does not have a spouse or children in which to invest herself, she needs to carefully guard against drawing an inordinate sense of identity from her work. Many missionaries tend to be task-oriented by nature, and singles may unwittingly overextend themselves in their work because of the deep sense of purpose and significance their work provides, especially in the absence of family relationships.

For married missionary women, they sometimes feel that being a mother and homemaker relegates them to the sidelines of mission decisions and responsibilities. Though these women may have chosen mother and homemaker roles as their primary roles for a period of time, they still want to be given a voice in mission planning and decisions. Many missionary wives keenly desire to make their own contribution to the mission cause, serving not just in a supportive role to their husbands, important as that role may be.

The need to be validated tends to be even greater for those missionary women living in countries that typically devalue women. In Muslim countries, for example, where women are generally considered inferior to men, missionary women frequently report a stronger need for validation. Single women, especially, can find this a challenge in the Muslim culture.

Healthy Relationships in the Missionary Community

A need for healthy relationships among coworkers also ranks high on the list. A missionary community is rarely a homogeneous group, but one often comprised of different organizations, denominations, nationalities, ethnic groups, and subcultures, each with its own values, beliefs, norms, and customs. Add to that mix all the individual personalities, temperaments, and family backgrounds involved, and one can well imagine the challenge in trying to integrate the myriad of differences. Conflicts, misunderstandings, rejection, betrayal, and criticism can mark the missionary community just as any other group of people living and working together. Not surprisingly, it can be quite disillusioning for missionaries to recognize their coworker's feet of clay—and to see their own as well.

Women quite often acknowledge they inadvertently began their missionary experience with totally unrealistic expectations. They just assumed missionaries would get along well with each other because of laboring together in the work of the Kingdom. "After all, we're all Christians!" What they sometimes find instead, however, is a heightened potential for conflict because of rubbing shoulders closely in the missionary community in the midst of difference, without having good communication and conflict-resolution skills. Missionary women frequently express a need to rework unrealistic expectations in the interest of building relationships.

Spiritual Nourishment and Support

Sadly, missionary women's own needs for spiritual input and growth can easily get lost in the shuffle of ministering to others' needs. "To experience more of God's presence and his love in the midst of my mission work" is the cry of many women longing for a deeper relationship with God, while immersed in unending ministry around them. They long for spiritual nourishment to renew and restore their souls. They crave more biblical teaching in their own language, quality worship that ministers to the depth of their soul, and fellowship that encourages them in their spiritual journey. Many women express a need for help to work through issues of faith that get presented on the mission field. One missionary poignantly writes:

> There's a sadness and depression that comes from dealing with constant poverty of soul, spirit, and material things surrounding most missionaries. Coping with these often requires spiritual contortions. How do we not be overcome with sadness and depression when we offer only a tiny drop of help in the sea of human misery? These are VERY real issues! Being compassionate means daily hurting for all the hurts around you.

Indeed, the numerous hurts confronting missionaries can be potentially corrosive to their faith and spirit. Not surprisingly, missionaries often wonder how to maintain a spiritual and emotional balance through the many challenges presented.

To help navigate these rough waters, many missionary women express a need for pastoral care. They long for someone to give them perspective on their questions and struggles, to assist them in refocusing, to help them sort through the tough issues on the mission field, to guide them in their mission experience as they pass through the different seasons of life. Often mentioned is a need for a mentor—such as an older, wiser woman to come alongside to provide encouragement and support, spiritual direction, and accountability in issues of spiritual disciplines and personal sin. The growing emphasis on member care in the missionary community in recent years has begun to address this need for pastoral care in very positive and constructive ways.

Time Alone

A related need is rest from continually giving out to others—time to nurture body, soul, and spirit. Though this is a universal need, it seems all the more critical for missionary women because of their intense involvement in the lives of others. They need regular times to escape the demands of those around them, to have a private getaway spot where they can replenish their own emotional and spiritual resources. Many women feel they are giving out all the time, or "dying on the vine." Yet, because of the tremendous needs around them, women often have difficulty giving themselves permission to set aside those needs and nurture themselves without feeling guilty. One missionary woman wistfully states that what she is most eagerly anticipating on her upcoming furlough is the freedom to close her windows in the middle of the day to take a nap without village people huddling outside the door wondering why she is shunning them.

Missionaries also need time away from each other. For those who live and work closely together, privacy can be a real challenge to find. Nonetheless, it must be found, and without guilt, if they hope to function at their best.

Maintaining Close Contact with Family Members Living Elsewhere

For those of us who are not missionaries, we often fail to understand the sacrifice those in mission work make in leaving behind beloved family members. Good-byes become tearful partings, not just because parents, grandparents, children, and other relatives may not be seen for a long time, but also because some of these loved ones may never again be seen this side of heaven. Relationally oriented as most women are, separations from family members can be very difficult. This is especially the case when the separation is from their very own children or grandchildren. No matter how clearly a woman may know it is God's will for her to be on the mission field, it still can be an intensely painful struggle for her to deal with the reality of being separated from family. To maintain close contact with beloved family members and nurture strong relationships with them from afar is a tremendous challenge for missionary women. Email and Skype communication in recent years have tremendously helped in this area, but still cannot replace having loved ones there in person.

No one pulls harder on the strings of a missionary woman's heart than her own children. Many mothers on the mission field grapple with the pain of their children living away from home. Some of their children may be attending boarding school elsewhere or may have returned to their home country to attend college or to find employment. Missionary women often tearfully speak of the challenge in trying to meet their children's needs long-distance or of having to place them in the care of another person. They recall wiping their tears as many times they watched a plane take off with its precious "cargo" headed off to boarding school, knowing it would be months before they would see their children again. And now as the mission field more than ever draws its new recruits from the age fifty-plus crowd, many grandmothers join the ranks of women leaving behind beloved family members to set off on mission ventures.

Being Understood by People Back Home

Missionary women often feel it is hard for people who have never lived on the mission field to understand their needs or relate to their struggles. Sums up one missionary, "It's the rare lay person who understands what I'm experiencing and who understands my emotional needs. When I finally drum up the courage to share, I find that some spiritualize my needs, some give pat answers, and some empathize."

Missionary women need the freedom to share deeply from their hearts without people quietly dismissing their struggles or without granting them a super spiritual status. One woman sadly expresses,

> Genuine sharing of needs back home somehow seems to result in us being given the label of "too emotional for our own good," like it's inappropriate to have those needs. And that's really painful because I so much want people to know what I struggle with. I'm not asking for sympathy, just understanding and a recognition of what we really grapple with on the mission field.

Women state they are more than willing to share the good missionary stories typically requested, as long as they are free to share their real life struggles as well. They long to be seen as real people and have others connect with them in their challenges of life.

EMOTIONAL NEEDS UNIQUE TO SINGLE WOMEN

As one veteran single missionary wryly states, "The hardest part of singleness on the mission field is being single!" Here is how various single women describe their needs:

- Learning to go it alone
- Finding acceptance in cultures where singleness is an anomaly
- Finding acceptance in the missionary subculture where singleness is not the norm
- Coming to terms with the possibility of never getting married
- Developing healthy relationships with men
- Dealing with the issues of sexuality in a healthy way
- Giving and receiving physical touch
- Good living arrangements

Learning to Go It Alone

Perhaps the greatest need and challenge for singles is that of learning to function as a solo on the mission field. As mentioned previously, a single woman does not carry her support system with her to the mission field. She has left family behind and typically goes totally alone to establish a new life. When she has decisions to make, other people may pray for her and support her, but the weight of decisions rests primarily on her shoulders. She typically has no one constant person with whom she can bounce off ideas, who will act as a sounding board for her. In difficult situations, there is no husband to protect her or fend for her; she has no male covering as does a married woman. Says one single woman, "A woman with a strong marriage can verbally process, pray, and share with her husband behind closed doors, whereas a single is primarily on her own." In short, the task of looking after herself is largely her own. This can significantly contribute to a sense of being isolated in her mission experience.

The single missionary must learn to meet her emotional needs in the absence of a spouse. Typically, there is no one particular partner she can rely on to love her, hug her, encourage her, affirm her, give her a shoulder to cry on, or simply be her cheerleading section. Other people here and there may provide emotional support, but she cannot necessarily count on that. Whether single or married, each woman must ultimately be responsible for getting her own emotional needs met, but it is especially incumbent upon the single woman to do so. Even if not comfortable for her, she must be willing to be intentional, decisive, and assertive about getting her needs met in order to survive well on the mission field. She must allow the Lord to become her husband, drawing on a close, intimate relationship with him for regular emotional sustenance. She must be willing to reach out to others and nurture herself in healthy ways.

Learning to successfully navigate the waters of loneliness is critical, no matter how difficult that may be. It is important that the single woman manage her alone time well, ultimately appreciating solitude instead of loneliness. She needs to guard against spending excessive amounts of time alone, exacerbating a sense of loneliness. She must learn to become a friend to herself and value her own company.

Out of necessity, the single missionary typically must function more independently than does her married counterpart. Depending on her situation, she may need to handle basic house and car repairs on her own. She must learn how to manage her home, handle herself in the marketplace, conduct business affairs in a foreign language, interface with local authorities, and deal with government red tape and hassles. Basically, she has to learn to become self-sufficient.

Singleness may call for some restriction of her activities, such as in the area of travel. In many countries, it is unsafe for a woman to travel alone, sometimes even with another woman, especially after dark. The single woman must be prepared to stay indoors after dark, or else find a male companion with whom she can travel without in any way raising suspicion in either the mission community or among the nationals.

Finding Acceptance in Cultures Where Singleness Is an Anomaly

In some cultures where singles minister, there is no such thing as a single woman category. Only the physically or mentally handicapped woman would ever remain single into her adult years in those cultures. In contrast, many women who go to the mission field are single and may remain so the entirety of their years on the field. The single woman may be seen as an odd entity in a culture that devalues unmarried women. Some single missionaries report being mocked in their host cultures because of their marital status. Comments one woman, "Where I live and work, women, especially single women, have no rank. With no husband or children to show the world, you're considered the absolute dregs of society. Much as I know in my head that that's not true, I really have to work at affirming myself."

Depending on the host culture, sexual harassment may be a real problem, particularly for the single missionary. One woman describes the challenge this way: "In the country where I serve, you're open to every conceivable lewd comment from the national men. When you go to the market, you just simply learn to expect sexual harassment. I often wish I had someone to stand up for me, to serve as a cover for me, so I wouldn't have to deal with this alone." Affirming her worth and specialness to God in these discriminating settings can present a challenging assignment for the single missionary.

Finding Acceptance in the Missionary Subculture Where Singleness Is Not the Norm

Fitting into the missionary subculture can also present a challenge for singles. Given that many mission communities are comprised primarily of couples and families, singles can sometimes feel like a social peculiarity—like the proverbial fifth wheel or the odd woman out. They sometimes wonder, "Is my singleness fully respected among my married coworkers? Where do I belong? Just who or what is my primary group? With whom can I vacation or spend the holidays? Is it indeed possible to develop a sense of family as a single?"

Singles sometimes grapple with feeling excluded from various mission social events, even looked down on, due to their marital status. Many find it hard to meet people as a single if not already part of an established unit. Some admit longing to feel "looked after" by other missionaries instead of having to fend for themselves much of the time. They sometimes have to fight against self-doubt or shame in the missionary community because of their marital status. Some speak of the unfairness of raised eyebrows if two single women spend considerable time together or in others not understanding the dynamics of long-term same sex friendships.

Coming to Terms with the Possibility of Never Getting Married

The plain reality is that if a woman goes to the mission field single, there is a high probability that she may leave the mission field still single. The sooner a woman can come to terms with her singleness, the less frustration she is likely to encounter in this area. For many singles, though, this issue tends to be a recurring one, rather than one that gets settled once and for all. This can be a difficult process, necessitating working through a multitude of painful feelings, such as sadness, grief, disappointment, despair, anger, shame, or bitterness. The biological clock ticking away does not help matters any as it reminds one of the passing of childbearing years. Singles at times struggle with God, wondering, *"Is this my reward for serving you faithfully? Is this what obedience to your call is all about?"* Hope and despair at times may alternate with each other as women struggle to make their experience fit their theology. Some women may have an opportunity to date and marry on the mission field, but that is generally far more the exception than the rule.

Recognizing that she may never marry invariably raises issues of security for the single woman. Questions present themselves, such as, *"If I stay single, who will take care of me when I'm older and possibly can no longer adequately take care of myself? Will I have someone with whom to retire? Will I have adequate resources in my later years?"* These questions can begin to hit hard, especially in mid-life. Not all mission boards provide for their missionaries after retirement, and the single missionary (unless married before) does not have the option of her children taking care of her. It is the rare missionary who has a large pension plan or a substantial Social Security savings account to handle financial needs in later life.

Another aspect of coming to terms with singleness on the mission field has to do with caring for one's aging parents. This issue is in no way limited only to single women, but it seems that they in particular agonize over the question, *"Where does my primary responsibility lie—with the mission field where I feel called by God to work, or with my parents back home?"* Regardless of the emotional or financial cost to her or of the proximity of other family members to the parents, it is often automatically assumed by married siblings (even if their own children are grown) that it is the primary responsibility of the single female offspring to provide care to aging parents. Even if she lives on the other side of the world, the single missionary may be expected to terminate her work and return home. In the absence of a spouse or children, her own calling is often given less weight by her family. I know of one missionary woman who had six married siblings, all with grown children, and all living within thirty minutes of the parents. Because she was the only single sibling, however, it was assumed she should be the one to give up her work and move back home to care for her aging parents thousands of miles away.

Developing Healthy Relationships with Men

Even if she has successfully settled the issue of singleness, the single missionary woman still needs opportunity to relate to men—both single and married, missionaries and nationals. She needs the opportunity to see life through a man's eyes and the male perspective that her female friends cannot give. Naturally, though, she needs to exercise a great deal of caution in this area. Because missionary wives may be involved primarily at home caring for their families, especially when their children are young, they are often less directly involved in mission work than are the single women, working right alongside the married missionary men. To avoid problems, singles need to keep their relationships with men out in the open, free of suspicion or misguided intentions. They must do their best to ensure that their manner of relating to missionary men is not questioned by nationals, even if that behavior may be considered totally acceptable within the missionary subculture. In relating to national men, the single missionary must be especially sensitive to cultural cues concerning decorum in male-female relationships. With God's grace, she can rise above the frustration that often comes in having to continually scrutinize her behavior so as to avoid suspicions. She needs to decide whether or not she will date national men and to understand the implications of doing so.

Dealing with the Issue of Sexuality in a Healthy Way

Handling sexuality can be a special challenge for single women. Questions are raised, such as, "Can one truly be sexually fulfilled as a single? What are appropriate ways to meet sexual needs? How does

one commit to moral purity for the long haul? How does one subli-
mate sexual needs or desires in healthy ways? Is masturbation a sin?
How do I handle my guilt from impure thoughts?" Unfortunately, this
topic rarely gets addressed openly on the mission field or in pre-field
training. Sensing that the discussion of sexuality may be off limits for
Christians, some single missionaries repress their sexual feelings and
drives, even asking God to remove them.

To avoid dealing with the area of sexuality in a healthy manner, however, only invites potential problems for single missionaries. They may
live with continual frustration and tension that rob them of joy and
vitality. They may attempt to hide the issue behind excessive weight or
may minimize their femininity in appearance and behavior. Some may
become totally absorbed in their work in an attempt to suppress this
conflictual area. For yet others, the outcome is more serious if they
become entangled in immoral relationships.

Through the years, I have counseled a number of women whose missionary careers came to a crashing halt because of immoral relationships
in which they had become entangled. One particular woman became
sexually involved with a national man out of her intense loneliness. Totally
driven by her overwhelming need and too embarrassed to acknowledge
it to fellow missionaries, she fell prey to the solicitous attention of a
kind, non-Christian man in her village. She quietly began dating him, all
the while trying to convince herself that her strong faith and high moral
standards would safeguard her from any inappropriate behavior. Only
too late did she realize how desperately vulnerable she had become, and
she returned to her home country as a broken woman.

I have also counseled several women who became sexually involved
with other missionary women. These women were not homosexual
in orientation, by any means, but they had never learned how to appropriately acknowledge and address legitimate emotional needs that,
over time, became sexualized. I might comment here that rarely ever
are moral failures, whether heterosexual or homosexual, simply issues of meeting sexual needs. Instead, they are primarily attempts to

meet deep underlying emotional needs that in the absence of healthy awareness and addressing of these needs find expression over time in a physical/sexual involvement. Singles need to embrace their sexuality, acknowledging their sexual needs and feelings as God-given, and learning to express them in healthy, creative ways.

Giving and Receiving Physical Touch

A single woman has no spouse or children of her own to caress her, hug her, cuddle up next to her, or rumple her hair. It has been said that to be emotionally healthy a person needs eight to twelve hugs a day. Singles may literally go for months without a single hug, depending in part on how their host culture or mission group views hugging. Even a "holy hug" from a Christian brother or sister may raise eyebrows. Whenever a single missionary has physical contact with another adult, she needs to be fully aware of her needs and motives and be sensitive to cultural and mission norms concerning the propriety of such behavior. She needs to recognize that physical touch, even something so seemingly innocent as a back rub or neck rub given by another woman, can potentially lead to inappropriate behavior. A single status in no way, though, eliminates a God-given need for touch. It just means a single person must find creative ways to get this need met.

Good Living Arrangements

Quite often single missionaries feel that their needs in living situations are assigned a lesser priority than those for families and couples. On the mission field, there is sometimes the misconception that any two singles should be able to live together and adapt to each other, despite differing personalities, temperaments, or personal habits. Unfortunately, disastrous consequences can result when singles are arbitrarily placed with each other or assigned to live with families without having any prior relationship with them.

Singles at times feel they are the ones most expected to move or to have others move in with them, and as singles come and go, so their roommates come and go. One single missionary woman told of sixteen different roommates in eighteen years! For those single women experiencing a multitude of changes in living arrangements, home hardly feels like a stable refuge. Singles find it takes tremendous emotional resourcefulness to establish close relationships with roommates when they come and go so frequently.

Because her living situation is often temporary (recognizing that permanency is hardly characteristic of any facet of missionary life), the single woman may simply decide to treat her home as a temporary residence, decorating it only minimally and withholding placing her "personality stamp" on it. As a result, her living quarters may feel more like just a house rather than a home. One particular single missionary humorously describes her experience this way:

> Even when I do decide to decorate, the decor keeps changing as roommates keep changing! Conceivably one could argue that all the adjustments and readjustments of singles' living situations are simply a refining tool of God to help produce flexibility and adaptability, but after awhile, these changes feel far more chaos producing than character producing!

EMOTIONAL NEEDS UNIQUE TO MARRIED WOMEN

The emotional needs of missionary wives are not essentially different from other married women, but the particular demands and stresses on the mission field seem to invariably heighten their needs and present additional challenges in meeting them. Here are some of the common needs expressed by married women:

• Maintaining emotional equilibrium in multiple roles
• Taking care of herself in the midst of meeting her family's needs
• Contributing directly to the cause of the mission

Maintaining Emotional Equilibrium in Multiple Roles

Balancing the juggling act of wife, mother, and homemaker can be a challenge of the highest order on the mission field. Missionaries typically comment that simply the act of living requires much more time for them, and perhaps no one feels it more than the missionary wife and mother trying to manage a busy household in a foreign land. Depending on how primitive her setting is, she may need to heat water on the stove for family baths, wash clothes by hand, grow much of their food, boil their drinking water, soak all fresh produce in chlorine to eliminate parasites, cook food from scratch, bake their bread, and possibly even kill and clean the chicken for dinner. Convenience foods and time-saving appliances that we take for granted in the industrialized Western world may be almost nonexistent, and what appliances are available may break down on a regular basis. Refrigeration may be limited, necessitating daily shopping that can take literally hours. In certain areas of the world, it is culturally unacceptable for men to shop, so the missionary wife cannot count on shopping assistance from her husband. Depending on how well she knows the language of her host culture, communicating with nationals can present a real challenge as she carries out her daily responsibilities. In addition, she must observe and learn all the cultural customs and norms while out in the public eye.

If she has young children at home, she is likely the parent most involved in their day-to-day care while her husband is more directly involved in mission work (with him sometimes gone for days or weeks at a time). Babysitting, day care services, or other support services are typically very limited. Having grandparents around to help babysit is a luxury that has to wait until furlough. If she homeschools, she adds to an already demanding job description the role of teacher, often having only limited educational resources with which to work. If her children attend boarding school away from home, she may struggle continually with a sense of loss and the challenge of trying to nurture them long-distance.

In the midst of caring for her family, she needs to work on keeping her marriage strong and growing, even fresh and exciting. She needs to focus on her husband and ensure that he does not get lost in the shuffle of life. She needs to let her husband know her needs and not let herself get lost. She needs to find time and energy to do her part in re-vitalizing this most important relationship on a regular basis, no small challenge given the typical limitations of both time and energy. She needs to help create a space and time for a healthy sexual relationship with her husband. Otherwise, it becomes far too easy for marriages on the mission field to just coast in neutral because of so many other demands being placed on them. Unfortunately, missionary couples are not spared the pain of divorce just because they are in full-time ministry in foreign lands.

Given that medical care is often limited on the mission field, handling health issues becomes yet another responsibility for the missionary wife/mother, regardless of her training. She frequently needs to serve as the "resident doctor" for basic medical problems in her family. Dealing with illness or injuries tends to fall much more on the shoulders of a missionary woman than on those of her non-missionary counterpart.

As if these responsibilities were not enough, the missionary wife may have a steady stream of nationals coming to her door, asking for help of various sorts or just stopping by to visit. Due to cultural norms in her host country, she may feel little freedom to decline assisting them or to ask them to come back later, however graciously presented. Privacy can be a scarce commodity in a missionary home.

Dealing with visitors from back home also becomes part of her juggling act. Much as she may dearly love and welcome visitors, enter-taining them for a period of time in her home can add a tremendous load to her responsibilities, if not handled sensitively and wisely.

Taking Care of Herself in the Midst of Meeting Her Family's Needs

In the midst of all of the above, the missionary wife/mother must still pay attention to her own needs if she is going to thrive on the mission field. It can be tempting for her to expect her husband to meet her needs, rather than assuming responsibility herself, no small challenge in a foreign setting. Besides having no ready access to babysitting services, she may also not have available to her adult educational classes, a local YMCA, good bookstores or libraries, shopping malls, coffee shops, bathtubs in which to relax, a place to be alone, or friends close by. It may not even be safe to venture outside just to take a walk by herself. She may need to become extremely creative in finding ways to take good care of herself.

Contributing Directly to the Cause of the Mission

Despite her important and demanding roles of wife, mother, and homemaker, she still needs to feel she has something of significance to contribute to her mission. As mentioned earlier, some wives and mothers struggle with knowing how to fit into the mission, uncertain how to connect to the larger cause. One missionary woman writes, "Sometimes I wonder if I'm even a missionary because I function just as a mom who simply happens to live on the mission field. My role can be very confusing. What am I? I need to feel like I have a purpose in this mission beyond my role in the home. But what is that?" Yet knowing that larger purpose can sometimes create a difficult dilemma as she tries to figure how to integrate that purpose into her extremely busy days.

WAYS TO ADDRESS EMOTIONAL NEEDS OF MISSIONARY WOMEN

Permit me to speak directly to missionary women in this section, pooling their ideas along with some of my own, on how to meet emotional needs. Much more could be said about each of these ideas, but space allows for addressing them only briefly.

1. Recognize that no matter how healthy you may be, you will still have emotional needs as a missionary.

Being a committed, godly woman called to God's service on the mission field will not exempt you from emotional needs. Having emotional needs is normal, natural, and legitimate. God created all of us with these needs to keep us ever mindful of our need for relationship, first and foremost with himself, then with others and ourselves. You will at times experience loneliness, discouragement, and misunderstanding. Count on it! That's simply part of the human experience. The question is not, "Will you have needs?" but "How will you handle them?"

One veteran missionary woman summarizes her thoughts on this subject in this fashion:

> The idea that we are anything different as missionaries in another culture than we are here at home is not true. In fact, what we are seems to intensify in another culture; i.e., if we are selfish, giving, lonely, hospitable, reclusive, etc., we will be even more so where we are the "revered American missionary." If we have problems with relationships here—in or out of the home/church—we will find those same problems overseas, only again, more so.

Don't be surprised if you discover needs on the mission field you had not even realized beforehand that you have. The stress of missionary life may bring out needs and reactions in you that leave you totally reeling and dumbfounded initially.

Be assured, there is nothing spiritual whatsoever about trying to ignore one's emotional needs and just live by faith instead. To deny one's needs in a vain attempt to live above them is a sure way to become enslaved and controlled by them—to be need-driven rather than faith-driven. Having emotional needs is not the antithesis of faith nor is the absence of needs the hallmark of a godly saint. One need only look at the life of David, "a man after God's own heart," to understand this. The Psalms are replete with David emotionally crying out to God time and time again in the rawness of his deeply felt needs.

2. As much as possible, get your emotional needs in good order before even going to the mission field. Develop a healthy self-esteem.

If you have not yet begun your mission work, consider postponing an assignment until you have taken care of your "emotional baggage." Taking unnecessary "baggage" to the field with you only serves to compound the inevitable stresses and strains of missionary life, ultimately limiting your effectiveness. Become as emotionally healthy as you can on this side of an assignment. Whatever troubles you have at home will become magnified on the mission field— guaranteed! Anticipate what emotional needs you will have, and begin now to prepare for them. Before heading overseas, work hard at developing a strong support system of healthy relationships in your home country. You will reap the benefits for years to come. Make any unresolved issues a serious matter of prayer and have a few trusted friends commit to pray for you. Face directly any issues that need to be confronted and don't allow yourself to run from the pain or discomfort of them. Consider support groups and/or counseling as necessary. If you're already in mission work and have "emotional baggage" that needs to be addressed, begin taking steps immediately to work on the issues.

Do all you can to develop a healthy and accurate self-esteem before beginning your mission work. Make a serious study of the character of God. Learn to know within the depths of your soul your identity in Christ and how he sees you. Ask God to root out the lies and misconceptions about yourself that limit your potential. Learn to know yourself as much as possible, both the healthy and the unhealthy parts. Identify and come to terms with your strengths and weaknesses, meanwhile continuing to work on them. Accept what you cannot change about yourself and learn to become comfortable with yourself. Continually trust God to complete his good work in you, even while fully seeing all that still needs to be done. The value of a healthy, solid self-esteem cannot possibly be overestimated if one is going to survive successfully on the mission field.

3. Be sure of your calling to the mission field. If possible, exercise choice in your mission assignment.

Know without a shadow of a doubt that God has called you personally to the mission field. If you are married, a husband's call alone is not sufficient; you need your own. Without this calling, it is too easy to quit later when the battle intensifies, when you wonder whatever could have possibly motivated you to sign up for mission work.

Exercise choice, if you can, as to where you go on the mission field. Try to choose a mission setting that supports healthy friendships among women. To choose an isolated situation where you would be mainly on your own could be a real setup for defeat. Do some homework on your part first. If possible, visit a potential mission setting before making a final decision.

To those who are single, try to go to the mission field as part of a team. (Some organizations send out singles only in pairs.) Avoid the "going-it-alone" route as much as you can. If possible, choose a place that is accepting of single women, allowing freedom to move about on one's own.

4. Cultivate a close personal relationship with the Lord.

Make this relationship an absolute priority, despite whatever else may be going on in your life—and don't wait until you get to the mission field. Learn how to have intimate fellowship with the Lord, drawing from him—not from your spouse or your friends—as your primary source for meeting emotional needs. This is especially true if you are single. Wisely writes one missionary, "The Lord must be your strength, your joy, your everything—even if you are married." Do not make the mistake of assuming that your service for the Lord substitutes for time alone with him. Schedule time in your day for him as this time may not happen otherwise; do not allow busyness to crowd it out. Jealously guard your time with him. Do not allow yourself to feel guilty, though, especially as busy mothers, when your quiet time may get shortened or sometimes simply lost in the day. Just start over the next day.

5. Recognize that YOU are the one human ultimately responsible for getting your emotional needs met. Give priority to meeting your needs.

As you seek the Lord's help in this area, he will guide you and give you wisdom, but it is you who needs to take the primary human initiative to get your needs met. Do not assume people around you will meet your needs; you could be very disappointed or disillusioned otherwise. You are responsible for you—not your spouse, roommate, prayer partner, mission leader, friends, or anyone else. One seasoned missionary woman emphasizes, "You can pray for, long for, or hope for someone else to help meet your emotional needs, but you *cannot* expect it or demand it." So be willing to accept responsibility for getting your own needs met. Develop a plan; be proactive and assertive. Make getting your needs met enough of a priority that you are willing to invest time, energy, and money in seeking solutions. One missionary wife speaks from the voice of experience as she comments how taking initiative has been her primary lifesaver. She states,

> No one is going to observe my need and take steps to meet it. That's my responsibility. This includes taking initiative to make time with friends, to take time to read, to include fun and relaxation, to pursue potential friendships in unlikely places—among single women and with women both younger and older than myself. If I don't bear responsibility to do these things, no one else will either. So if they aren't important to me, they simply won't happen.

Do not wait until everyone else's needs are met before you begin thinking about your own. As women, we tend to be nurturers by nature, often to our own detriment. We look after everyone else's needs first, then tend to ourselves, *if* there happens to be any time or energy left over, which often there is not. What comes to mind here are the instructions typically given by airline personnel to flight passengers just before takeoff. The message goes something like this: "If oxygen masks are needed, please place your mask on *first*, and then assist children or others around you who may need help." Whether on or off an airplane, we are of virtually no help to anybody else around us if our oxygen supply is dangerously depleted.

The plain, perhaps somewhat harsh, reality of mission life is that it requires a tremendous measure of emotional resilience or hardiness if one is going to endure the course well. Taking ownership and responsibility for your own emotional needs will go a long way in strengthening your internal resources.

6. Identify your own specific needs and feelings, and give yourself permission to express them.

Learn to recognize what triggers your needs and what intensifies them; then work with that knowledge accordingly. Honor your needs and limitations. When I was a missionary in Japan, I lived right in the midst of a Japanese community and totally immersed myself in every way possible in the Japanese way of life. I typically loved this immersion, but about every three or four months, I suddenly found myself feeling as if I were drowning with anything and everything Japanese. At those times, I had a desperate sense of needing to come up for air by escaping to familiarity for a while. Fortunately, I had wise missionary relatives living in Tokyo who understood my need, so at those critical times they would invite me to come visit them. They graciously allowed me to hide away in their house for several days and return to all my familiar American ways as much as I could. Quite miraculously at the end of this self-imposed "house arrest," I would emerge thoroughly refreshed and rejuvenated, ready to reenter the mainstream of Japanese life for another few months, until the process started all over again.

Learn to say "I'm lonely," or "I'm hurting," or "I need…" Allow people to reach out to you. Don't build a tough shell around yourself. Make an absolute commitment to share yourself and your struggles, even if you cannot choose the friends you would ideally like. Admonishes one missionary: "To not communicate one's inner self condemns one to a downward spiral of loneliness and depression, or to becoming hardened in a way that restricts the flow of Christ's love in us." Commit to becoming vulnerable, to taking risks in sharing. Exercise discretion, though, in what and with whom you share.

Choose to stay open in relationships, despite the mobility and transitions so typical of missionary life. It does indeed hurt to say good-bye over and over again, but the loneliness of walling oneself off from potential friendships simply to protect against the pain of more good-byes hurts far worse. The price to pay for staying involved and open in quality relationships on the mission field is decidedly far less than choosing to close off to others.

Consider journaling as an excellent tool to help express your feelings, to sort through what's going on in your life and give clearer perspective. A journal can become a type of best friend who will allow you to pour out your heart and share your innermost secrets in full confidence.

7. Come to terms with the reality that some of your emotional needs may go unmet for periods of time.

Hard as that may sound, there will be times when you simply have to live with unmet needs—and be content in the process. It would seem that Jesus himself had unmet needs while on earth, and so will each of us. Deliberately and intentionally choose to trust God for grace and strength, even joy, during these difficult times. Trust that if God indeed has brought you to the mission field, he will provide for you during those dry stretches. He will meet you in the midst of your unmet needs and will make himself sufficient during those times. One former missionary, single at the time, shares her thoughts about her own unmet needs on the mission field: "I never stopped longing for relationship, or affirmation, but I learned to be content without my needs met." Following is an excerpt of an email message she sent after her return to the United States to a new missionary struggling with loneliness:

> I think what you are going through is very normal. To be very honest, I never got over the loneliness I felt most of the time I was there. I learned to accept it as part of what God had called me to, but I never got over it. The Lord and I had some very long conversations over it, and many nights, especially out in the village, I cried myself to sleep.
>
> So I can't give you any easy answers as to how I overcame the loneliness, because I didn't. I do know that the Lord showed himself in some very special ways during that time, and he himself comforted me.
>
> I remember one particularly bad day when I was really struggling with adjusting to village life alone, living with a local family. I got so frustrated that I remember going out behind the village, sitting on a hill and crying, "Lord, here I am in the middle of nowhere and no one knows what I am going through right now. No one cares!" Then I opened my Bible to Psalm 103:11–14, and 1 Peter 5:6–7. I had to be reminded that God did care. It didn't mean I ever felt good about being alone. I just knew that I could cry out to God and he did hear me, but that for the moment this is what he had chosen for me.
>
> So I am afraid I have no solution for loneliness. I eventually learned to live with it, accept it, and no longer fear it. I took comfort in knowing that God brought many of the great men of biblical times—Abraham, Moses, Joseph, Jesus—through times

in the wilderness. (By the way, the main semantic component for "wilderness" is a "lonely place.")

I did discover one thing that I grew to love, and that was the seawall down by the bay. I used to walk down to the wall and then jog along the wall. I let myself just walk on the beach or sit on the rocks if I was either really hot or really tired. Many times I lingered and sat and watched the sunset. But the seawall became my time with the Lord, often kind of a hug from the Lord each day. I miss that, I miss that very much.

Another missionary woman writes, "I believe the fact of living in a foreign country presents some emotional needs which cannot be really met…but one must accept and find the Lord sufficient." Yet another one muses, "I believe I've learned that God does not promise to meet all our needs by immediate answers to our prayers, but knowing he is at work to develop character and a deep spiritual walk with him has made the loneliness worthwhile." You may not always have a profound sense of needs being met in the moment, but looking back, you will likely be able to see that God gave exactly what was needed to persevere through those difficult times. Those periods of unmet needs provide an excellent opportunity to depend on God in ways not otherwise experienced.

8.With God's help, learn to change loneliness into solitude.

Recognize that loneliness is not caused by isolation or singleness per se, but by the mind-set that says, "Someone ought to be here." Loneliness has been described as being alone with oneself while solitude is being alone with God. Loneliness is simply part of the human experience and part of what drives us to a deeper relationship with God and other people. Ask God to teach you how to spend time with him as a friend. Remember that you always have the freedom to choose your own attitude, regardless of what may be going on around you. Viktor Frankl in his book *Man's Search for Meaning* (first published in 1946), stated that even though he was a prisoner in a Nazi concentration camp, he was freer than his guards because he found they could not take away his right to decide his attitude. He wrote, "Ultimate freedom is a man's right to choose his own attitude." Recognizing this freedom can be a tremendous way to avoid self-pity.

While learning to enjoy the company of God, learn to enjoy time alone in your own company as well. Develop the art of becoming your best friend! Put yourself on your list of people with whom you enjoy spending time.

9. Keep expectations realistic.

Recognize the emotional drain on you that the myriad of cross-cultural stresses and demands of missionary life creates. Allow yourself the freedom to make mistakes, to live with your imperfections and limitations. Give yourself time to adjust to the differences in your host culture. However interesting newness may be, it can be very wearing. Don't try evaluating yourself or your world when you're tired, sick, angry, pressured, or depressed! Be careful not to compare yourself with others. The better you know yourself—your strengths, abilities, weaknesses, limitations, trigger points, and temperament—the more effectively you will be able to set realistic expectations. If it is hard for you to identify your unrealistic expectations, ask someone you trust to share what they observe about you or how they experience you.

Be careful about expectations you assume for your workload. Allow me to share the counsel of my wise mother years ago as I was just starting my counseling practice. She stated, "No matter how many clients you see or how hard you work, there will always be many more people with many more needs than you can possibly ever meet." So pace yourself accordingly. There's no special merit in burning out for the Lord!

Work diligently to keep your expectations of other people realistic. They also are finite, imperfect, flawed beings. Simply count on the fact that they will hurt you and disappoint you at times.

10. Make a conscious choice to actively pursue developing several key friendships on the mission field.

Seek out fellowship with other Christian women and intentionally start cultivating friendships. Even though the pool may be small from which to draw, don't become discouraged. You might be surprised at how a friendship develops, even from what perhaps initially seems like an unlikely match. If you live in an isolated setting and no particular friendship seems possible naturally, ask the Lord to bring a friend across your path. When you find a possibility, deliberately pursue this friendship, even if long-distance. Write letters; make telephone calls; send email messages; Skype; schedule trips into town together at the same time; plan vacations together. Do not allow distance or busy schedules to force you to neglect developing and nurturing friendships. As one woman states, "No matter what it costs to say hello and good-bye, make friends and keep them; be a good friend."

If possible, meet together with several other women on a regular basis. Get together to celebrate holidays, birthdays, engagements, babies, or any other special occasions. Create reasons! Share struggles, pray together, swap news from back home, help each other with house projects, or in teenage parlance, "just hang out." If one of these women is an older woman whom you deeply respect, consider asking her to become a mentor to you. If no one close by can fill that role for you, consider email mentoring.

Be aware of emotional dependency in your friendships, however. Because no one friend can meet all of your emotional needs, avoid the trap of trying to jealously possess the time and attention of any one particular friend. Seek out at least several friends to help meet your needs for friendship and intimacy. Learn how to set appropriate boundaries.

Listen to one single woman's story of how she dealt with the need to cultivate friendships on the mission field:

When I worked in Kenya, I lived in a little house by myself. People asked me if I were lonely, and I'd say, "No, the Lord lives with me." But later during my furlough, a counselor told me, "You are intensely lonely." I replied, "Oh, really? I tell people that I'm not lonely, and I thought I was telling the truth."

The counselor helped me see that God is a relational God and that we are made in his image. Therefore, quality relationships are part of the package if we are going to be emotionally whole. He told me that I should spend 30 percent of my time in in-depth relating. Prior to this, my priority list had looked like this: 1) my personal relationship with the Lord, 2) my health, 3) my office job for which I had come to the mission field, and 4) personal outreach in my free time.

Relationships weren't even on the list. So I made a list of my favorite people in town. And I would make a plan to spend a substantive amount of time with one of them every day. For example, Suzie's two-year-old went down for a nap at 1:00 every day. So I would drop in to see Suzie at 1:00. Ruth was single, so I'd ask her if we could do something together on our day off. I really enjoyed my boss. So I invited his family of five to dinner, and we spent a whole evening together. Seven days a week I made appointments. If I saw one of my favorite people as I was running errands, I gave myself permission to forget about my to-do list and to linger and enjoy a conversation with that person for as long as it worked out.

I had to interview people in my job. Prior to this, when the interview was over, I would chat a little bit so as not to be abrupt and then go my way. But now, if I especially liked the person, I would linger and just enjoy spending time with him or her. After a few months I realized that I was much happier. I wasn't spending as much time visiting my non-Christian friends to witness to them in my free time, but I felt like I was living life more as God had intended it to be.

11. Broaden your circle of friends.

Do not limit yourself to just your own team, your own mission, or the mission community for friendships. Reaching out beyond your familiar world can expand your thinking and protect you from tunnel vision. Besides, a friend outside your own group may feel like a safer person with whom to share your heart, as there is less likelihood she is socializing with other people you know. Reach out beyond the missionary community to the larger expatriate community as well—to the foreign business and academic community, if available.

Intentionally seek to develop friendships with nationals. Though cultural differences may limit deep friendships from developing, you could be delightfully surprised. Comments one woman, "God redefined what I thought of as needs and brought much satisfaction through relationships with nationals." In reality, there's probably no better way to win nationals to the Lord than to first develop friendships with them. If unsure, ask God to show you how to develop friendships with nationals.

12. Develop good relational skills.

This is especially necessary if you are an introvert and relating to others doesn't come naturally for you. One truly can learn how to become a good communicator and friend. Observe carefully people who have good relational skills. Practice on safe people around you. If you're considering going to the mission field, work hard at developing good relationships first. If you don't have good friendships at home, you won't automatically start making them on the mission field. Good relationships are *absolutely* essential to being successful in mission work. One missionary advises, "Don't go to the mission field until you have first figured out how to initiate, develop, and grow in healthy intimate relationships. You need them to be successful on the field. You need them to grow in your walk with the Lord. You need them to glorify the Lord in your life." The ability to develop and maintain friendships is one of the greatest personal and ministry skills a woman can have, let alone one of the greatest gifts she can give to herself.

13. Develop a strong, healthy support system back home.

Make sure you have at least a few people back home with whom you can fully share what's really going on with you—the good and the bad, the joys and the sorrows, the victories and the struggles. Communicate regularly with these people and allow them to be a real support to you. Many missionary women happily report finding compassionate and empathic responses when they relate openly with a few deeply trusted friends. As appropriate, share from your heart with your larger body of supporters. (You may need to educate them on how to care for missionaries.) Though you may feel vulnerable, you may be surprised by how much some people can identify with you. One particular woman commented on her joyful surprise in finding her supporters so open to her struggles. She attributes their receptivity to her frequent communication with them in which she tries to be as accurate and as positive as possible.

With the introduction of email communication, later Skype, and more recently, social media such as Facebook and Twitter, one can now keep in contact with people at home in a way never dreamed possible by early missionaries. When email communication first became available, one missionary stated: "Email is the absolutely most wonderful invention since sliced bread! Utilize fully." Whether by email, "snail mail," Skype, faxes, phone, texting, Facebook, or Twitter, people need to hear regularly from you to continue as a support base for you. Do your best to talk some of these people into visiting you on the mission field. Grandmas and Grandpas are a must!

Of critical importance, develop a good solid prayer base back home. Form a prayer team of faithful intercessors who will commit to pray for you on a regular basis. You cannot possibly make it on the mission field for long without a strong prayer covering. Keep your prayer team informed regularly of your prayer concerns and praise reports.

14. Take good care of yourself.

Eat healthy foods; get adequate rest and sleep; exercise regularly. How we care for our bodies has a direct impact on our emotional well-being. Give yourself permission to relax and have fun. Laugh a lot. Learn how to play and enjoy life. Pursue outside interests such as mountain climbing, photography, bird watching, flower arranging, or coin collecting. Be sure to take regular vacations. If you are single, take them with your best friends. You may find limited choices due to fewer resources, cultural restrictions, and safety issues, so prepare to be extra creative, imaginative, and flexible as you seek outlets for fun. Take advantage of any good books, CDs, and videos you can find.

ADDRESSING THE EMOTIONAL NEEDS UNIQUE TO SINGLE WOMEN ON THE MISSION FIELD

1. Take the initiative to make friends with roommates or other singles, missionary wives, couples, and families, and develop appropriate friendships with men.

Commit to developing friendships with those in your community, both single and married, male and female. Don't wait for others to initiate and don't automatically assume they may be too busy or not interested. Entertain others in your home; practice hospitality. Become an "honorary auntie" to the missionary children around you. This provides an opportunity to meet some of your own needs for relationship with children and gives parents a much-needed break.

Work hard to develop good relationships with roommates, whether or not you had a choice in living together. Plan regular times to talk, pray, play, or travel together. Commit to becoming as good friends as possible, regardless of the length of time you may be roommates. Guard against becoming emotionally dependent on each other, however. Be prepared for the reality of conflict. Just as in marriage, you will invariably have clashes with each other. Resolve to address the issues together and prayerfully work through them. Seek outside help, if necessary, but with each other's permission first.

Exercise the utmost of wisdom and discretion in developing friendships with men, both fellow missionaries and nationals. If the men you relate to are married, draw their wives into your friendships. Doing so can serve as a powerful deterrent to feelings of jealousy or exclusion on the part of the wives or to any inappropriate behavior between you and the men. Make sure that your manner of relating to male coworkers, even if totally appropriate by your own culture's standards, does not clash with the host culture's standards on male-female relationships. Be especially sensitive to cultural cues in relating to national men.

The extent to which you reach out and develop relationships, seeking to build a sense of community, will have a major impact on your effectiveness and sense of well-being on the mission field. Just because you are single does not mean you must live out your mission experience feeling alone or lonely. Your singleness in no way lessens your need for relationship. You just may have to work harder at creating community.

2. Limit how much time you spend alone.

Don't unnecessarily exacerbate your sense of aloneness. Spending inordinate amounts of time alone is a guaranteed setup for loneliness. Learn to develop a good balance between "alone time" and "people time," regularly offsetting one with the other. Learn to recognize what times of the day or what days of the month you may have the hardest time by yourself; then plan accordingly.

3. Acknowledge your own "nesting" needs.

Being single doesn't exempt you from these needs. Make your living place look and feel like home, no matter how temporary your living situation may be. Decorate it attractively to express your personality. Take several favorite items with you from home to add to your new setting. Even a few small treasures can help bring a sense of continuity to a totally new environment, making it feel more familiar and inviting.

4. Come to terms with your singleness before going to the mission field.

For many singles, this issue tends to be a recurring one, rather than one that gets settled once and for all. Whenever the issue resurfaces, pour out your heart to God and find a trusted friend with whom you can share freely. Make regular acts of committing your singleness to God. Recognize that a woman does not have to be married in order to be happy and fulfilled. God has made you whole just as you are, and you do not need a husband to be complete. The ultimate issue is faithfulness to God—living out his will in our lives, walking in obedience to his spirit—regardless of marital status.

Be careful not to idealize marriage. Believe it or not, a husband isn't the answer to life's problems! And no, singles do not have the corner on frustration. A single woman myself, I have often said that one of the best things that helps me keep a healthy perspective on my own singleness is doing many hours of marital therapy through the years! Do not go to the mission field expecting to find your husband there; you could be sorely disappointed. God may indeed bring you a mate on the mission field, but just don't plan on it.

5. Honestly acknowledge and address your sexual needs and feelings.

Acknowledge these needs and feelings as God-given and as part of the way God has created you. Learn to express them in healthy creative ways. If properly channeled, your sexual energy can become a tremendous source of productive creative energy. Enjoy being feminine in both appearance and behavior; revel in being the woman God has made you to be. Just because you do not have a sexual partner does not mean your femaleness must be ignored or hidden. Discuss the area of sexuality openly with a counselor or trusted female friend and make it a real matter of prayer.

Commit yourself to absolute moral purity. Do not set yourself up for unnecessary temptation. Hold yourself accountable to someone you trust. Be careful of your vulnerability, especially when feeling emotionally needy. Ask a more experienced missionary woman to help you become aware of the sexual nuances and subtleties in your host culture. Learn what unintended messages you could innocently be giving off to men. Actively and intentionally monitor your thought life. Carefully guard against involvement in any form of pornography or in attempting to find pseudo-intimacy through avenues, such as an unbridled fantasy life, excessive reading of romance novels, or inappropriate Internet "chat rooms."

6. Find healthy ways to meet your need for touch.

Develop healthy relationships with missionary and national children whom you can hug freely. They'll love you for it! Take appropriate advantage of physical touch that may come naturally with greetings or farewells. Ask your married female friends for hugs. Consider a pet. There's nothing like a huggable little dog waiting for you at the front door who can't wait to jump all over you when you come home!

ADDRESSING THE EMOTIONAL NEEDS UNIQUE
TO MARRIED WOMEN ON THE MISSION FIELD

1. Do not expect your husband to meet all of your emotional needs.

No one spouse can possibly meet all the needs of the other spouse. One sure way to cripple a marriage is to place the primary burden of meeting needs on the spouse's shoulders. *You* are the one, with the Lord's help, who must assume primary responsibility to get your own emotional needs met. This doesn't mean withholding expression of your needs to your husband; just be realistic how much he can meet.

2. Commit to building a strong marriage.

Seek to establish a good foundation in your marriage before going to the mission field. Deal with any problems that need to be addressed. Marital problems will not cease just because you have chosen to serve the Lord in full-time ministry. One missionary woman points this out so well as she emphasizes, "Married women without a good marriage are *miserable*." Whatever marital problems you have back home will only intensify on the mission field—guaranteed! If you're already on the mission field, openly address the problems with your husband.

Discuss with your husband how you both intend to build and maintain a strong marriage that encourages friendship, good communication, and healthy intimacy. Resolve to work through any conflicts that arise. Set aside regular times to talk. Passionately admonishes one missionary wife,

Communicate, communicate, communicate with your husband. Build bridges instead of creating schisms in your relationship with your husband, as this relationship will be your primary source of life. If this relationship breaks down, both of you might as well pack your bags and go home, as there is no ministry that will be effective on the field (or at home) when this vital link is broken.

Resolve to be your husband's biggest encourager. Plan dates with him. No matter how demanding missionary life may be, you must spend time alone with your husband if your marriage is going to thrive. Allow sufficient time to play together, despite the workload. This isn't a luxury, but a vital necessity.

If possible, discuss in advance potential sources of marital conflict you may experience on the mission field. Develop a plan to deal with problems that may arise as a result of the particular stresses of missionary life. Ask a seasoned missionary couple to share with you some of their struggles and how they dealt with them.

3. Intentionally affirm your value during those years when your primary role in the mission setting may be that of mother and homemaker.

For those of you who spend most of your time with your children, recognize you have absolutely no less value than those women directly involved in mission work. Don't in any way underestimate that role. Fully affirm yourself as you help to shape the lives of those precious little ones. Watch for opportunities to minister to other people in the midst of raising your children. Wisely advises one woman, "If you have young children, don't feel you are not fulfilling your missionary role. Make these roles a route for ministry. Befriend a national mother and teach her, by example, how to live out biblical roles of wife and mother. She may never have seen these before."

4. Don't allow the demands of home and family to isolate you from other women.

Regardless of busyness, you still need female friendships. Find quality time to develop and maintain friendships with other women. Be willing to take the initiative to do whatever is necessary to plan time together. Save energy for these friendships! As one busy missionary mother encourages, "Rest enough so you have sufficient physical energy to pursue friendships. Don't put it off because of fatigue." This is especially true if you are homeschooling your children.

Seek to develop friendships with single women. You may be delightfully surprised to discover how much you have in common with them and how much you may have to offer each other. Consider "adopting" one into your family, but recognize her role is not just to babysit (and don't take her on as a project or out of pity). With God's help, choose not to become threatened by your single coworkers. One particular single comments, "Don't be afraid of the single missionary. She's not after your husband. She's probably already had opportunities to be married."

5. Make a life for yourself and continue to develop yourself as a woman.

States one missionary mother, "Don't take all your identity from your husband's role and don't let being a mother consume you—the kids will be gone someday and you'll still be a person. Then what?" You are more than your husband's wife or your children's mother, important as those roles are. Utilize your God-given gifts and abilities as much as possible. Stretch your mind. Read books that spark your interest. Pursue personal goals you've dreamed of for a long time, such as taking a correspondence course, learning to play the guitar, getting into an exercise routine, or writing poetry. Even if time limitations mean having only a few minutes here and there to pursue these goals, do so anyway. This is not selfish! You will have more to give back to your husband and children emotionally if you allow time for yourself. You can't give out of an empty well. Remember your oxygen mask! Find snatches of time alone whenever possible just to catch your breath, to think, even to nap.

Recognize, however, that you may simply need to live with some of your needs going unmet for periods of time, especially in those years of having young children at home. Remember, this is a season of your life. Life won't likely always feel so demanding. Your children will be gone from home in a matter of time. Trust God more fully than ever to get you through those stretches where your needs take more of a backseat. And get your praying friends to diligently commit to praying you through those stretches!

6. *Ask your mission leadership to articulate their expectations concerning wives and mothers in ministry. Seek opportunities to contribute to the larger cause of the mission with your particular gifts and abilities.*

Find out what roles and responsibilities you are both expected and permitted to assume on the mission field, and if possible, do this before even accepting a mission placement. If you are uncomfortable with what is outlined, discuss openly your feelings and concerns with your leaders. Be able to articulate clearly with them what you need.

Use your gifts and abilities as time allows to make your particular contribution to the mission. Take the initiative to create opportunities. Remember, though, that even during those stretches of time when all your energy seems to be going into maintaining your home, you are still making an immense contribution.

WHAT HAPPENS WHEN EMOTIONAL NEEDS ARE NOT MET?

An entire book could be written addressing this particular question, but suffice it here to briefly say that there can be a huge price to pay for sustained unmet needs. To ignore emotional needs or to live with them unfulfilled for long periods of time can set up any person for a host of problems—physical, emotional, relational, and spiritual. Missionaries may be especially vulnerable because of all the unique challenges the mission field presents. Potential problems may include discouragement, depression, despair, debilitating loneliness, explosive anger, panic attacks, dutiful but joyless work, lost vision or purpose, addictions, interpersonal difficulties with coworkers or nationals, marital or family problems, divorce, health problems, financial problems, moral failures of various types, pornography, spiritual lethargy, dryness, or—in the most extreme of cases—even suicide.

It is utterly heartbreaking to see missionaries return home virtually broken and burnt out after having invested tremendous amounts of energy and time preparing for their missionary calling, to say nothing of the tremendous financial loss involved. I have worked with a number of such missionaries as they sort through dashed dreams and hopes after excruciatingly painful experiences, assisting them in picking up the broken pieces of their lives and slowly beginning to heal. God is so faithful to redeem their pain and rebuild their shattered lives, but, oh, the utter agony they often experience in the process.

PRACTICAL APPLICATIONS

This chapter is not meant to be an exhaustive study on the emotional needs of missionary women, by any means, but hopefully it can serve as a beginning point of discussion on this subject. Possibly several applications can be made.

For Those Women Considering the Mission Field

Before committing oneself to mission work, ask yourself the following questions with honest soul-searching:

1. What are my emotional needs now? Am I able to clearly articulate them? What am I currently doing to meet these needs? How well am I succeeding in meeting them? Which, if any, are unfulfilled? What blocks their fulfillment? What specific steps can I begin taking to get them met?

2. Is there any "emotional baggage" in my life that needs to be addressed? If so, how can I begin to deal with it now? Should I consider counseling? Am I truly open to resolving any unfinished issues in my life? If not, why not?

3. What kind of support systems do I already have in place? Will they continue for me on the mission field? How can I strengthen these systems? Do I need to develop them further or expand them?
4. How can I begin preparing now to deal with the emotional needs I will likely experience on the mission field?

You may want to consider discussing these questions with someone who knows you well and who would give you honest feedback. Make your emotional needs a regular matter of prayer.

For Women Already on the Field

Consider the above questions and do your own soul-searching, asking for input from a trusted friend or two as well. If needed, consider counseling. It is never too late to begin addressing needs. Make your emotional needs a regular matter of prayer.

For Mission Organizations

I would encourage you to carefully review your mission's policies and practices related to the women in your organization. In what ways does your organization contribute toward women addressing their emotional needs? How is sensitivity demonstrated toward them? Are women encouraged to expend time and energy meeting their needs? Despite the inevitable demands and busyness of mission life, is ample opportunity provided for women to develop close friendships with other women? In what ways are they encouraged to fully develop their God-given potential? What is your organization doing to ensure that women do not inadvertently experience discrimination based on gender or marital status? How are mothers who stay at home given input in ministry decisions? Are couples given adequate time away from their responsibilities to nurture their marital relationships? Are there any changes that might need to be made in any of these areas? If so, what steps are necessary to make these changes?

I would suggest that the material in this chapter be discussed in pre-field training and orientation. Have candidates grapple individually with these questions as well as discussing them in small groups. Have couples discuss together. Help men become sensitized to the emotional needs of women.

Consider offering a seminar, workshop, or retreat on the mission field where women can deal openly with the topic of meeting their emotional needs. It is the rare woman who would turn down an opportunity to share her thoughts and feelings on this subject. Provide a setting for the men, as well, to talk about the needs of their wives and how to relate to them.

For the General Reader and Mission Supporter

Could I boldly challenge you to ask the Lord what personal application he would have you make as a result of reading this chapter? I, for one, come away with a decidedly renewed commitment to pray more faithfully and fervently for missionaries, as well as to encourage a number of specific missionary women I know quite well by emailing them on a regular basis. Here's to doing our part to support God's faithful servants on the front lines of battle!

SUGGESTED READING

Anderson, N. 1993. *Living Free in Christ.* Ventura, CA: Gospel Light.

Andrews, L., ed. 2004. *The Family in Mission: Understanding and Caring for Those Who Serve.* Palmer Lake, CO: Mission Training International.

Bowers, J. 1985. Women's Role in Mission: Where Are We Now? *Evangelical Missions Quarterly,* 21(4): 352–362.

Brestin, D. 1988. *The Friendships of Women.* Wheaton, IL: Victor Books.

Cloud, H., and J. Townsend. 1992. *Boundaries.* Grand Rapids, MI: Zondervan Publishing House.

————. 1999. *Boundaries in Marriage.* Grand Rapids, MI: Zondervan Publishing House.

Coffman, C. 1997. *Weary Warriors: Lessons from Christian Workers Who Burnt Out.* Norman, OK: Apples of Gold.

DeMoss, N. L. 2001. *Lies Women Believe.* Chicago, IL: Moody Publishers.

Echerd, P., and A. Arathoon. 1989. *Understanding and Nurturing the Missionary Family.* Pasadena, CA: William Carey Library.

Eenigenburg, S., and R. Bliss. 2010. *Expectations and Burnout: Women Surviving the Great Commission.* Pasadena, CA: William Carey Library.

Eldredge, J, and S. Eldredge. 2005. *Captivating: Unveiling the Mystery of a Woman's Soul.* Nashville, TN: Thomas Nelson Publishers.

Eldredge, S. 2007. *Your Captivating Heart: Unveiling the Beauty, Romance, and Adventure of a Woman's Soul.* Nashville, TN: Thomas Nelson Publishers.

Foyle, M. 2001. *Honorably Wounded.* Grand Rapids, MI: Monarch Books.

Frankl, V. 1984. *Man's Search for Meaning: An Introduction to Logotherapy,* 3rd ed. New York: Simon and Schuster.

Gish, D. 1983. Sources of Missionary Stress. *Journal of Psychology and Theology,* 11(3): 238–242.

Hansel, T. 1991. *Through the Wilderness of Loneliness.* Elgin, IL: David C. Cook Publishing Co.

Harley, W. 1986. *His Needs, Her Needs.* Old Tappan, NJ: Fleming H. Revell Co.

Hawkins, K. 1994. Missionary Super Moms. *Journal of Applied Missiology,* 5 (2).

Jeremiah, D. 1983. *Overcoming Loneliness.* San Bernardino, CA: Here's Life Publishers, Inc.

Koons, C., and M. Anthony. 1991. *Single Adult Passages: Uncharted Territories.* Grand Rapids, MI: Baker Book House.

Leverington, R. 2006. Preparing Women for the Realities of Life on the Mission Field. Paper presented at the Mental Health & Missions Conference, Angola, Indiana.

Mohline, D. and J. Mohline. 1997. *Emotional Wholeness.* Shippensburg, PA: Treasure House.

Neff, M. 1983. *Women and Their Emotions.* Chicago, IL: Moody Press.

O'Donnell, K., ed. 1992. *Missionary Care: Counting the Cost for World Evangelization.* Pasadena, CA: William Carey Library.

————. 2002. *Doing Member Care Well.* Pasadena, CA: William Carey Library.

O'Donnell, K., and M. O'Donnell, eds. 1988. *Helping Missionaries Grow: Readings in Mental Health and Missions.* Pasadena, CA: William Carey Library.

Patterson, V. 1989. Women in Missions: Facing the 21st Century. *Evangelical Missions Quarterly,* 28: 360–364.

Powell, J. B., and J. M. Bowers, eds. 2002. *Enhancing Missionary Vitality: Mental Health Professions Serving Global Mission.* Palmer Lake, CO: Mission Training International.

Schubert, E. 1993. *What Missionaries Need to Know about Burnout and Depression.* New Castle, IN: Olive Branch Publications.

Seamands, D. 1988. *Healing for Damaged Emotions.* Wheaton, IL: Victor Books.

Smith, M. 2005. *Through Her Eyes: Perspectives on Life from Christian Women Serving in the Muslim World.* Waynesboro, GA: Authentic Media.

Swenson, R. 1992. *Margin.* Colorado Springs, CO: NavPress.

————. 1999. *Overload Syndrome.* Colorado Springs: CO: NavPress.

Taylor, W., ed. 1997. *Too Valuable to Lose: Exploring the Causes and Cures of Missionary Attrition.* Pasadena, CA: William Carey Library.

www.missionarycare.com

www.mmct.org/#/resources/communique

www.mrnet.org

www.peter'swife.org

www.womenoftheharvest.com

NINE

Combating Chronic Stress
by Restoring God's Image
Sheryl Takagi Silzer

P rior to a diagnosis of a chronic illness, I never considered in what way my theology might be faulty or how my particular personality traits contributed to chronic stress in my life. However, after serving twenty-five years with a major American mission board and working in four different countries, I experienced two years of intense stress. Following these two years our family returned home for furlough, and at the end of that furlough year I was diagnosed with breast cancer.

My first response was that I should have expected it because my mother, her sister, and my maternal grandmother all had breast cancer. However, my mother was over seventy when she was diagnosed and I was not yet fifty. It did not seem fair that I should get it so soon or that I should even be having cancer since I had faithfully served God for twenty-five years doing mission work. Things did not seem fair or right. Looking for a solution for the problem, I went to the library and read books on stress and cancer. That is when I discovered that cancer was one of the most common chronic illnesses and that ongoing unresolved stress reduces one's immune system, making a body susceptible to whatever disease was in one's family, like cancer in my family.

In addition to books on cancer, I started reading various articles and books on missionary stress. It seemed like overseas missionaries suffer from more stress than their counterparts back home due to the number of new situations—new home, new language, new food, and new friends, in addition to the loss of all those familiar things (Loss 1983). Another writer thought that missionaries were hit with an occupational disease called "culture shock" which went through stages (Oberg 1960). He suggested that once the missionary maneuvered these stages, she would arrive at adjustment. Along the same lines, some felt that the first term was the most critical and if the missionary finished the first term, he or she would be able to continue on with mission work. Others felt that women more than men suffered from culture shock since their particular roles entailed more changes in learning different cultural customs, compared to the man's work role, which is basically a change in office location (Chester 1988).

Another study revealed that there were a number of different factors that contributed to missionary stress, and the most common was interpersonal communication problems with coworkers, nationals, and constituents (Gish 1983). One missionary doctor explored the stress that arises from various kinds of interpersonal relationships and gave practical suggestions for learning how to handle stress (Foyle 1987). If missionary stress was not properly addressed, it could easily lead to burnout and depression (Schubert 1993).

Having been a missionary for twenty-five years I had no problem recognizing that missionaries lived with chronic stress each day of their lives. I had even postulated that missionary women live on the edge and it only takes one more thing to push them over. It had been a regular practice of mine to live on the edge and have that feeling of being pushed over the edge by one more thing. After recalling many stressful incidents in my missionary life, I concluded that it is surprising that more missionaries do not suffer from chronic illness.

I also read books and articles about missionary attrition. It appeared that the most frequent reason given for attrition was health reasons that were also associated with difficulties in interpersonal relationships and sometimes character issues. I also discovered that attrition studies were not popular in mission organizations. First of all, most of the articles were based on the author's own perspective rather than on carefully developed statistical studies. Secondly, mission organizations used different types of categories so that helpful comparison of attrition between missions was not possible. Furthermore, I also discovered that some agencies did not have a standard method of recording attrition so that even the studies conducted within a mission agency were not reliable.

The definition of attrition was also ambiguous. Some defined attrition using the category of acceptable and unacceptable. However, each mission organization defined these categories differently and intended to reflect the reason for attrition, but the reasons were symptoms rather than causes. The definitions were further complicated by differences in the length of missionary service—whether it was a short-term missionary or a career missionary. The reasons for attrition also were multiple, reflecting issues that had been long-standing and difficult to resolve. There were also different reasons given by different people—the mission agency, the sending church, mission colleagues, or the missionaries themselves. In spite of all the differences in dealing with attrition and the reasons given, there did seem to be a pattern—many missionaries went home for health reasons that were related to interpersonal difficulties and character issues (Taylor 1997). Attempting to address this problem, another study was conducted to compare the differences between newer sending agencies and older sending agencies in regard to missionary attrition (Hay et al. 2006).

A study conducted by a number of medical doctors found that although malaria and hepatitis were the most common medical complaints, mission agencies had few strategies to minimize the risks of these illnesses. Another problem they discovered was that missionaries themselves tended to deny the importance of illnesses. Missionaries were also more prone to accidents than other populations (Lange et al. 1987). There were also differences in how mission organizations addressed health issues. Some left the decision up to the individual while others took more responsibility (Johnson 1995). It seems like missionary health is an issue that has not been readily addressed by mission organizations or by missionaries themselves. Offering improved medical preparedness training for their missionaries would be one way of addressing the health issue (Buckley 1993).

Over my twenty-five years on the mission field I had seen many of my colleagues return home early. Many had returned due to physical health, and poor health was often accompanied by stressful interpersonal relationships and unresolved conflicts. I had no trouble associating my cancer with unresolved stress and difficulty in interpersonal relationships, particularly with authority figures. However, I had not been able to understand theologically why I should have cancer.

My cancer had been diagnosed after I had decided to return to school. In one of my classes the professor asked a question that I had not considered during my time as a missionary. He asked us to consider what it meant to be made in the image of God (Silzer 2011b, 9–19) and challenged us to imagine how it would be different if we reflected God's image in our lives. Being in the midst of chemotherapy, this question was quite challenging. In what way did my having cancer relate to my ability to reflect his image? Was God punishing me for not measuring up to being a good missionary and therefore he had allowed me to have cancer?

I began to think back over a number of events in my life as a missionary. I remembered that I had joined this particular mission because of its goal—Bible translation. My own experiences as an ethnic minority—Japanese-American—had developed a desire in me to reach out to other ethnic minorities that did not have God's Word in their own language. In high school I was attracted to the minority group in the area—Hispanics. I began to study Spanish and decided to major in Spanish in college. Although I did not speak Japanese, knowing Spanish helped me develop an interest in languages. I also remember my father saying that he wanted one of his children to be a missionary. There were four of us children—three brothers and myself. My older brother decided not to enter mission work, and perhaps unconsciously I felt it was my responsibility to fulfill my father's wishes. This is typical in an Asian home for the children to submit to the directives of their parents.

Then I became aware of a mission organization that focused on learning languages and doing Bible translation. Their goal was to provide translated scriptures for language groups that did not yet have them. The end goal was usually the completion of a New Testament and sometimes the Old Testament.

I went to the mission field just out of college as a single, which was a big step for me. Prior to this I had not traveled outside of the United States. I did speak Spanish and was assigned to a country in Latin America. I remember traveling alone to one country and then to another. God provided a contact in both countries, but being on the plane alone was very scary. Perhaps it was a mixture of the fear and the excitement of the unknown. I finally arrived in the country I was assigned, and shortly thereafter another single woman and I were assigned to a group of people who lived in the Amazon jungle basin. Shortly after I arrived in that country I remember my father asking me if I worked eight hours a day for the mission. So I made sure that I spent at least eight hours a day doing mission work.

The people we were assigned to readily welcomed these two strange women and began to help us learn their language. After struggling to learn to speak the language, we started to record the sounds and the grammar of the language. We had just passed the mission requirements to begin doing Bible translation when my partner and I were asked to take the summer off and teach at our training schools in North America.

Although this was an enjoyable experience, it took time away from the work of Bible translation. However, it turned out that I met my future husband at this school. After we had decided to spend our lives together, we struggled with the question of where we should work. Should we continue with the same group working with my partner, or should we go to another country that was just opening up for mission work? It turned out that we felt God leading us to this new country, and we began making plans to get married and begin preparation for this new country.

We were delayed a number of months in arriving at our new assignment as we were waiting for visas. Because of this we took a six-month temporary assignment in a nearby country. When we finally arrived in the country, it seemed like things went very quickly. A well-known linguist was coming to lead a workshop, and we were encouraged to choose one of two languages to work on during that time. We were both excited to be finally beginning language work as a couple after being delayed over a year waiting for a visa.

My husband trekked out to the village and arranged for a man to come to the workshop and help us learn his language. My excitement started to rise again as I felt the thrill of being able to do Bible translation work. During the workshop we completed the beginning work on the sound system and the grammar of this new language. However, shortly after the workshop was over, I came down with a bad case of malaria and it turned out I was also pregnant with our first child. The doctor prescribed medication for me, but I was not responding and my malaria got worse. Finally, it was decided that I should make a trip to see the doctor and discovered through blood tests that my hemoglobin was very low. I was taken as soon as possible to the nearest hospital in the neighboring country. This led to an extended stay in that country recuperating and giving birth to our first son.

Upon our arrival back my husband made a series of visits to several villages and found that the language we had started to study was that of an isolated village and not closely related to the other languages in this group. The mission director strongly felt that we should move to another language group and begin over again. I was not real happy to be starting over as this was the third time that I had begun work in a new language. However, it sounded like a logical reason to make a change.

This time we were placed in a lovely village on the coast where palm trees were softly swaying in the breeze. I felt like we finally reached the place where we could begin and complete a translation of the New Testament. Working hard in order to make up for lost time in the other language group, we jumped into language learning and attended regular workshops provided by our organization. Before long we were at that longed-for-stage—Bible translation. This time both my husband and I were able to work on this. He began with the Gospel of Mark, and I began with a series of stories on the life of Christ. A real thrill came over us as we finally reached the point that we both had aimed for since joining the organization. Our two young boys did not hinder our progress as child care was arranged for them half a day and they enjoyed playing with their friends the rest of the day. Our dream had finally come true.

About the same time we began the process of translating scriptures, our organizational sponsor was putting out a request for members who had higher educational degrees. Although my husband only had a bachelor's degree, he was asked to consider a doctoral program. After a period of consideration and praying, my husband was accepted into a program that bypassed a master's degree. So our long-awaited goal of doing Bible translation was once again put on hold by a four-year study program. One benefit of this program was that we were able to spend half of that time continuing in language study and doing some Bible translation.

The day finally arrived when my husband finished his study program. We had taken a short furlough and were ready to renew translation work. Again the excitement was building as we arrived back in the country. On the way to our accommodations, the director asked us to take an important position for two years—associate director over twenty-five other language teams doing Bible translation. Although the temporary position sounded interesting, our enthusiasm to continue Bible translation was dampened by this offer. We felt guilty when we heard that if my husband did not take this position, they would have to ask another family to come out of a village program to do this job. So we took this job, and the two-year temporary position grew into three and four years until my husband was asked to take the job permanently. For a couple of years I tried to work on the project by myself, but felt unable to deal with the stresses and strains of family life at the same time.

This change affected me more than my husband as he already had been in his new job several years. Although I shifted to a job at our mission office, I still felt a loss of the job that I had joined the mission to do. I did not realize how much this affected me until we took up a new assignment in the capital city and I was not able to have an official job for the mission due to a number of circumstances. I began to feel stressed out, and every little thing bothered me. I began to complain about my situation in a number of different ways. I thought that my household helpers (eleven different ones in twenty months) were keeping me from doing official mission work. I complained about the administrative structure of the mission that was not able to find a job to fit my gifts or my situation. I could not find a place where I thought I fit, and I did not feel good about myself. I felt that if I had an official job for the mission, God might be more pleased with me. I also did not think that anyone else really understood my situation.

I knew that I was experiencing stress because I would have a hard time sleeping and I'd wake up early in the morning brooding about my situation and what I could do to change things. My friends knew that I was out of sorts, but they humored me and thought that things would change in time. My children asked me why I was so stressed out, and I did not have a very good answer for them. I really felt that if my household help could learn their roles I could make a contribution to my mission. In a sense I blamed them for my situation. As a household employee left every two or three months, I would periodically have to spend extra time looking for and training a replacement. I thought that my sixteen years of experience in this culture and language would enable me to function in this new location. I was greatly disappointed when it looked like I could not handle anything at all. Of course, this did not make me feel any better about myself.

Several years later in one of my classes, I was instructed to meditate on my family and the situations that God brought to my mind. It was during this time of reflection that God brought together a number of situations in my family and he began to help me put them together. First, it became apparent that it was important for me to please my father, and I transferred that into my role as a missionary. Part of the reason I became a missionary was to please my father, and working eight hours a day was essential to this purpose. As long as I was able to have an official job with the mission and a full workday, I felt good about myself. I also thought he was more pleased with me by making this kind of mission contribution. Pleasing my father was tantamount to pleasing the mission, and since making an official contribution was important to God, I thought he was displeased when I did not work for the mission. I did not realize how my identity was associated with completing a New Testament, so that beginning three translation projects and finishing none was devastating to me. To top this off, when I did not have an official mission job I really began to fall apart.

God began to show me that my relationship with my own father shaped my view of God and my relationship to him. My desire to please my own father drove my desire to please God by doing mission work, including reaching the mission goal of completing a New Testament. I also had trouble saying "no" to numerous requests for jobs that sounded like what a missionary in my situation should do. I never had told my own father "no" except in defiance and was quickly punished for disobeying. My inability to say "no" did not develop discernment in knowing which of these jobs God actually wanted me to do. If a director asked me to do something, I felt it was the same as God wanting me to do something. I also was influenced by my coworkers who suggested I do things as well. I could not say "no" to them because I wanted to please them in the same manner that I tried to please my father. Eventually, it was impossible to fulfill all the requirements that the director or coworkers suggested, and this created anger against them. However, I could not express this anger directly to them, but instead I would suppress these feelings inside me. The suppression of this anger affected my immune system, and one day the good cells turned to cancerous cells. The result of the chronic stress of wanting to please my father and please others affected my interpersonal relationships and eventually my own health.

God began to show me how my actions came out of my cultural background and experiences. A good Asian person followed the Confucian value of respecting one's parents and submitting to their direction. My inability to confront or express my disagreement came from this value of respecting authority figures. Another Asian value was wanting to please the members of the group by doing what they suggested. Although both of these values are in the Bible—honoring your parents (Eph 6:1–2) and thinking of others as better than yourself (Phil 2:4)—I interpreted these cultural values as biblical values. I thought that these values were clear and unmistakable. I tried to honor my parents and to think of others as better than myself. I interpreted "honoring my parents" as obeying everything they asked me to do. I never considered it necessary to ask God if obeying a request from my parents was the way he wanted me to honor my parents. I never considered that my parents' request might not be what God wanted for me.

However, I also did not correlate my poor health with blind obedience to authority figures and the suppressing of negative emotions. Although I knew that my parents and authority figures were not always right, I did not think it was my place to point out my disagreement. Yet by regarding them as always right, I had created the false belief that some people were right just like God and that I was always wrong. Since this belief was false, the consequences would be any kind of expression of sin—anger, bitterness, envy, hate, jealousy, etc. Holding on to this belief enabled the devil to get a foothold (Eph 4:27). The longer my anger stayed, the more it seethed inside of me and began to turn to resentment toward all authority figures. My speech began to be more negative, and there was very little that appeared to be positive in my life. I could not find anything for which to be thankful, and I passed this dark cloud to all those around me.

It was this scenario that produced chronic stress that affected my immune system, reducing its ability to fight off the growth of cancerous cells. This stress was based on an incorrect view of humanity and, in particular, my parents and authority figures. This false view of humanity also created a false view of a God who was distant from me and a God who punished those who did not obey. I believed in a God who was pleased when I worked eight hours a day for the mission and as a result a God who was not pleased with my roles as a woman, a wife, a mother, and a homemaker. Therefore, fulfilling these roles caused me much stress.

When contemplating my value as a person made in God's image, God began to show me that my value was not through my role as a mission worker working eight hours a day for the mission, but it was through my role as a woman made in his image. This role was not to be in competition with other men and women in the role of doing Bible translation, but it was to be in the role of male and female in complementation reflecting God to others (Gen 1:26–27). God did not say that each person had to complete a specified workday or assignment for the mission, but that each person was created to reflect and glorify God and not glorify humanity. Whatever I did each day should be done to the glory of God and not for the glory of humanity. This means that my role as a mission worker might not fit the agency's goal on a day-to-day basis, but it means being open to what God has for me every moment of the day. God knew that there were times when I could not make a contribution to the goals of the mission organization. In fact, he provided a ministry for me with the eleven different people in my household. However, I could not see those people as part of my ministry because I had been blinded by following the guidelines of the mission—doing Bible translation. I had replaced God's standard with human standards.

As a result of these reflections on my missionary stress and the things God taught me about my cultural self-identity, I have developed a six-day workshop for on-field missionaries to go through a process of cultural self-discovery. I have led these workshops in Asia, Latin America, and the Pacific (Silzer 2011a).

This case study raises a number of questions to be explored in regard to the theological implications of chronic illness and the mission world.

- First of all, the relationship of missionary stress and chronic illness needs to be examined. What is the incidence of chronic illness among missionaries? What kind of chronic illnesses are affecting missionaries, and what are the factors contributing to it? Is there a relationship between missionary stress and chronic illness?
- Secondly, in what way is chronic illness related to stress in interpersonal relationships, particularly in relation to authority figures? How can interpersonal relationships be improved to reduce the incidence of chronic illness?
- Thirdly, what is the missionary's view of God and self? How does the missionary perceive him or herself to be or not be reflecting the image of God? In what ways can mission agencies foster a better view of God among their members?
- Fourthly, in what way can mission agencies and mission training programs help each missionary to discover his/her view of God and promote a greater reflection of the image of God?

It has been a revelation to me to understand how my own stress came from a faulty view of God that I picked up from my relationship to my father and how that relationship was shaped by cultural beliefs, particularly Confucianism. I understand how this stress affected my body by preparing the way for chronic illness—in my case cancer. As I have contemplated who God is and what it means to be made in his image, God has helped me change my beliefs and that has led to greater health. Although being cancer-free for almost twenty years came at that time through surgery and medication, I believe the greater healing came through spiritual healing of my false view of God and in turn a false view of myself.

My prayer is that anyone who reads this chapter will be challenged to consider 1) their own personal view of God, 2) how this is related to stress that affects interpersonal relationships, and 3) how God can reveal to them how to make the appropriate changes to reflect God's image more clearly.

REFERENCES

Buckley, D. W. 1993. Medical Preparedness of Overseas Missionary Personnel. Paper presented at the Third Conference on International Travel Medicine, April 25–29, Paris, France.

Chester, R. 1988. Stress of Mission Families Living in "Other Culture" Situations. In *Helping Missionaries Grow: Readings in Mental Health and Missions,* ed. K. O'Donnell and M. O'Donnell. Pasadena, CA: William Carey Library.

Foyle, M. 1987. *Overcoming Missionary Stress.* Wheaton, IL: Evangelical Missions Information Service.

Gish, D. 1983. Sources of Missionary Stress. In *Helping Missionaries Grow: Readings in Mental Health and Missions,* ed. K. O'Donnell and M. O'Donnell. Pasadena, CA: William Carey Library.

Hay, R., with V. Lim, S. Hay, and R. Ketelaar. 2006. *Worth Keeping: Global Perspectives on Missionary Practice in Missionary Retention.* Pasadena, CA: William Carey Library.

Johnson, R. O. 1995. Rethinking our Stewardship Responsibilities: Stewardship of Human Resources. Paper presented to the Keeping International Staff Healthy, AERDO Forum, Eatonville, WA.

Lange, R., et al. 1987. Missionary Health: The Great Omission. In *American Journal of Preventive Medicine,* 3(6): 332–338.

Loss, M. 1983. *Culture Shock: Dealing with Stress in Cross-Cultural Living.* Winona Lake, IN: Light and Life Press.

Oberg, K. 1960. Culture Shock Adjustment to New Cultural Environments. *Practical Anthropology,* 7(4): 177–182.

O'Donnell, K. S. 2002. *Doing Member Care Well: Perspectives and Practices from Around the World.* Pasadena, CA: William Carey Library.

———. 2011. *Global Member Care: The Pearls and Perils of Good Practices.* Pasadena, CA: William Carey Library.

Schubert, E. 1993. *What Missionaries Need to Know About Burnout and Depression.* Newcastle, IN: Olive Branch Publications.

Silzer, S. T. 2000. Work and Identity: A Personal Reflection. *Evangelical Missions Quarterly,* 36(3): 342–345.

————. 2011a. A Multicultural Team Building Workshop. In *Reflecting God's Glory Together,* EMS: 19. Pasadena, CA: William Carey Library.

————. 2011b. *Biblical Multicultural Teams: Applying Biblical Truth to Cultural Differences.* Pasadena, CA: William Carey Library.

Taylor, William, ed. 1997. *Too Valuable to Lose: Exploring the Causes and Cures of Missionary Attrition.* Pasadena, CA: William Carey Library.

TEN

Helping Finishers Bridge the Gap
Dianne B. Collard

As Staff Development Consultant with an established mission agency, I had the opportunity to work with missionaries throughout the entire life cycle of their ministry, from appointment to the field until their return home. In the late 1990s I observed a new trend among people coming to the field. There is an increased number of the so-called second-career people in their forties, fifties, and sixties becoming missionaries. As I assisted in their preparation and monitored their adjustment upon arriving on the field, I was left with a distinctly favorable impression of this relatively new source of laborers. Granted, there are obstacles to be overcome facing both the mission agency and the new (albeit older) missionary, but the benefits for the Kingdom are worth the effort.

In this chapter, I will offer an overview of the "Finishers" movement, followed by some specific considerations for women who are planning to go to the mission field in their second-half stage of life. These suggestions grow out of my personal experience of becoming a missionary during the decade of my forties, as well as the observation of and interviews with second-career women on the mission field.[12]

---

12 The author has conducted numerous personal interviews with women missionaries in the second-career category, all of whom wish to remain anonymous.

SECOND-CAREER MISSIONARIES AS FINISHERS

It is clear that this chapter is less about what is than what may be in the future. A significant but quiet transition has occurred in the missionary work force as we entered the new millennium. For the first time in history of modern missions, there is the possibility of a large number of first-time missionaries being appointed who are near or at the (previously) normal time of retirement. This phenomenon in the United States has adopted the nomenclature of Finishers.[13]

The driving forces behind this transition shift in missionary recruitment are simple. First, there is an expanded understanding of what God meant in the biblical challenge to "send forth laborers," which no longer confines such laborers only to young people with forty years of service ahead of them. Secondly, the availability of such a second-career labor force is greater than any time in history.

Nelson Malwitz, Finishers Project[14] founder, made this conservative prediction.

Over the years from about 2000 to 2020, there will be about 40,000 people available for mission organizations to assimilate and assign (i.e., an average of 2,000 per year in that 20-year span). (1998, 2)

An important demographic shift is pending. In fact, it is beginning as those 55 to 65 and retiring now are making their way into

---

13 The term "finisher" is derived from these two verses—Acts 20:24: "if only I may finish the race and complete the task the Lord Jesus has given me—the task of testifying to the gospel of God's grace"; and 2 Timothy 4:7: "I have fought the good fight, I have finished the race, I have kept the faith" [emphasis mine].
14 The original proposal prepared April 1996 is revised December 2001 and the online version and current information about the Finishers Project are found at their website: http://www.finishers.org. New sites such as http://www.mid-life.com are being created (July 2003) to facilitate the over-forty group finding suitable ministries and mission opportunities.

the service of the church and missions… This category will be the most educated and healthiest retired class in human history. (Malwitz 1998, 2)

In addition, studies have indicated that this baby boomer generation is looking for significance, and as one pastor advocates, the general openness to the challenge is their way of contributing to an "eternal legacy" (Malwitz 1998, 4). This is facilitated by the twenty-eight years added to the life expectancy in the past century, as well as a marked increase in financial stability (ibid., 3, par3–4).

There is now a concerted effort to recruit these people, and mission agencies are revising outdated policies and procedures in order to appoint and direct them. Frequently mission agencies have made and must continue to make a major cultural shift in their thinking (Malwitz 1998, 1).

The proposal for the first conference of Second-Career Ministry in July 1996 gave this stirring mandate:

With the leading edge of the boomer population approaching early retirement years beginning about 2000, the church faces an unprecedented opportunity to harness the pool of dedicated, experienced and life-qualified personnel in pursuit of the Great Commission. Will churches…and the present mission agency community be equipped to meet the challenge? (Malwitz 1998, 1)

The first conference, called Finishers Forum '98, was sponsored by the Finishers Project and The Navigators, and occurred on October 1–3, 1998, in Chicago. The stated purpose of these conferences is "to facilitate the establishment of an infrastructure designed to ease the way for talented, accomplished, mature, second-career people to quickly find an effective place of service in the cause of Jesus Christ in order to bring as many people as possible to Heaven" (Malwitz 1998, 1).

To the amazement of the planners for the 1998 conference, delegates attended from 38 states and five countries, with 200–300 late registrants turned away. Numerous sessions were held addressing various issues regarding integration into the missionary enterprise. Thirty mission organizations had displays representing approximately 15,000 second-career opportunities, with another 20 mission agencies unable to exhibit due to lack of space. The movement had taken shape and was off to a significant beginning. At the final session over 100 delegates indicated their commitment to serve in missions. Six months later 90 of these delegates were either on the mission field or had committed to join a mission organization.[15]

The Finishers Project website clearly states that this organization is a "matching service, not a sending agency" (http://www.finishers. org/). By 2011 there were over eighty missionary agencies participating in the Finishers' Project. According to Don Parrott, Finishers Project president, there are currently over 16,000 opportunities for service listed (2011, http://www.finishers.org/home/video).

It behooves a mission agency to seriously consider the procedures and policies that will either hinder or facilitate the placement and effectiveness of such Finishers. Changes in recruitment, appointment, and attitudes of field leadership will be necessary for the mission agency seeking to effectively use this labor pool. It is a major shift in how the task of missions will be accomplished, and it will require serious consideration and adjustment. Nelson Malwitz stated in 2011 that the three biggest issues in effective placement were 1) matching the abilities to the assignment; 2) aligning the appointees' expectations with the reality of field ministry; and 3) preparing the team to receive second-career people and use them wisely (2011 personal interview).

---

15 This is a deduction made by analyzing the entire survey (Nelson Malwitz, personal communication, June 16, 2003).

THE VALUE OF FINISHERS IN THE MISSIONARY TASK

Space allows only a cursory consideration of the many benefits of second-career missionaries, or Finishers. Within most of the cultures outside North America, respect and honor is given for maturity, rather than youth. Numerous Christian leaders around the world have expressed to mission agency leaders, "I appreciate the enthusiasm of the young people you send, but where are the people with the experience and wisdom of age?" Finishers come with over thirty-five years of work experience, and often forty or more years of spiritual maturity, as well as a deep knowledge of themselves and God. Their influence can be significant.

The struggles of a young family, with their educational and social needs, will not be an issue for Finishers. They can focus fully on ministry without the distractions that often plague a younger person. Financial pressures that burden many missionaries will not be as great due to the availability of retirement income and savings.

Finally, most Finishers offer a deeper understanding of their calling. There is a sense of urgency to finish well—doing something significant for eternity. Life has often produced an expanded ability to love people—even the unlovely or those very different from themselves. My observation is that this expressed love overcomes many of the obstacles associated with language learning difficulties or acculturation issues, so Finishers become excellent missionaries.

CONSTRAINTS AND CONCERNS

As great as the issues are at the meta-level of mission agencies, so are the challenges facing the individual older woman missionary who arrives on the mission field for the first term. Each woman's experience is unique, and yet a similar theme surfaced through my numerous interviews. The single most significant difficulty expressed by these women was a profound loneliness.

The loss related to the leaving of family and friends is a reality for anyone leaving their home to live in a foreign country. But it is observed that the experience of this loss is even greater with second-career missionary women. The friendships forged over the many years in their home country are deeply missed and not easily replaced. Communication by email, Skype, letters, and phone calls helps, of course. But trying to build close relationships with nationals and even other missionaries seldom supplants the deep feelings of being alone and often ends in frustration.

Related to this is the misconception that adult (college-age and above) children are less of a concern than younger children. Every woman interviewed told stories of one or more of her children who was struggling in some manner, expressing the need for the parent to be available. Some adult children deeply resented the parents and accused them of abandoning them. Such was the response of my twenty-one-year-old son when we left for the field. This contributes to the difficulty of the second-career woman on the mission field. Along with this, it was often difficult for the younger team members to comprehend or empathize with the woman grieving over the missing of her older children. Even further complicating this issue is the struggle to be a (very!) long-distance grandmother. Debbie Lamp, a leader of Barnabas International's women's ministries, gave this explanation of the struggles for these women: "In my experience the biggest issue that all the "Finisher" or second-career women have to face is leaving adult children and grandchildren behind, especially when those children are twenty-somethings and not settled into a career and life yet. The responsibilities of parenting from a distance are just as difficult for these women as for the career missionary mother who sends children home for college at eighteen. Second issue on the list has to be caring for their aging parents" (July 12, 2011 personal correspondence).

In addition to this struggle, other issues surfaced as the discussion continued with Finishers on the field. These women, with their husbands, commit to the field often with an idealistic view of missionary life and what their role would be. They are frequently highly experienced and often successful in their careers. Suddenly they find themselves in the low-person position on a missionary team. This results in feelings of being unappreciated and underutilized. The wife, especially, may feel she is overlooked as placement on the field is determined by her husband's expertise. She may feel neglected and of little value. Many women expressed resentment that their husband was underutilized as well. Dr. Gregory Holden's research discovered that finding suitable roles within both the national churches and the sending mission agency is the source of extreme stress in the second-career missionaries sampled (1994, 289).

A key issue that becomes an obstacle is language acquisition. While experts debate whether or not age is a determining factor on the ability of learning a language, research does indicate that learning a new language is "significantly more stressful for the older group than the younger group" (Holden 1994, 288). In addition to the stress factor, the older missionary is often not allowed adequate time or resources to learn the new language well due to shortness of their term of service or the demands of the assignment. It does not mean that ministry cannot be accomplished, but not being able to communicate contributes to the feelings of isolation of the older person, plus it may undermine other team members' fully accepting them.

All the women interviewed expressed a disappointment with the relationship with other team members. One missionary wrote, "Probably my biggest disappointment is seeing missionaries fail to get along to the point of adversely affecting their ministries" (Holden 1994, 298). Undoubtedly this is a reaction to unrealistic expectations in this area and could be helped by adequate pre-field preparation. But it also reflects the (often unspoken) assumptions of a traditional field missionary in defining what is a real missionary.

One forty-five-year-old woman, a gifted evangelist, was told upon her arrival on the field, "You shouldn't expect to do any real missionary work. Find your fulfillment in supporting the other members on the team and being a grandmother to our children." This is NOT why she had come to the mission field, and she proceeded to prove them quite wrong, winning scores of people to the Lord!

A crucial stress-producing factor in the life of the woman Finisher is the care of aging parents, which younger missionaries do not face. Often, the second-career woman hesitates to engage in missions with the dual concerns of adult children AND her parents, finding herself in the so-called sandwich generation.

Stress management is a major issue to be considered by a Finisher woman. While her coping mechanisms may be adequate in her pre-missionary life, the addition of changing careers, intercultural adjustment, and the above-mentioned issues can overload even the healthy woman. Preparation must be made to provide assistance in handling such stress.

A woman in the Finishers category must also consider any special dietary and health needs that may be more difficult to handle on the mission field. Medical and dental care varies greatly from one country to another, plus it is a daunting task to communicate such important information in a language other than your own.

OVERCOMING OBSTACLES

The need for quality pre-field training and on-field orientation is crucial. Realistic expectations and cross-cultural adjustment preparation will facilitate effectiveness. Dr. Holden concludes his study with an emphasis on four factors important to a successful missionary experience (1994, 302):

1. The degree of their preparedness
2. The accuracy of their expectations
3. The degree of stress
4. The missionaries' relative success at handling the transitional issues

While these may seem common to all missionaries, this study found that they were especially significant for second-career people. They must not be ignored.

Serious consideration needs to be given to the possibility of Finishers requiring more frequent trips to their home country to care for family and health needs. This has both financial and policy ramifications that must be settled before the Finishers leave for the field. In addition, funds and time should be allocated for the adult children to visit the field as soon as possible. The understanding and involvement of such children will facilitate the adjustment of the woman in the Finisher category.

THE CHALLENGE

At the first Finishers Forum attendees were challenged with using the mandate from Luke 14:23:

> The opportunities are plentiful. We are the healthiest and best educated generation of forty-,fifty-, and sixty-year olds to ever walk the face of the planet. As a generation of Christians there is still plenty of time to act on the challenge of Jesus to "Go out into the highways and hedges, and compel them to come in, that my house may be filled" (KJV). (Nelson Malwitz, personal communication, June 16, 2003)

The rewards are great and the obstacles can be overcome with awareness and preparation. Thousands of women may answer the call. May we as mission agencies and field personnel be ready to join with them to accomplish the goal of reaching the world for Christ.

REFERENCES

Finishers Project. http://finishers.org/home.

Holden, G. 1994. Crossing the Missionary Boundary: The Role of Personal Expectations in the Transition to Cross-Cultural Ministry. PhD diss., Fuller Theological Seminary, School of Intercultural Studies.

ELEVEN

High Alert to Enemy Attacks
Marguerite G. and Charles H. Kraft

C onnie is a bright, vivacious missionary, a mother of four, deeply loved by coworkers and local people alike in the country in which she and her husband have been serving. In order for her husband to assume administrative responsibilities, they were asked to move to a city, into an apartment across a narrow alleyway from a mosque.

It was a fine apartment, but Connie and Bob (fictitious names) noticed a kind of heaviness in the rooms closest to the mosque. So they prayed in those rooms against any enemy influence on themselves and their family. They felt the oppression lighten after that, but within a few months of their moving to the city, Connie began to fall into what soon became a deep depression. Bob and the children seemed to be fine, but in spite of much prayer, Connie just couldn't shake the depression. After eleven months of this ongoing depression, the mission leaders had decided that Connie and her family would have to return to the States to try to find help for her there.

At this point in Connie's story we arrived in their city to conduct a seminar for the missionaries on inner healing and deliverance. We were asked to pray for Connie, and by the grace of God, she found healing from a number of emotional wounds and was set free from the demons that were attached to those wounds. She and her family did not have to leave the field and, though in a different locality, are missionaries to this day, over twenty years later.

There are a number of things in Connie's story that seem to have happened due to a depth of spiritual sensitivity that is quite usual in women but rare in men. For a start, Connie had experienced a difficult childhood. Her father was an alcoholic, making her early life quite unpredictable. Her husband had had his own difficulties in childhood, but without the kind of sensitivity that Connie had, he did not experience the same intensity of hurt.

In her home, then, Connie as the oldest daughter was forced to carry from an early age far more responsibility than a child ought to have to carry. And it came out as we ministered to her that she had been deeply wounded spiritually as well as emotionally. She, probably like most women, had been very sensitive to her mother's pain and also the injustice of the responsibility she was forced to assume for her younger siblings. She carried out her duties quite well, apparently, but sustained a good bit of damage in the process.

Though the wounds were there and were deep, the enemy was not able to use them to cripple her as long as she was in the familiar cultural setting of her home country. She had become a Christian early in life and had grown strong enough spiritually to suppress the pressure of the demons of anger and shame that she was carrying. But now, though her faith was still strong, the cultural stress, the responsibility for her family, plus her own spiritual sensitivity probably connected with new intensity with her early wounds. This made her more vulnerable to the demons inside that had gained new power by connecting with the dark angels from the mosque next door to break through her defenses.

Unfortunately, Connie was quite unaware of most of the factors involved in her situation. She did not know, for example, that she, like many with her kind of background, was carrying deep wounds to which demons were attached. She knew there were tensions inside related at points to her childhood experiences. But she thought she had outgrown or overcome the power of those memories through her

Christian growth. And, as is usual in missionary preparation, Connie had learned nothing about the spirit world and how it works in her mission's pre-field training program. So no one was more surprised than Connie to discover, as we did in ministry, that the "garbage" of those early reactions was being used by demonic "rats" to keep her and her family from their mission work (C. Kraft 2011).

When men and women respond to God's call and move into missionary work, they become a great threat to Satan and his kingdom. This kind of commitment indicates obedience to God in being willing to serve on the front lines in expanding his kingdom. Leaving the security of home and its comforts, adapting to a new way of life and new surroundings, and finding a place within a new community to effectively serve present an unbelievable amount of stress on the cross-cultural worker and give great opportunity for the evil one to move in and distract in God's work. In this chapter we will be focusing specifically on the areas where women are especially vulnerable. This is particularly relevant since studies have shown that "wives are often the determining factor for families staying or leaving the field" (Lindquist 1982, 22).

Satan, full of anger toward God and the humans he created, is determined to break the loving relationship that God intended to exist between himself and human beings. Missionary women are some of his prime targets. Women, both married and single, throughout the world are key in the nurturing role that God has given them. Satan is jealous over women being able to create a new life. He cannot create, only damage and destroy what already exists. So we often find enemy attacks especially on women. He has found that great damage can be done to the entire family by keeping the wife and mother from functioning effectively.

Too often Christians see Satan as simply a pervasive influence of evil in the world, not as a being or personality determined to get at and destroy those who are furthering God's work. The Bible speaks of the spiritual battle that exists and the weapons we have at our disposal to be victorious (1 Pet 5:8; 2 Cor 10:4; Eph 6:11–18; 2 Cor 4:3–4).

For too long Satan has benefited from our lack of focus on his tactics for battle. Our lack of awareness, along with failure to avail ourselves of biblical guidelines for spiritual battle, results in great destruction and heartache in life and havoc on the frontlines.

Ruthanne Garlock uses the illustration of the Spanish conquering the Mayan Indians in the early 1500s to illustrate what often happens in spiritual warfare:

> The Mayan Indians—who fought with bow and arrow—were known to be brave, fierce warriors. But the Spanish soldiers had a distinct advantage because they wore armor, and they had horses and guns. Horses were unknown in the Western Hemisphere at that time. So when the Indians saw one of these swift-footed beings with an armored soldier attached, they thought it was all one creature. They aimed at the horse, not realizing that the real enemy was the soldier astride the horse. Their arrows felled the horses in great numbers, but the armored soldiers jumped from their mounts and shot the Indians with their muskets. The Mayans were massacred by the hundreds and the Spanish easily seized control of the entire region. (Sherrer and Garlock 1991, 35)

The Indians failed to recognize the real enemy riding on the horse's back, and that brought their defeat. Garlock comments, "That's exactly what happens to countless Christians. They shoot at one another instead of fighting the devil" (Sherrer and Garlock 1991, 35).

Women tend to be more sensitive to spiritual things than men. As we look at spiritual activity the world over we find that women outnumber men regularly in the places of worship. A great number of spiritual leaders such as spirit mediums, shamans, diviners, and fortune-tellers of any given society are women. It may be due to this sensitivity that Satan works extra hard to influence and misguide women. However, when God gets hold of this female sensitivity and women's expertise and loyalty in interpersonal relationships, he has a potent weapon on his side to fight the enemy. Sherrer and Garlock's book (1991) shows how specific women using their spiritual gifts to fight the enemy have prevented suicides, saved lives, broken addictions, and conquered disease.

SATANIC ACTIVITY

Because of such activities our enemy, Satan, and his demons are very active in their attempts to counter even Christian women. They are also very active in and through the women they influence in the societies in which we work. In what follows we will deal with these two areas. It is important to deal with the first area to help women get free from any satanic activity in their lives so they are able to carry out their ministries to which God has called them. The second area, then, is important because the people to whom we are called are also under attack by the forces of Satan.

The Scriptures portray the life and ministries of Jesus and of his followers as taking place in a world ruled by Satan (John 14:30). This means that we who are of the kingdom of God live in a context of spiritual warfare. As the Apostle Paul states, "For our struggle is not against flesh and blood, but against the rulers, against the authorities, against the powers of this dark world and against the spiritual forces of evil in the heavenly realms" (Eph 6:12). We live and work, then, in a world full of satanic activity.

Given this fact, what can we learn about these activities? Do these affect us? Are spiritually minded, dedicated women affected by satanic activity? And can such women be effective in fighting the enemy?

The satanic kingdom is alive and well in the world today. In some areas of the world it is quite obvious that the enemy is strongly present. There are people all over the world who worship gods and spirits (demons) and live lives as committed to those gods and spirits as we are to the true God. These peoples may quite openly give Satan full reign in their lives.

But, less obviously, our enemy works to tempt, harass, disrupt, and do whatever else he can to gain influence even in the lives of God's people. We would expect this, since it is God's people that he hates most. It is those committed to Christ who can really hurt him and hinder the working out of his plans in the world.

How, then, do satanic forces work in the lives of Christians? We've mentioned temptation. Satan and his helpers are the agents of temptation. Women are tempted as are all humans. Women are particularly prone to envy, pride, gossip, doubt, criticism, mistreatment of their husbands, children, and coworkers, and a myriad of other sinful behaviors. The Bible doesn't allow us to avoid responsibility for such behavior; it shows us what happens to people like Eve, King Saul, Jezebel, Judas, and even King David, who allow satanic temptation to get the best of them.

And there are many other scriptural examples of Satan's working in what looks like an extreme case. God allowed the "thorn in the flesh" into the Apostle Paul's life as a "messenger of Satan" (2 Cor 12:7), to aid him in controlling his pride. We don't know exactly what the "thorn" was, but the fact that it is identified as coming from Satan should help us to recognize that God sometimes uses satanic activity to teach us. Similarly, God brags to Satan about Job and then gives Satan special permission to attack him. In addition, a demonic being was allowed to hold up the answer to Daniel's prayer (Dan 10:13), showing us that demonic beings can affect the timing of the answers to our prayers.

Further, we learn from the accounts of the ministry of Jesus and his disciples that people can have demons living within them. This led to deliverance from demons being an important part of the ministry of the disciples, with statements such as that in John 14:12 and 20:21 indicating that this is to be a part of our ministries as well. In John 14:12, Jesus predicted (prophesied), "anyone who has faith in me will do what I have been doing. He will do even greater things than these, because I am going to the Father." And in John 20:21 Jesus said, "As the Father has sent me, I am sending you." From this and other passages it is clear that Jesus intended us to continue every aspect of his ministry, including attacking and defeating demons that live in people.

Due to the ignorance of Western Christianity concerning demonization, however, we tend to ignore this part of the ministry Jesus gave us. The result is twofold in the lives of Western missionaries: we don't know what to do about demonization either in the people we go to or in missionaries themselves. We, the authors, have had experience with several hundred missionaries and other Christian workers who were carrying demons. They were usually quite unaware of this fact until we challenged the demons, but they were very glad to get rid of them! We speak below of a variety of reasons why missionaries might be demonized.

Some Christians don't think that believers can carry demons. Often this contention comes from taking the mistranslation "demon possession" seriously. This mistranslation gives the erroneous impression that a demon has more control over the person it lives in than is usually the case. The Greek terms in the New Testament do not mean demon possession. They merely mean "have a demon," with the implication that the demon is living inside the person. There is a big difference between having a demon and being possessed by a demon because the latter mistakenly implies ownership.

Clinton E. Arnold, a noted theologian and authority on the New Testament and spiritual warfare, explains how when one becomes a new Christian, one's identity changes and one becomes pure and holy as the Holy Spirit takes residence within the person (1997, 84). However, the continued struggle with sin and the propensity to do evil is still present as corrupt thoughts and desires come from within.

> Demonic spirits seek to exert their influence in the same way and in the same places that the evil impulse does. They attempt to reassert their control over the mind, will, and emotions of the individual in a variety of insidious ways...

The difference between a believer and a nonbeliever is at the core of their being. The believer has an entirely new nature because he or she has been brought into a relationship with Jesus Christ and endowed with the Holy Spirit. Demonic spirits cannot penetrate to the core of this person's being and snatch away what belongs to God. A believer may yield to the evil impulse or to a demonic spirit, allowing it to assert a dominating influence over mind, will, emotions, and even the body. But the person's new identity as a child of God cannot be erased or stolen. Nor do demonic spirits have the ability to evict the Holy Spirit of God. (1997, 85)

After discussing the biblical basis for the activity of spirits, Arnold concludes:

The theological and historical evidence suggests that Christians can be profoundly influenced by evil spirits—even to the extent that it can be said that they are inhabited and controlled by demons. (1997, 88)

Since believers have the Holy Spirit within, they have the means to defeat both sin and demonic spirits. It is helpful to understand, as Arnold points out, that the enemy asserts his influence in three different ways: 1) through evil inclinations (the flesh), 2) through the cultural environment (the world), and 3) through demons (Satan's direct activity) (ibid., 90). Each of these will take as much governing power as the believer allows them to take.

Our experience with well over one thousand cases of demonized Christians has clearly proved to us that demons can live inside of Christians. These demons usually have come from their pre-Christian life and have been banished from their human spirits at conversion. They can, however, continue to live in body, mind, emotions, and will until they are cast out (C. Kraft 2011, 71). We believe also that most of those Jesus freed from demons were people of faith. Quite often when a person came to Jesus for healing, he states that it is the faith of the person that has made him/her whole (e.g., Mark 10:62; Luke 7:50). What he meant was that that person had come to the right person for healing. It was faith in Jesus that had brought the healing. Faith in Jesus is what saves a person. We conclude, therefore, that since those Jesus healed had faith in him, they would classify today as Christians.

So the first order of business is to get the missionary cleaned up. The second thing to discuss is how missionaries can deal with demonization among the people they work with on the field. We discuss both of these topics below.

SPECIFIC PROBLEMS NEEDING ATTENTION

Today's missionary women have many unique difficulties that need to be addressed in the context of spiritual warfare. These include home and career pressures, coping with addictions either their own or those of children or spouses, cultural pressures, adjusting to losses in life, being at a distance from the usual support system, marital pressures, and many others. As human beings we are all susceptible to enemy attacks, and we are no match for the evil one if we are operating merely in our own strength. The difficulties we face in life may be normal problems that God can use to test us and make us strong, or they may be Satan's attempt to destroy us and our work. The same occurrences can be used by Satan or by God, depending on whether we partner with God or with Satan. Satan is busy especially in Christian circles to get us to partner with him to hinder God's working. God has given us free will, and we can choose at any time not to obey him and not to avail ourselves of the power of the Holy Spirit within us. Wrong choices increase our vulnerability.

Women, as well as men, have many emotional problems to deal with. Many of the more serious of these problems have developed in childhood or even before birth. When, then, these problems are not dealt with, they fester inside of the person, making life difficult. If the problems are not dealt with, they can strongly influence the person in a wide variety of ways. It is often the case that a person is not conscious of the influence of these problems in her adult life. The result is that the damage often is great and rooted so deep inside that she has no ability either to assess the damage or to get it healed. And many churches are clueless to bring her the healing she needs.

The existence and effects of such childhood problems are widely recognized. What is not so widely recognized is that when an emotional problem is not dealt with, demonization can result. Demons are like rats, and rats feed on garbage. The garbage of emotional wounds, if not dealt with, gives demonic rats a legal right to enter and live inside a person (C. Kraft 2011). Thus, though Christians are often able through Christian growth and spiritual discipline to weaken and suppress any demons living inside them, they often have not been able to get completely free of them.

So, among the problems to deal with are the emotional wounds, received usually in the early years of life, and the possibility that there may be demons attached to them. In addition, many women (and men) carry demons that have come from inheritance, cursing, or soul-ties (see below). Though these also can be weakened through suppression resulting from Christian growth, they can still affect a person, especially when that person is out of her home territory and sensing the tensions and spiritual powers of another cultural situation.

Self-Worth

Women, more than men, are susceptible to depending on relationships for their sense of self-worth. We can assume, then, that Satan will attack women in this area. Carol Gilligan (1982), in her research on female personality and development, shows that relationships and care are key elements in woman's identity and definition of maturity. "Women not only define themselves in a context of human relationship but also judge themselves in terms of their ability to care" (ibid., 17). Women's sense of self is organized around making and maintaining relationships of care—caring for others and being cared for by others. Women have deep concern with both sides of an interdependent relationship and need to feel their own connectedness.

For many women the disruption in a relationship results in serious self-doubt. Thus, moving to a new location makes women highly vulnerable. This provides the opportunity for spiritual attack. Satan's lies begin to flow: "You are not worth anything here, you are a failure, nobody cares about you here, your husband/colleagues don't care about you." This can easily lead to depression, unmanageable stress, and physical illness to the point where one is not able to function in the new setting. It is easy to begin blaming others for this insecurity and unrest—husband, mission board, and even God. This may cause the woman to question her faith and spiritual health.

After working with hundreds of women to help them deal with internal issues, we have come to the conclusion that the primary attacks of Satan are in the area of self-worth. Many women, like Connie, have been brought up in homes where they have not been valued, except for their ability to provide services. They grow up, then, with the feeling that they are not worth anything as persons, only as servants. Somewhere along the line, though, they come to Christ and commit themselves to missionary service. If they marry, then, they see themselves as servants to their husbands. Often the mission structure reinforces this self-perception. If they are single, they may feel they have been missed and, therefore, not valued either by people or by God.

Not infrequently, then, a woman carries with her, deep within her earliest memories, the knowledge that she was not wanted. She may have been the product of an inconvenient pregnancy and experienced rejection in the womb because of that. Or the pregnancy may have been wanted but the parents strongly wanted a boy, not a girl. We have worked with many who were born the second, third, or fourth girls in their families who carry deep wounds due to such unwantedness. Not infrequently, then, such women have been unconsciously or consciously cursed or not infrequently curse themselves with a curse of not being wanted.

Or a woman may have been abused sexually, physically, or verbally as she was growing up, giving her the strong impression that she is merely a worthless object to be used and thrown away at the whim of a man. Approximately one in every three girls in the United States is sexually abused before she reaches maturity (Cunningham and Hamilton 2000, 17 citing Gavin de Becker). Though such women often can give the impression that they have it all together, the conscious or unconscious memory of such events takes an incredible toll on their psyches, resulting often in serious dysfunction, especially in their relationships with men.

Whatever the source, feelings of negative self-worth provide fertile ground for demonic activity in a person. The demon's job is to do as much as possible to cripple the person, rendering her unable to carry out what God has called her to do. He, therefore, lies to her concerning who she is and teaches her to tell herself these lies.

Self-Rejection

A natural outgrowth of self-worth problems is self-rejection. When a person carries memories of unwantedness or abuse, self-rejection is a normal response. The pattern of thinking that generates such a response seems to be, "Adults do not value me. Adults know what they are doing. Therefore, there must be something wrong with me that leads adults to reject me. This being (perceived as) true, I need to reject myself."

Such self-rejection, with what seems to the person as a solid basis in adult attitudes, can be vicious. We have dealt with women whose self-rejection was more like self-hatred or even self-loathing. They hate being women. They hate being alive. As one woman told us, she feels she has no right to exist, and feels she is just taking up space that really belongs to someone else. This woman, though a pastor's wife, was carrying a demon of self-hatred (and others as well) attached to her feeling of self-hatred—a feeling that dated back to her reactions to childhood mistreatment.

Another woman who had come for prayer ministry simply stated that her problem was that "I hate myself. I wish I had never been born." And many others have said the same thing in one way or another. We found the roots of this self-hatred in a family experience that alternated between abuse and neglect. The relationships she had a right to expect were defective in the extreme and she, in response to what she felt those relationships were saying about her self-worth, had developed a vicious self-hatred accompanied by deep-seated anger at God for letting this happen. And demons were having a field day at her expense, aiding and abetting her negative feelings toward herself and toward God.

Women strongly depend on interpersonal relationships. When they move to a new setting they often feel rejection and they reexamine their self-worth. They have worked hard to belong and be accepted as adults according to the opportunities and standards of their society of origin. Moving to a new society often brings problems of identity. She may no longer feel that she is valid for her own sake but is depersonalized and only known as being "mother of ———," or "wife of ———," or one who behaves modestly, or one who has no children, or one who supports (or doesn't support) her husband.

Single women often face criticism and constant rejection from the nationals who may look down on them or even have no place in their society for single women. Because of this the single missionary woman is personally weakened and feels rejection at the very core of her being. For example, we knew a missionary woman who had studied and had experiences in church planting. But she was treated by her superior, a national, as the one to make men comfortable (e.g., prepare the coffee, organize the office) and ignored when it came to discussing and lending her expertise in decision-making issues. Satan often uses these kinds of experiences of rejection to stir up trouble on the frontlines.

Shame and Guilt

Shame is feeling bad about who one is. It contrasts with guilt, the feeling that one has done something wrong. Shame is about *being*, guilt about *doing*. Typically, a person conceived out of wedlock or a person who has been sexually abused will carry memories of shame and probably also guilt. These memories, then, fester inside and affect the person's life and self-image in a variety of ways, working usually from below the level of consciousness.

The feeling of the lady referred to above that she had no right to exist is a typical fruit of shame. The feeling of one who is abused is often that she is ruined and worthless, like an old rag that is only good to be thrown away. Anyone conceived to parents that did not want her is likely to have picked up a spirit of shame in the womb. Words such as, "Shame on you" and "You ought to be ashamed of yourself" can contribute greatly to an attitude of shame, especially when they come repeatedly from parents or significant others.

We have found that spirits of shame can be vicious. Their job is to take away all sense of pride a child of God has a right to feel, so that a person cannot assimilate the scriptural truths about God's love, acceptance, and forgiveness or that he has adopted us into his family and made us his princesses (1 John 3:1–2). The lady mentioned above was so much a victim of the spirit of shame that, though she was the organist for her church, she felt so bad about herself that she literally sneaked to and from the organ to keep as much as possible out of sight of the church members.

And one or more deceiving and lying spirits usually accompany spirits of shame and guilt. Their job is to get the person to believe their lies about who she is and what others think of her. Such spirits often invade her self-talk so that she constantly hears herself saying negative things about herself, even though intellectually she knows these things are lies. But the voice that she thinks is hers continues to speak the lies against her will.

Fear, Insecurity, Worry, and Control

Many women live with a high level of fear, often manifesting itself as insecurity. As mentioned, a woman tends to take her cues from her perception of the relationships she has with those who are significant in her life. If, then, she does not feel secure in the way she is being treated by her husband or her coworkers, or if the way she is treated brings back memories of early abusive treatment in her childhood, she can be tormented by fear and insecurity.

Fear comes in a wide variety of types: fear of the future, fear of not being accepted, fear of authority, fear for family, fear of inadequacy, fear of not living up to the expectations of others, fear of failure, fear of singleness, fear of death, fear of traveling, and fear of heights. And each of these fears is likely to have its roots in family of origin issues.

The female brain, more than the male's, is structured to carry a universe of concerns all at the same time. The split brain of a man usually enables him to focus in on one thing at a time, without carrying his concern for everything else as he concentrates on any given issue. A woman's brain is, however, quite different, with more connections between the right side and the left. The result is that a woman carries just about all her concerns with her everywhere she goes. This sets her up to worry about one or more of a myriad of problems she knows about even as she attempts to focus on whatever she needs to be doing at any given time.

For example, I (Chuck) can get involved in what I am doing and completely put out of my mind all the other things that make up my life. Especially when I'm on a trip, I can forget my family, my other responsibilities, and any problems that face us, because I have a man's brain. Even when we're traveling, though, Meg has on her mind our family and everything going on back home plus whatever we have planned for the future, especially if there are any problems. That is to say, women tend to worry more than men do. And the enemy tests women at this point.

When a woman is fearful, insecure, or worried, it is easy for her to feel the necessity of asserting control over situations that she feels could become chaotic if she is not in control. In cross-cultural situations, mothers often over-control their children out of fear that bad things could happen to them if they are not under tight control. Women who have the gift of compassion, then, are especially prone to worry. Many women regularly take other people's burdens on themselves and get bogged down with other people's problems.

We worked with one pastor's wife who suffered from a thirty-year severe back problem. As we ministered to her, God led us to focus on the fact that she was like a sponge, soaking up all of the problems of the people in her husband's congregation. And, due to her female brain, she carried all of these worries with her at all times. There was even some domestic tension centered on the fact that she felt her husband was not concerned enough about the problems. As we helped her to give these other people's problems to Jesus and commanded the demon of worry to leave, however, she gained both emotional and physical freedom. The pain in her back disappeared completely and never came back.

Living in fear, insecurity, and worry provide fertile ground for demonic influence. We have met many demons whose job it was to aid and abet such feelings. They have found homes in unsuspecting women. The insecurities of living female in a society that often gives women very little room to wiggle can result in deeply felt fears that become congenial garbage for demonic rats.

Anger and Unforgiveness

Many women are angry. And, given their life situations, many of them have a right to be angry. The kinds of unwantedness and abuse, coupled with the unfairness and frustrating of expectations that life often brings, are more than enough to stimulate angry reactions to life. Many women carry unconscious bitterness over the rejection they have felt as little girls from parents who wanted a boy. Many carry anger over frustration of expectations they grew up with, the so-called glass ceiling in school, church, or the business world. Abusive relationships, either as children or as adults, including the breaking off of romantic relationships by men who may have used them and left them, are further causes of anger and unforgiveness.

Holding onto such anger, no matter how justified it may be, how-ever, results in the festering of the anger and provides an entry point for demons (see Eph 4:26–27). The issue that gives the demons rights is usually unforgiveness. Jesus said we are to forgive those who have hurt us as God has forgiven us (Matt 6:20). If we do not, the enemy has the legal right to enter us and to encourage the anger.

Loneliness

Life can be very lonely for men or women. Our society, while giv-ing us much freedom, seems to produce loneliness as a by-product. Women, since they are relationally oriented, become very lonely without meaningful relationships. Girls grow up with the expectation that marriage will solve their loneliness problem. But often this does not happen since husbands rarely know how to help the situation. Male coworkers are also usually blind to the relational needs of women.

Extreme loneliness can, whether consciously or unconsciously, lead to anger, bitterness, resentment, self-image problems, and just about any of the other problems mentioned above. When people hang on to these feelings, then, the result is demonization.

Inherited Demons, Curses, and Soul-Ties

Unfortunately, demons can be inherited. Or they can come in through curses if the person is otherwise vulnerable, or they can result from soul-ties. In our ministry we have dealt with many people who have inherited demons from parents or grandparents who were members of occult organizations such as Freemasonry, Scientology, Mormonism, or non-Christian religions such as Islam, Buddhism, or Hinduism. Like all demons, these like to lie low, never betraying their presence but subtly influencing the person in various ways. A typical influence is to create difficulty in reading Scripture and/or praying. Sometimes such demons work with others to push a person to consider or attempt suicide.

Curses likewise, whether coming from others or put on by the person herself, can affect women unconsciously. It seems from Proverbs 26:2 as though there needs to be some spiritual or emotional weakness in a person for a curse to land on the person. But the above list of women's problems provides enough potential garbage for curses to land heavily. One of the major sources of cursing we've found is self-cursing. Given problems of unwantedness and/or abuse, many women curse their bodies or parts of them somewhere along the line. The influence of the media and society's beauty standards often result in self-cursing. Statements such as "I hate my hips" or "I hate the fact that I have breasts" constitute curses.

One lady came to us asking for prayer after an X-ray showed lumps on her breasts. As it turned out, she had been sexually misused and the man focused on her breasts. This led her to say something like, "I resent the fact that I have to have these things that make me so vulnerable to men." In the power of Jesus we cancelled the curse and the next X-ray showed no lumps.

Soul-ties, then, are spiritual bonding that carry satanic power. They usually result from dominating relationships, often between mother and daughter, or from sexual relationships outside of marriage. When a person is in a very dominating church or other group, a soul-tie can result as well. They can be easily broken, as can curses, by simply repenting of them and claiming the power of Jesus Christ to cancel them. But they can be disruptive to our lives if we don't know they're there and, therefore, don't do anything about them.

WHAT TO DO ABOUT THESE PROBLEMS

Most Christians today have been conditioned to interpret all that happens to human causes and weaknesses. As a result, there is criticism of one another, a tendency to put one another down, gossip—all of these hindering the work to expand God's kingdom here on earth. What we so often fail to recognize is the work of the evil one determinedly attempting to keep God's work from moving ahead. To recognize this activity in daily life and to become more aware of spiritual warfare, the following reminder is helpful:

> My coworker is my coworker.
> My coworker is not the enemy.
> The enemy (Satan) is the enemy.

This concept is usable in so many situations—my husband, my neighbor, the national coworker, my child, the field director. This places the focus constantly on the behind-the-scenes actions of the evil one. Satan—not the other person—is our enemy and we must be on guard against his tactics. God has provided us with a part of himself, the Holy Spirit, who is within us and more powerful than any other spirit power. We need to be actively in battle in the spirit realm in order to more effectively work for the furtherance of God's kingdom.

So often Christians experience spiritual bondage to a variety of things that Satan uses to detract from our focus on God and sap our energy for serving him. Some of these may be depression, addictions, fears, self-pity, or even unchristian behavior. Sherrer and Garlock present the following steps for being able to walk free from the traps that can make us ineffective.

Ways to Effectively Combat Spiritual Bondage

1. Identify the problem. Ask the Holy Spirit to show you any areas of bondage you may have overlooked.
2. Confess and repent before the Lord the sins the Holy Spirit reveals to you.
3. Choose to forgive all who have wounded you; also forgive yourself. Release your anger toward God, your feeling that he "let you down."
4. Receive God's forgiveness and cleansing.
5. Renounce the sin and close the door in any area where the enemy has gained entry.
6. Ask the Holy Spirit to help you break the behavior and thought patterns you've become accustomed to (see Phil 4:7–9).

7. Allow the Holy Spirit to daily conform you to the image of Christ (Sherrer & Garlock 1991, 139).

We are God's children and Satan has no legal power over us, though he never stops trying to cause havoc in our lives. Jesus gave us the Holy Spirit, who is greater than any evil power (1 John 4:4).

In each of the areas discussed in the previous section, we are dealing with two issues: the human dimension and the spirit dimension. And they are connected. Not all human problems give demons entrance, especially if they are dealt with right away. If, however, the problem is kept for a period of time, such as from childhood into adulthood, it festers and creates emotional damage. When such festering happens, then, demons have a legal right to enter. Their job is to use the emotional or spiritual problem to harass the person, producing in the person as much disruption as they can get away with. As mentioned, though, people with Christian faith expressing spiritual discipline can often suppress demonic activity fairly successfully as they grow in their relationship with Jesus.

It is important that women who seek to serve Christ fully receive ministry to enable them to deal with each of these problems. They need inner healing to clear up emotional and spiritual damage they may have sustained (see C. Kraft 2010a). They may need deliverance to get rid of any enemy spirits that have taken up residence. It is our practice to help people in this regard by first dealing with the emotional and spiritual garbage, then challenging the demons. When the garbage is dealt with first, the demons lose their power. Thus, we very seldom have any violence from the demons, since they are so weakened by the time we begin dealing with them.

Though it is best to work with someone who knows how to do inner healing, much, if not all, of the healing needed can be brought about for most persons by following the guidelines in C. Kraft 2010b, 2011, and 2012. A woman called me (Chuck) from Baltimore one time thanking me for one of these books and letting me know that she had bought a copy for a friend, asking her to "Read it and do me." The friend read the book and each of them worked on each other, both getting freed up from emotional and spiritual problems as well as demonization. A similar call came from another woman who had asked her pastor to read the book and follow the directions there. That worked also.

MINISTRY IN A CONTEXT OF SPIRITUAL WARFARE

Demonization is quite common among the people we go to as missionaries. So is the need for emotional and physical healing. It is a shame that most of the Christianity we have taken to the world is virtually powerless (see C. Kraft 1989, 2002; M. Kraft 1995). This is especially regrettable since most of the peoples of the world are very concerned about issues that they understand to involve spiritual power. The women of non-Western societies are especially likely to be concerned about issues such as healing, their own fertility and that of their farms and animals, getting free from demons, attracting blessing from spirits for themselves and their families, protection, preventing misfortune, and many other such things. Though our primary concern as Christians needs to be with the relationship of these people with God, Jesus showed us that we should not be unconcerned with issues involving spiritual power.

And Jesus said we would do what he did (John 14:12) and gave us the same Holy Spirit who empowered him to enable us to witness like he did in love and power (Acts 1:8). We read, therefore, that while he was on earth Jesus gave his disciples "power and authority to drive out all demons and to cure diseases, and he sent them out to preach the kingdom of God and to heal the sick" (Luke 9:1–2). We have learned to take the preaching part of that commission seriously. Why have we usually neglected the healing and deliverance part? When there are problems we have tended to offer secular medicine and psychology, even to people who know that at least a major part of these problems is spiritual. In most non-Western societies dealing with the spiritual forces is an essential part of their daily existence.

We have noted that women are often especially sensitive in spiritual matters. God has frequently gifted women with discernment, both natural and spiritual, to notice when people are in difficulty. If, then, a missionary woman has herself experienced inner healing and deliverance, she can, with her gifting and a little training, minister quite effectively to those who are hurting in the society to which she is called. It has been our experience that gifted women can be mightily used by God in such ministry.

Indeed, we know of a couple who worked in Indonesia who decided to make this kind of ministry their primary approach to evangelism. They worked with a people who believe in healing and deliverance and used their own gifting in this area to attract seekers. Though they were working among a male dominated people, the wife was well accepted when she took the lead in ministering to those who were hurting. These missionaries were under no illusion that healing and deliverance alone would be enough to bring people to Christ. After all, it is a relationship with Christ, not healing from him, that saves. And even Jesus was not always successful in moving people from healing to conversion. Furthermore, people in a power-oriented society are quite ready to accept healing from any source without feeling an obligation to commit themselves to that source of blessing. So these missionaries offered inner healing and deliverance as Jesus did, to attract people into a relationship.

Intercession is another facet of spiritual warfare that women are often gifted in. Prayer, especially intercessory prayer, is an act of warfare. When we pray, we are aligning ourselves with God in the partnership he seeks, inviting us to assist him in doing what he would like to do in the human context. For he seems to have made a rule for himself that he seldom works in the human context without a human partner. When, however, we join with him in obedience by praying for ourselves and others repentantly and seeking his face in humility, he promises to forgive our sins and heal our land (2 Chron 7:14).

It has been our experience that many women have the gift of intercession. Often women, more than men, are sensitive to the Holy Spirit, hearing from him whether in words or in pictures (e.g., dreams and visions). Their praying, then, both brings clarity concerning the leading of God in ministry and the attacks of the enemy who seeks to hinder that ministry. There is no estimating the amount of spiritual power that is generated when groups of dedicated women get together to intercede for the work of God.

Both a healing ministry and a prayer ministry fall into the category of ground-level spiritual warfare. There is also cosmic-level spiritual warfare. This consists of attacking the cosmic-level spirits spoken of in Ephesians 6:12. The basics of such warfare, however, involve what humans do at ground level. When people repent, when Christian leaders unite, when people, especially Christians, forgive each other and reconcile, when people unite in humility and prayer as God recommends in 2 Chronicles 7:14—when these things happen, God brings revival of Christians and enables them to be more effective in reaching the lost. Women can have a great ministry in this area, even if for cultural reasons they have to work in the background.

Prayer walking is an important activity in cosmic-level warfare. This involves one or more persons laying claim to a certain territory that they regularly walk around and pray over, claiming that territory and the people who live in it for Christ. The usual territory is a neighborhood or small village. It is good to do this in a group rather than just as an individual. And it can often be done without much fanfare and by people who do not hold official positions in the church. Since the spirit world works according to authority relationships, however, if those who do have official positions are involved, either as participants or as sponsors, such acts of spiritual warfare carry more weight (see C. Kraft 2012).

There is much in Scripture concerning the importance of territory to God. Claiming territory spiritually, then, should be a part of our attacks on the enemy. Satan claimed in tempting Jesus that the kingdoms of the world had all been handed over to him (Luke 4:6). We know, though, that the territory he claims really belongs to God and that we are commissioned by God and given his authority to take it back.

Steve Nicholson, a Vineyard pastor in Evanston, Illinois, who became discouraged over the lack of growth in his church, took this mandate seriously and began praying over the area in which his church was situated. As he prayed, he felt led to specify the exact area from such and such a street on the north to such and such a street on the south and likewise from east to west. After several weeks of such targeted praying, then, he was visited by a demonic spirit who said, among other things, that he was a spirit of witchcraft and that he refused to give him that much territory. Steve persevered, however, continuing to claim all of the territory he had specified and eventually felt the breaking of the demonic spirit's power. His church then began to grow, with many of the converts coming to Christ from witchcraft (Wagner 1991, 30–31). Women, especially with permission from church or mission leaders, can assert such authority to extend the kingdom of God into enemy-occupied territory.

Another aspect of spiritual warfare relating to territory is the need to take authority over our homes, places of work, churches, and the like—in short, any place that we would like to take away from Satan's power. Our homes need to be dedicated in whole and in part, in the present and in the past. What we mean is that we ought to be claiming the presence and power of God in these places to displace any enemy rights. We were ministering to a missionary lady in Papua New Guinea once and found that a demon had rights in her life due to the fact that the previous owner of the home she lived in had committed adultery in that home. Quite innocently, this woman had moved into the home without claiming her spiritual authority as the new rightful owner to break the power the enemy had been given by the previous occupant. Once we claimed the power of Jesus to break that power, Satan had no more legal right to that home. At that time we also cancelled additional enemy rights over the home that had come through the earlier history of warfare, including bloodshed, on the land on which the home was built.

On another occasion, we worked with a missionary family serving in Kenya who found that one side of the room in which their children slept was dangerous. Whoever slept in that part of the room experienced strange evil dreams, including the mother who, doubting her children's story of bad dreams, tried it out herself. We assumed that there was some kind of curse on that part of the home or the land on which it was built and claimed the power of Christ to cleanse it spiritually.

A similar thing was reported to us by a missionary working among Native Americans concerning a house in which some of his colleagues had lived. He reported that over the past thirty or more years, whoever lived in that house had had to leave quickly after a relatively short period of time due to sickness, accident, marital discord, or other such problems. He asked us, "Do you think that house may be cursed?" We responded that we suspected that there might indeed be a curse. So this man, who was the leader of the mission, asserted his authority in Christ to cleanse any past or present curses that might be on that house or the property on which it stood and, to date, no more such problems have occurred among those living in it.

On another issue, there are many places that we go into that are controlled by Satan. We should calmly claim the protection of God as we go into such places. Indeed, we should always claim such protection no matter what we are doing or where we are going. God gives his people a certain amount of automatic protection, we believe. But, especially when we suspect the places we are going into are under strong demonic influence, we should claim additional protection. Among such places would be temples, shrines, homes and property of spirit practitioners, and, in our home countries, bookshops selling occult materials, buildings of occult organizations, and the like.

In addition to the spiritual warfare over territory that we can engage in, it is important for us to continually claim spiritual protection for our children and husbands, letting the enemy know that we as parents are the gatekeepers into our families. One of the things we recommend is that parents say to the listening spirit world something like, "We (the parents) are the doorways into this family and you (enemy spirits) cannot enter this family except through us. We open our doors to the Holy Spirit but close them tightly against all representatives of Satan. In this regard, we forbid any satanic spirits to go over, under, or around us. You can only gain access to our children by going through us, but we are not allowing that to happen. Instead, we claim total protection of Jesus Christ, King of kings and Lord of lords, for ourselves and our children."

One more area to mention is that any material items that we may have in our homes that came from the people we serve need to be prayed over to cancel any enemy power that they may contain. It is the custom of many of the peoples of the world to dedicate things they make to enemy gods and spirits. When, then, we purchase or are given these things, they carry demons into our homes. We should not get frantic about this. Nor should we destroy most of the things that have come from non-Christian sources. We simply need to claim our authority in Jesus Christ to cancel any enemy power that has been invested in these things and then bless them with the power of God and all will probably go well. In some few cases, asserting God's authority in this way doesn't seem to work. If one suspects that that is the case with any given items, simply destroy them. Keeping items that have been given us as gifts rather than destroying them can be an important testimony to those who gave them to us. So, only destroy such items as a last resort.

CONCLUSION

Whether at cosmic-level with housing or families or taking territory for Christ, or at ground-level in freeing people from inner problems and demons, women can play an important part in spiritual warfare by asserting the authority given us by God to take back his world from

Satan. A book that can be helpful in these areas is *I Give You Authority* (C. Kraft 2012). It is a sad thing that for lack of understanding in these areas we often let the enemy do whatever he wants to do in our lives and ministries.

In this brief introduction to spiritual warfare, our aim has been to enable you to be more aware of the spiritual battle going on and what to do about it. We are in a war zone, behind enemy lines. Whether or not we like it, we all wear uniforms and all are targets of an unseen enemy. We know from the Bible that our side of the war gets to win. But we don't know whether we will emerge victorious in any given battle. Being on the front lines is a privilege, but we must be prepared and alert.

REFERENCES

Arnold, C. 1997. *Three Crucial Questions About Spiritual Warfare.* Grand Rapids, MI: Baker Books.

Gilligan, C. 1982. *In a Different Voice: Psychological Theory and Women's Development.* Cambridge, MA: Harvard University Press.

Cunningham, L., and D. J. Hamilton. 2000. *Why Not Women? Biblical Study of Women in Missions, Ministry, and Leadership.* Seattle, WA: YWAM Publishing.

De Becker, G. 1999. *Protecting the Gift.* New York: The Dial Press, Random House.

Kraft, C. H. 1989. *Christianity with Power: Your Worldview and Your Experience of the Supernatural.* Portland, OR: Wipf and Stock.

———. 2011. *Defeating Dark Angels,* rev. ed. Ventura, CA: Regal Books.

———. 2010a. *Deep Wounds, Deep Healing,* rev. ed. Ventura, CA: Regal Books.

———. 2012. *I Give You Authority,* rev. ed. Grand Rapids, MI: Chosen Books.

———. 2002. *Confronting Powerless Christianity: Evangelicals and the Mission Dimension.* Grand Rapids, MI: Chosen Books.

————. 2010b. *Two Hours to Freedom*. Grand Rapids, MI: Chosen Books.

Kraft, M. G. 1995. *Understanding Spiritual Power: A Forgotten Dimension of Cross-Cultural Mission and Ministry*. Maryknoll, NY: Orbis Books.

Lindquist, S. E. 1982. Prediction of Success in Overseas Adjustment. *Journal of Psychology and Christianity*, 1(2): 22–25.

Sherrer, Q., and R. Garlock. 1991. *Woman's Guide to Spiritual Warfare: A Woman's Guide for Battle*. Ann Arbor, MI: Servant Publications.

Wagner, C. P. 1991. *Engaging the Enemy: How to Fight and Defeat Territorial Spirits*. Ventura, CA: Regal Books.

TWELVE

In the Line of Fire
Steve Hoke and Judith E. Lingenfelter

A cursory reading of any major news magazine or newspaper headline reveals a world in turmoil. The 9/11 disaster in the US introduced the word "terrorist" into our daily vocabulary, and exacerbated the tensions that already exist in the missions world. Subsequent terrorist bombings at uneven intervals in every continent, and the Arab Spring of 2011, have thrown the world into a state of unease and concern. Do we evacuate or stay? Which is more important, the safety of our families or the work we are doing with nationals? Do we fear because our faith is not strong enough, or do we take foolish risks and feel that God will take care of us? These issues have jumped to the forefront of our consciousness as church bombings in Pakistan, kidnappings in the Philippines, and rapes of Chinese Christians in Indonesia capture our attention.

Except for natural disasters, most settings of danger and stress put the missionary family in the line of fire and create moral dilemmas for churches and agencies alike regarding their safety and care. Such settings call for the courageous and the strong at heart, and impact women in unique ways. Missionary wives often work separately from their husbands during most of day, and are stretched between the conflicting demands of home, children, ministry, and safety, while single women juggle delicate gender issues and heightened feelings of vulnerability because of their visibility in such tenuous situations.

WOMEN'S UNIQUE CONCERNS IN THE LINE OF FIRE

What are the pressure points that are unique to women in such situations? What are the issues that women have to face? While unstable situations affect men and women alike, this chapter focuses on women for two specific reasons: 1) they are usually more relational in their understanding and dealing with events, and 2) mission leadership is still overwhelmingly male, and many women feel their voices are not heard. Our recent conversations with women around the world reveal several critical concerns. Each concern is listed below with a comment from different women we talked with via email.

Concern for Children and Family

> I don't know if women feel it more than men, or if their maternal instincts are greater than those of their husbands, but if the safety of a woman's child is in jeopardy, it will greatly influence decisions she makes in a crisis.

Women may want to stay with their husbands in deteriorating situations, but the safety of the children becomes a paramount consideration, because the children bear the consequences of the choices that are made for them. In addition it does seem evident that the Holy Spirit has wired women with a sensitive danger sensor that most men do not have installed, or have let the batteries lapse. It is wives who more often have the first and more consistent intuitive caution that something is amiss, that there is danger lurking, that the children may be at risk. I think too often we have not seen this "maternal compassion" as a gift from the Spirit, but another example of a mother's frailty. Nothing could be further from the truth. Families and organizations need to honor a woman's intuitive "read" of an emergency, and at least listen for what the Spirit may be saying.

Churches and mission agencies could do more to prompt dialogue among couples and probe for great theological reflection about issues of family safety and security before deployment than is presently done.

Physical Safety and Security Issues

> One thing I can share since I've been on the field is that though I am not afraid of traveling, I am very uncomfortable traveling the train at night. Since I am a former rape victim I am very cautious as I walk the city at night and use common sense traveling in lighted, touristy areas…Many women shrug these dangers off as they don't want to think it could happen to them and prefer their independence. However, explaining that no one is exempt and training them in preventive measures will help prevent serious problems from occurring in the future.

An increasingly volatile issue is the range of concerns connected with women working in unstable Muslim areas of the world, particularly in Central Asia. One agency reports that their families in Turkmenistan, Kazakhstan, and Uzbekistan are constantly under threat of expulsion, depending on the shifting political environment of the day.

A CRM missionary writes, "I have very close friends who served in Central Asia for a long time and were expelled from two different countries (along with their four kids). They are now working out of the organization office with missionary families traumatized by the effects of political and social unrest and focusing especially on the spiritual warfare aspects of these types of situations that often get little attention."

A mother of three writes,

> We are dealing with a high number of missionaries living with the threat of expulsion since we are right across the channel

from North Africa. They are either living with the constant un-
certainty/fear of expulsion or have just been expelled and are
now trying to regroup and figure out a new place to serve. They
may have been denied reentry to the culture and weren't able
to go back home for their belongings or they were given a few
hours to pack and were escorted to the border without time
to say good-bye to anyone. Expulsion without warning usually
means there was not time for healthy closure with relationships
and ministry...It's very difficult.

One of the divisions of ministries within Church Resource Ministries
is an order among the poor called InnerCHANGE, who work among
the world's poor. Because they expect to be in unsafe places, they try
to prepare their staff to be "street smart." In some areas these teams
have emergency and debrief plans laid out which are shared with all
teammates in the case of a crisis to an individual, the group, or in
the context. Too often mission agencies omit crisis forethought in the
training or in individual and team planning. However, we must also
recognize that God has wired us differently, and while some women
can deal with daily threats against them with seeming equanimity, others cannot. For example, a single Chinese missionary working in the
Philippines had her apartment broken into three times by the same
men who were friends of the local police. While she survived those
robberies, the day she was beaten and robbed on the way to work
finally took its toll, and she finally decided after seven years of this that
she could not take it anymore. She returned home to Singapore.

Relational Issues

A pressure that women can face as missionaries is that they may
be undervalued by their supervisors, and not taken seriously in
terms of key decision-making. Married women with kids may
feel the pressure to abandon or alter a sense of call to full-time
active ministry in order to "stay at home" or to live in safer areas

of the world. Single women may feel pressure from family and friends to not be living in "dangerous neighborhoods" alone.

When the mission is focused on church planting or Bible translation, the woman who stays at home with small children can be ignored. I (Judith) still remember meeting a German missionary working with YWAM in Hong Kong. She felt marginalized because caring for an infant excluded her from the street ministries that others were involved in. However, she lived in one of the many high-rises in the area and had to wash clothes in a common area. Pretty soon she had met all the women who came to wash clothes regularly and had started a Bible study. Her male team leader told me that it was nice that she could be so productive, but the implication was that she wasn't doing real ministry.

Emotional Issues Involving Uncertainty and Guilt

These issues are not the same as for men. From Siberia a woman writes:

> How do you interact with the women who are waiting to pick through your garbage as you take it to the dump? How about always having an evacuation bag packed? Women need to be shepherded. They need a special connection to the home office, and I believe they need their own woman VP or director to look out for their interests. It seems obvious to me that all the guys in charge are just that—guys. I know that they are wise and godly guys, but the addition of a female to oversee the spiritual, emotional, intellectual, and physical well-being of the women missionaries would be great.

We in North America are unprepared for the dire poverty we confront in so many situations in which wars and political changes have caused whole economies to collapse. It causes its own culture shock, and women especially need others to help them process their emotions as they encounter the economic disparities that make them feel guilty for what they do have.

Cross-cultural and Gender Issues When Under Stress

A single woman missionary writes:

> My US male coworker talked with one of the Russian men on staff before he left on furlough. He told him not to pursue a relationship with me. The Russian waited a whole three hours after my teammates had flown out before showing up at my doorstep.

Her suggestion is to have some accountability structures in place that the team has agreed on and to have some prayer cover in place so women wouldn't have to think on the spot in some situations, "Should I or shouldn't I?" Shortly afterward the Staff Development and Care Team designed a four-pillar support system to provide foundational support for every missionary on staff (see article by Steve Hoke and Myra Perrine, "Designing Your Thrival Strategy" 2009).

Another suggestion for both single and married women is to make sure that the women cross-cultural workers have a way of talking with each other regularly about the challenges of dealing with men in cross-cultural settings in order to think through strategies, become aware of one's boundaries or when boundaries have slipped, or simply to be listened to and validated for the stress these kinds of situations place on women.

It would also help if the men on a mission team were aware of how they can be good brothers to the women on the team and help be a buffer and protect them. It's also important that women, both single and married, have a clear sense of their boundaries with men, especially with men in cross-cultural situations. This would take processing with the men and women on the team ahead of time before such situations land in front of workers.

Vulnerability to Physical Attack and Danger in War-Zones

> When the war in Serbia and Kosovo broke out, we in Romania discussed what we would do if our safety were to be threatened. The question was whether we would evacuate or remain. We

praise God that the situation never got to the point where we had to make that decision. However, as I considered our options, I was torn between the safety of our children and wanting to remain with the Romanian people we love and minister with. When I voiced my thoughts to a Romanian friend, she responded, "Why would you leave if it was unsafe, when we would have to remain?" Why, indeed? The only reason might be because being Americans might make us more of an enemy to those who possibly threatened the country. I probably would not have wanted to remain with our Romanian brothers, sisters if I did not identify somewhat with them.

In recent years this woman's conflict has been repeated in many contexts. When teams are extracted from a country in conflict. When spouses are injured or killed, as in the case of Tom and Libby Little in August 2010 in Afghanistan. Women want to know…Are we expendable? Should we stay? Do we endanger the nationals by staying? Mission agencies and mission teams need to have policies in place which all agree to BEFORE such decisions need to be made.

Team members need to have discussed such scenarios together face-to-face so there is trust. At these times it is difficult to actually weigh and make decisions, and decisions that are not thought through ahead of time can be filled with emotional reactions that can be regrettable.

A Sense of Helplessness When Excluded From Decision-Making

Lack of inclusion of women's and children's voices in decision-making shows that male leaders are more interested in getting a decision made than listening to others and making a wise decision. It's as if they are saying, "We're not interested in others and we consider ourselves more important than others." It also means that those leaders have been impacted by a North American cultural value of efficiency, which is not a high value in many contexts in the majority world.

A basic need for any woman is a need for security. She needs to know that the mission agency LISTENS to her and takes her seriously. It is important that a woman perceives the agency as coming alongside in such a way that it is safe for her to ask for what she needs. Does she have an advocate? Does the agency see her as a partner with her husband on the field...or is she just "the wife"? If she is seen as just a wife then she may not feel that she has the credibility and thus the leverage to suggest change. It is interesting to note that one gift many women have is to sense something is not quite right long before her male counterpart is sensitive to it. This is an important gift that may make a difference in deteriorating situations. If the males around routinely screen her out and her response is to talk more, then that gift is marginalized.

These issues are certainly not new. Dana Robert's book *American Women in Mission* opens with a chapter on missionary wives which says, "The premature deaths of so many of the early missionary wives were caused not only by fever-laden tropical climates, but by fatigue brought on by doing and wanting to do too much. Few missionary wives had the time to write memoirs or theoretical treatises that summarized their missionary experience. As women and as laity rather than clergy, the 'assistant missionaries' had neither voice nor vote in discussions of mission theory and strategy" (Robert 1996, 4).

The Apostle Paul in 1 Corinthians 12 clearly states that EVERY part of the body is crucial to being the body of Christ. First Corinthians 12:22ff says that even the weakest parts of the body we consider as most necessary; that we regard them with MORE honor. Inclusion in communication, decision-making, problem solving, and strategy are all body life issues. When one significant segment of the body is repeatedly and regularly neglected or omitted, it belies the high theology of those who talk it. True biblical body life teams would share every aspect of cross-cultural teamwork. But this is not yet the case among most North American mission organizations.

The way mission executives and team leaders do decision-making and lead teams has a direct connection to how a mission team will express the body of Christ in a context. Can you imagine the impact if team leaders were inclusive of all parts of the team and what the ripple effect could be to nationals in that context? Our ways as missionaries do bleed or ripple out into the context in which we live. A CRM leader asked: "Why is it difficult to comprehend that our leadership expresses a DNA that the national local leaders see and take in? What do we want local national leaders to see in us? How are we replicating the DNA of the body of Christ in the context by the way we lead (including or excluding members of our own body in decision-making)?"

Some things HAVE changed: Almost all North American women have more of a voice in mission, although that is generally not true of some of our Two-Thirds World colleagues whose journey in missions has been of far shorter duration. Their experience can often be captured in the rest of Robert's quote: "As they sat silently at the missionary meetings, the movement of their sewing needles substituted for their voices."

Women polled suggested several other issues that are not physically life-threatening but are vital to cohesion for couples and families. We list them here to aid in a healthier field experience.

Discerning the Call Together
Mission organizations have typically focused more on the gifts and passions of the husband than on the gifts and passions of the wife. When that is the case, the dynamics of blended ministry—how do our gifts and passions blend, complement, and differ from one another—are rarely explored. Navigating theological differences in teams around the issues of authority and leadership of women are often neglected or ignored.

Ministry and Motherhood
Many couples desperately need assistance in evaluating the advantages and challenges of women attempting to stay engaged in ministry during the child-rearing years. Many younger women of the recent

generations (even in the church) are being raised with a "you can have both" mentality. This often results in what can be called "opportunity overload"—too many good choices in addition to primary family responsibilities. Many women struggle in sorting out the options, benefits, and costs, and hearing from God to discern their path.

Cultural Shift and Age Differences

Not dissimilar to the generational differences experienced in decades past is the challenge in communication and decision-making when team or field leadership is from one era and the newly arriving candidates are from another. It takes insight, gifting, and sensitivity to negotiate how to "seed" change in organizations around women's issues and generational style issues. There is an increasing need for organizations to look to other organizations for models and patterns for women serving in missions.

WHAT AGENCIES AND CHURCHES CAN DO PRE-FIELD

Sending/supporting churches and cooperating mission agencies can provide considerable pre-field orientation briefings and training to equip missionaries for potentially explosive situations. *Evangelical Missions Quarterly* (EMQ) has addressed this issue at various times within the past decades. In April 1994 Phil Parshall wrote that missions should have general evacuation policies. However, it is important to recognize that "one size doesn't fit all." Multi-option crisis management plans should be in place before they are needed. Since 9/11 numerous agencies have moved to requiring teams to develop such crisis contingency plans *before* they are deployed or shortly *after* arriving and settling in, to ensure an intentional and appropriate "exit strategy" is in place as soon as possible. This team exploration of what crisis might look like in their setting also leads to updated and appropriate safety precautions for children and women as well.

In particular, missions need to identify who has the decision-making power and whether there are options for individual choice or not. In the heat of an explosive political situation, women often feel torn because they get caught in the middle of conflicting ideas about staying or evacuating. Parshall also says that there must be accommodation for those who do not feel they can enter a violent area. Each family situation has its own dynamics, and there should not be any hierarchy of missionary sainthood because some choose to stay and some do not. Finally, Parshall writes that one of the important components about risk-taking relates to the opinions of nationals in the country where missionaries serve. Sometimes staying puts our national colleagues in more jeopardy, whereas in other situations they feel that we abandon them because they would be glad to leave if they could.

In the July 1994 issue of EMQ Karen Carr, writing on post-traumatic stress syndrome, suggests that debriefings should be mandated following any traumatic event. "Missionaries may not feel they need the debriefing, or they may feel that there is a stigma associated with attending one. A mandated directive from the administrator gives the missionary the opportunity to get help and bypasses initial resistances." To add to Carr's idea, it is equally important to have separate briefings for women and any child over the age of five. Often women do not feel free to contradict their husbands, but the stress they have suffered needs to be articulated in order for healing to begin. Children, too, suffer traumatic reactions and need to be listened to and allowed to verbalize their fears.

Bob Klamser of Crisis Consulting International says that there are some common characteristics that mission organization leadership would do well to understand and consider in caring for their personnel.

1. Missionaries often tend to accept danger, and especially steadily increasing danger, as a normal part of the environment until a critical mass is reached.

2. Unless that critical mass has been pre-determined or pre-defined, the most common action is for individual missionaries to tough it out and accept levels of danger they are personally uncomfortable with in

the absence of leadership guidelines to the contrary. In such a situation, however, when the individual missionary finally determines that the danger level is unacceptable, the reaction is often hasty and ill-considered.

3. In the absence of contingency plans and pre-determined action points, when danger does impact the missionary team, one of the almost inevitable consequences is a crisis of confidence in leadership. This often results in long-term organizational concerns that are more significant, in terms of ministry disruption, than the original danger.

4. In each of these profiled situations the author is convinced that the organizational consequences could have been significantly reduced, and the overall health of the affected missionaries significantly protected, with more effective and more proactive crisis management capabilities by the organization's leadership (Klamser 2001).

These are very strong words coming from someone who works with missionaries in crisis situations, and Klamser's comments set the stage for separating out the need to listen to the women who are often caught in the middle of policies they had no participation in making.

WHAT AGENCIES AND CHURCHES CAN DO IN-SERVICE

There are a number of substantive changes both churches and agencies could make to provide an environment that is both just and careful. Steps toward increased participation and leadership development should include the following.

1. Invite input in policy setting and decision-making from men and women alike. More complete representation will ensure that affective concerns, in addition to the usual logical, cognitive issues, are surfaced and dealt with adequately.

2. Involve all representative people in the decision-making process. Women are quite often excluded from the policy making that the men engage in, even though it is their fates that are the issue in focus. It was a typical Old Testament pattern that women and children were simply expected to go along (or in some cases thrown to the lions along with their husbands!), but we are in a New Testament world now, and if Jesus in Luke 10:38–42 encouraged Mary to use her mind and learn, how can men today ignore the voice of the women who serve alongside them?

3. Don't presume or prejudge the responses of your staff in stressful situations. In particular, clarify before team deployment if you have the right as a team to make separate decisions, or if the team must act as one.

4. Move immediately toward women serving in leadership roles and participating in leadership teams on the field. This is the most important way to ensure that the women's perspective and voice is heard in all major decisions regarding mission-ministry. For those of you who still struggle over the issue of women in leadership, one of the best new books out on the subject comes from Loren Cunningham and David J. Hamilton (2002) called *Why Not Women?* I (Judith) have read many of the books debating head vs. source, and this seems like one of the clearest explanations I've read in quite some time. Both Steve and I are committed to qualified women in leadership, because as an integral part of the body of Christ, they should be heard.

In fact, in the last five years we have seen several missions who have set as a critical objective greater inclusion of women in leadership and in the decision-making process make substantial steps forward. Key women have been included at the board level, and not just a single, "token" representative, as well as in executive roles over ministry, finance, development, mobilization, and field training.

5. Encourage women missionaries to seek out friends, confidants, and mentors within and outside the organization with whom they can process issues and emotions. Too often we go to a cross-cultural setting without sufficient emotional support systems. It's crucial that women workers develop clear mentors and friends who will walk with them in their struggles so that there are outlets beyond their ministry team. Ideally, having confidants and mentors from within the same organization (but not the same team) can be a tremendous source of encouragement.

6. Develop direct linkages with other agencies and advisors with expertise in the areas of refugees, civil war, expatriate evacuation, medical airlifts, etc. Every mission agency should draft its own emergency procedures for dealing with catastrophic situations on any of its fields. However, often a mission is not the only one working in a particular city or country, and agreeing beforehand on how to work together in a crisis can facilitate the process. An Asian colleague relates how devastated he was by the unilateral evacuation of his teachers by their expatriate mission organization in response to rioting which was taking place in another city, not theirs. He felt betrayed, because their actions indicated that their own safety was more important than the work they were doing with his national mission entity. One organization that exists to help mission agencies in working through these policies is Crisis Consulting International, headquartered in Ventura, California (www.cricon.org). They can offer much needed help in areas where mission agencies may be unsure how to proceed.

7. Develop diversity and sensitivity training for everyone in the church and mission regarding issues of women in ministry and women in leadership. Men often need training in dealing with emotions and feelings (it's not a fluke that a book entitled *Men Are from Mars, Women Are from Venus* was so popular a few years ago!). It has taken years, for example, for me (Judith) to help my husband understand that sometimes I don't

want him to DO something about a problem: I just want him to listen as I vent my frustrations. These same gender misunderstandings happen in mission leadership, and often male leaders feel inadequate to understand and help female colleagues, especially because they need to be cautious that too much concern may be misinterpreted as sexual interest. Conversely, I have heard men get impatient because women tend to deal with issues of the heart first, then with programmatic concerns, while men feel like they are wasting time.

Developing a biblical body life theology as a foundation for all our teamwork that is balanced, healthy, and inclusive takes work on everyone's part. One theme comes through loud and clear: women need learning communities that are safe, confidential, and nurturing to men and women alike. Brainstorming creative ways to establish these communities should involve everyone on a team, and should encompass some trial and error as the strategies are developed.

Issues like gender inclusiveness need to be purposefully addressed, yet women also need to walk awhile in a man's moccasins, and realize the enormity of the pressures and expectations that men often have to face without much support.

One kind of in-service training might be to regularly drill routines so they become automatic. Whether it is an evacuation procedure or knowing instantly what to pack into one suitcase, it is far easier to think things through without the pressure of a crisis clouding judgment and raising adrenaline levels. However, training needs to be structured either in preparation for a potential crisis or in the debriefing after a major event. It is vital to recognize that using an intensive training module only once will not cement the information permanently.

A Filipina literacy colleague told me that she makes all her literacy workers go through each course four times. I was astonished…why so many times? "Well," she replied, "the first time they get the big picture but the details don't sink in. Each succeeding time they focus on different parts of the course. The best workers get it in three times, but most take four to really make the principles and teaching methods their own." My colleague recognized something that too often impatient Westerners do not: doing a workshop on an important issue once is not enough. It would be far better to be creative in presenting critical material using several different methods over a longer period of time.

Finally, all the preparation in the world will not substitute for the personal security that flows out of intimacy with Abba. A rock-solid relationship with the Lord is primary and foundational to all we have discussed in this chapter. While it may be a cliché to say that safety is not the absence of danger, but the presence of the Lord, that does not make it any less true. Stephen Lawhead's novel *Byzantium* is a story about an Irish monk who loses his faith because he keeps asking where God is and why God did not protect him from all the dangers he endured. At the conclusion of the book, one of his early converts, a Dane, reminds him of what the Christian life is all about. With great excitement he tells the Irish monk how he can't wait to "sail into heaven" because he will meet Jesus, who also suffered. Jesus will understand what they went through, and he will welcome them home.

Regular prayer meetings that focus not only on safety but also endurance to face whatever might happen should be regular routines to establish. In addition, biographies like *The Heavenly Man* (Yun and Hattaway 2002) remind us that memorizing Scripture passages or books rather than just isolated verses means that God's Word is not dependent upon our physical possession of a Bible, but can become much more embedded in our hearts to be retrieved in times of stress. That book also reminds us that compared to the suffering that Chinese Christians are facing regularly, our fears seem paltry.

Cross-cultural ministry is an incredible crucible for character development. Frontline ministries in times of political instability affect men, women, and children, and this chapter reminds us that too often the women and children have no voice in the decisions that affect them. Mission agencies would do well to include their voices in both the pre-field and in-service components of their work. In today's world of exploding missions (both literally and figuratively!), we can't afford the luxury of excluding half the mission force from the significant decision-making when a crisis affects them all. It is not only a gender inclusion issue. More significantly it is a Kingdom issue of body life stewardship with global Kingdom consequences. Steve and I believe we need to listen to the women and add their wisdom to that of the men who are trying to do what is best for everyone.

REFERENCES

Cunningham, L., and D. Hamilton. 2000. *Why Not Women? A Biblical Study of Women in Missions, Ministry, and Leadership.* Seattle, WA: YWAM.

Hoke, S., and M. Perrine. 2009. Designing Your Thrival Strategy. In *Global Mission Handbook: Your Guide to Cross-cultural Service,* ed. S. Hoke and B. Taylor. Downer's Grove, IL: InterVarsity Press.

Carr, K. 1994. Trauma and Post Traumatic Stress Disorder among Missionaries. *Evangelical Missions Quarterly* 30(3): 246–255.

Klamser, R. 2001. Caring for Those in Crisis. In *Caring for the Harvest Force in the New Millennium,* ed. T. A. Steffen and F. D. Pennoyer. Evangelical Missiological Society Series, Vol. 9. Pasadena, CA: William Carey Library.

Lawhead, S. 1997. *Byzantium.* New York: Harper Collins.

Parshall, P. 1994. Missionaries: Safe or Expendable? *Evangelical Missions Quarterly* 30(2): 162–166.

Robert, D. 1996. *American Women in Mission: A Social History of Their Thought and Practice.* Macon, GA: Mercer University Press.

Yun, B., and P. Hattaway. 2002. *The Heavenly Man: The Remarkable Story of Chinese Christian Brother Yun.* Grand Rapids, MI: Monarch Books.

SCRIPTURE INDEX

Genesis 1:26-27 .... 4, 21, 217
Genesis 2:18-22 25

2 Chronicles 7:14 252-53

Psalm 103:11-14 186
Psalm 139:13........................ 17

Proverbs 6:20-23 4
Proverbs 26:2 247

Isaiah 54:1-6...................... 115
Isaiah 56:2-6...................... 113

Lamentations 3:21 .... 22, 97

Daniel 10:13 236

Matthew 6:20 247

Mark 10:62 239

Luke 2:49-51...................... 119
Luke 4:6........................... 254
Luke 7:50 239

Luke 9:1-2 251
Luke 10:17-19 119
Luke 10:38-42 271
Luke 14:23 229

John 4:27 115
John 14:12 .... 236, 251
John 14:30 235
John 20:21 236

Acts 1 & 2........................... 24
Acts 1:8 251
Acts 2:17-18 24

Romans 8:17 23
Romans 12:1 26
Romans 12:10....................... 40
Romans 12:18....................... 25

1 Corinthians 1:31 111
1 Corinthians 7:34 115
1 Corinthians 9 40
1 Corinthians 12 266
1 Corinthians 12:11-27 23
1 Corinthians 12:22.............. 266

2 Corinthians 4:3-4 233
2 Corinthians 10:4 233
2 Corinthians 12:7, ... 236

Galatians 3:28 23

Ephesians 4:26-27 247
Ephesians 4:27 216
Ephesians 6:1-2 216
Ephesians 6:11-18 233
Ephesians 6:12 .... 235, 253

Philippians 2:4 216
Philippians 4:7-9................. 249

James 5:13-16..................... 117

1 Peter 5:6-7 186
1 Peter 5:8......................... 233

1 John 3:1-2 244
1 John 4:4......................... 250

INDEX

9/11, 259, 268

A

acculturation, 34–35, 37, 39, 41, 225
ACTS Seminary, 84
   Intercultural Ministry Centre, 84
Afghanistan, 265
Africa, 1, 39, 44, 56, 61, 127, 140, 149–50
   African, 42, 125, 134, 149–51
America(n). *See* United States of America.
anger, 34, 69, 76, 95, 131, 141, 172, 215–16, 232, 246–47
   explosive, 200
   toward God, 233, 243, 249
Anglican, 110
anxiety, 34, 36–37, 44, 62
Aquinas, Thomas, 97
Argentina, 110, 118
Arnold, Clinton E., 237–38
asexuality, 117
Asia, 44, 56, 217
   Asian, 210, 216, 272
Assemblies of God, 47

Attig, Tom, 96
attrition, 33, 40–41, 52, 121, 131, 208–09
authority, 2, 8, 11, 15–16, 51, 101–02, 109, 111–12, 119–22, 129, 138, 150, 163, 237, 251, 254–56, 267
   fear of, 245
   figures, 210, 216, 218
   male, 109, 119–21
   relationships, 119, 253
Aylward, Gladys, 27

B

Baltimore, 250
Barclay, Susan, 132
Barnabas International, 226
bereavement, 92–94
Bible, 21, 24, 28, 103–04, 108, 186, 216, 233, 236, 257, 274
   biblical
      complementary partnerships, 26
      concept, 40
      equality, 21
      interpretations, 110
      models, 22

perspective, 22
roles, 198
teaching, 21, 24, 165
theology, 85
values, 216
college, 45, 49
knowledge, 149
school, 48, 106, 111, 116
Scripture, 17, 21–23, 25–26,
  40, 111, 119–20, 122, 211,
  213, 235, 247, 253, 274
study, 9, 71–72, 106, 148, 263
translation, 58, 210–13, 217, 263
Bliss, R., 22
Boardman, Sarah, 132
Bolivia, 102–03, 111
  Bolivian, 106–07, 112, 114
Borker, Ruth A., 6
Bowers, Joyce, 130
Bowie, Fiona, 151
British Columbia, 84
Buddhism, 247
Buenos Aires, 110–11
burnout, 33, 79, 162, 208

C

California, 94, 102, 272
Canada, 84
  Canadian, 109–10
Carmichael, Amy, 132
Carr, Karen, 269
celibacy, 13, 113, 117
Central Asia, 261
Chicago, 223
children, 4–6, 9–10, 15, 39, 44,
  47–49, 57, 59, 68–69, 71–75,
  86–87, 91, 97, 104, 109, 112,
  114–15, 129–30, 140, 163, 167,
  170, 172–73, 175, 177, 184, 194,
  196, 198–200, 210, 226–27,

229, 236, 239, 245, 255–56,
  259–60, 263, 265, 268–69, 271,
  274
China, 28
  Chinese, 28, 147, 259, 262, 274
China Inland Mission, 27
Christian, 4, 16, 22, 26–27, 34,
  46, 51, 54, 93, 98, 117, 125–26,
  129–30, 136, 138–39, 143–45,
  147, 150, 156–57, 159, 164,
  174–75, 189, 225, 229, 232–40,
  248–51, 253, 259, 274
Christianity, 140, 237, 251
chronic illness, 207–08, 217–18
church, 16–17, 22, 27, 33, 39–41,
  44, 49, 51, 55, 61–62, 67–68,
  72–73, 81, 83–84, 86, 89,
  101–02, 104, 106–07, 109–10,
  121, 126–31, 134, 136, 138–41,
  143, 145, 148, 150–51, 156,
  180, 209, 223, 227, 240, 244,
  246, 248, 253–54, 259, 261,
  268, 270, 272
  home, 59
  indigenous, 40, 44, 49, 62
  institutionalized, 27
  national, 33, 68, 86, 227
  planter, 27, 93, 104, 106–08,
    138, 142, 145–46, 243, 263
Church Resource Ministries
  (CRM), 261–62, 267
Clark, Karen Kaiser, 96
Colorado, 52
communication, 5, 8, 17, 40, 42–
  43, 74–75, 80, 104, 160, 165,
  167, 192, 208, 226, 266, 268
complementarian, 22, 26–27
conference/seminar series, 56
control, 2, 8, 12, 15, 53, 93, 97,
  234, 237, 244–46
coping strategies, 67, 72, 75, 95, 97

methods, 134–37, 139–42, 144, 149
Crawford, Nancy, 22, 42
creativity, 4, 101
Crisis Consulting International, 269, 272
Crossman, Meg, 149
cultural
adjustment, 132, 142, 228
cross-cultural
adaptation, 111
adjustments, 132, 142, 228
challenges, 129
circumstances, 118
experience, 34
interactions, 17
ministry, 84, 122, 151, 274
setting, 8, 14, 272
situation, 245, 264
stress, 57, 156
workers, 1, 233, 264
differences, 36, 46, 68
influences, 2, 17
isolation, 83
re-entry, 37
trauma, 34
culture
host, 33–34, 36–37, 39–40, 46, 55, 60, 68, 70, 79, 125, 129, 138–39, 142, 149, 151, 170, 175, 177, 188, 194, 196
shock, 34–37, 41, 43–44, 57, 61–62, 92, 114, 142, 151, 208, 263
six aspects/stages of, 35–36, 92
Cunningham, Loren, 17, 21–22, 26, 271
curses, 241, 247–48, 255
soul ties, 240, 247–48

D
Daniel, 236
David, 180, 236
Deborah, 24
Deen, Edith, 22
demonization, 237, 239–40, 247, 251
demons, 231–33, 235–38, 240, 242–43, 246–47, 250–51, 254–56
depression, 35, 165, 185, 200, 208, 231, 241, 249
Dharmaraj, Glory E., 144, 147
discouraging women, 28
diversity, 272
Donovan, Kath, 131
Duvall, Nancy, 37, 46
Dzubinski, Leanne, 148

E
Eastern Europe, 39, 44, 59–60, 127–28, 140, 143
Easton, Susan, 47
Edwards, Jonathan, 28
Edwards, Sarah, 28
Eenigenburg, S., 22
egalitarian, 8, 22, 50, 117, 120
emotional, 4, 22, 34, 40, 54, 72, 93, 95–96, 109, 114, 118, 131, 135, 145, 158–60, 162, 165–66, 168–69, 172, 176–77, 184, 188–89, 193, 200, 231, 239–40, 246, 248, 250–51, 263, 265, 272
baggage, 162, 181, 201
needs, 155–57, 159, 168–69, 174–76, 179–85, 187, 189, 193, 197, 200–03
dealing with, 157, 250
trauma, 76
English, 71, 103–04, 129–30
English, Laura L., 131–32, 141, 148

equality, 1, 3, 8, 18, 21, 25, 46, 50
Escobar, Samuel, 66
Esther, 24
Eurasia, 44
Europe, 45, 56
evangelical, 22, 49, 58, 66–67, 83, 108, 117
Evangelical Fellowship of Canada, 73
Evangelical Missions Quarterly (EMQ), 268–69
expectations, 37, 40–41, 44, 46, 51–53, 60, 62, 71, 74, 76, 83, 129, 131, 141, 189, 200, 224, 228, 245–46, 273
  role, 35, 129, 134–35, 150
  unrealistic, 35, 117, 164–65, 188, 227

F

fear, 71, 115, 139, 186, 211, 244–46, 249, 259, 262, 269, 274
feminine, 8, 14, 117, 196
  culture, 6
  identity, 12
  socialization, 5–6
finishers, 222–26, 228–29
  movement, 221
Finishers Project, 222–24
  Forum, 223, 229
Frankl, Victor, 188
Freemasonry, 247

G

Garlock, Ruthanne, 234–35, 249
gender
  biases, 130, 133, 145, 151
  biological differences, 4
  constraints, 68, 71
  distinctives, 3
  equality, 18, 46, 50

identity, 11–12, 102, 116
  inclusive, 23, 273
  issues, 55, 59, 87, 122, 127–28, 151, 260, 264, 273
  methods for coping with, 135
  roles, 23, 33, 40, 43, 57, 107, 116, 144
  science, 3, 17
George, Pamela, 137
German, 103, 107, 263
Gilligan, Carol, 2, 240
Gilmore, David D., 12
God's calling, 61, 78, 81, 84, 88, 120, 136
God's image, 4, 21, 190, 207, 210, 217–18
  reflection of, 210, 218
Goldschmidt, Walter, 2
Great Commission, 18, 148, 156, 223
grief, 92–98, 172
Grunlan, Stephen A., 133–35, 137
guilt, 15, 41, 73, 166, 174, 243–44, 263

H

Hales, Dianne, 3, 17
Hall, Elizabeth, 37, 46
Hamilton, David J., 271
Hausa, 11, 15
Hawaii, 102
Head, Jim, 94
headship, 39
healing, 117–18, 145, 218, 231, 239–40, 250–52, 269
  ministry, 48, 253
Hinduism, 247
Holden, Gregory, 227–28
Hong Kong, 263
Humphrey, Geraldine M., 94

I

identity crisis, 51, 114, 121
Illinois, 254
Inca, 106
India, 47, 147
    Indian, 137
Indonesia, 252, 259
insecurity, 241, 244–46
International Foreign Mission
    Association, 46–47
interpersonal
    conflict, 76
    constraints, 75
    difficulties, 201, 209
    encounters, 34
    feedback, 36
    relationships, 40, 68, 74, 76, 149,
        208, 210, 215, 218, 234, 243
    skills, 84
Irian Jaya, 57
Islam, 247
    Islamic, 39

J

Jakarta, 57
Janssen, Gretchen, 34
Japan, 184
    Japanese, 184, 210
Jayawardena, Kumari, 137
Jeremiah, 97
Jezebel, 236
Job, 236
Johnstone, Barbara, 13
Jones, Marge, 52
Joyner, Rick, 24
Judas, 236
Judson, Ann, 132
justice, 1

K

Kamwe, 12
Kassian, Mary, 27
Kazakhstan, 261
Kenya, 125, 127, 147, 190, 255
King Saul, 236
kingdom of God, 21, 23, 40, 59,
    67, 71, 82, 164, 221, 233, 235,
    248–49, 251, 253–54
Klamser, Robert, 269–70
Korea, 1
    Korean, 121
Kraft, Charles H., 250
Kraft, Marguerite G., 149

L

Lamp, Debbie, 226
Langley, 84
language, 4, 6, 24, 27, 65, 68–70,
    73, 77, 83, 86, 93, 121, 128–29,
    132, 159, 165, 170, 177, 208,
    210–14, 225, 227–28
Latin America, 1, 15, 110, 211, 217
Lausanne Forum for World
    Evangelization 2004, 89
Lawhead, Stephen, 274
loneliness, 50, 95, 105, 116,
    159–60, 162, 169–70, 174, 180,
    185–87, 194, 200, 225, 247
loss, 35, 71, 92–98, 177, 208, 214,
    226, 239
    coping with, 91, 94–95
    definition of, 92
    in relationships, 71, 92
    occupational status, 93
    plan for recovery, 97
    treasured objects, 93

M

machismo, 107
male
  authority. *See* authority.
  chauvinism, 136
  domination, 2, 8–9, 45, 252
  influence, 83–84
  leadership, 80, 107, 117, 129,
    145, 150, 260, 263, 265, 273
  perspective, 2, 173
  values, 9
Maltz, Daniel N., 6
Malwitz, Nelson, 222, 224
Mandarin, 27
marital
  conflict, 198
  obligations, 163
  problems, 197, 201
  role, 68, 70
  status, 45, 56, 68, 70–71, 101,
    103, 112, 170–71, 195, 202
marriage, 10, 12, 33, 43, 46,
  49–50, 59, 61, 111–13, 159,
  169, 177–78, 194–95, 197–98,
  247–48
Mary, 27, 271
masculine, 2, 117
  communication, 5–6
  socialization, 6, 14
Mayan Indians, 234
Mayers, Marvin K., 133–35, 137,
  139, 141
McGee, Gary, 132
McNeil, Melanie, 146
Mennonite, 103–04, 107, 110
mentoring, 146, 189
Meyerson, 87
ministry, 21–22, 24–27, 34, 39,
  41–42, 44, 47–49, 54, 58–62,
  65, 67–77, 79–88, 101–04,
  106–15, 117–18, 120, 122,

125–26, 128–29, 131, 133–34,
  140–41, 143, 145, 149, 151–52,
  157, 162–63, 165, 178, 192,
  197–98, 200, 202, 217, 221,
  224, 227, 233, 236–37, 243,
  247, 250–53, 259, 262–63, 267,
  270–72, 274
  women in. *See* women.
mission
  agency, 22, 33, 35, 37, 41,
    45–46, 49, 52–53, 56–59, 61,
    88, 96, 110, 118, 129, 131,
    143–44, 148–49, 209, 218,
    221, 223–25, 227, 229,
    261–62, 265–66, 268, 272,
    274
  boards, 46, 55, 66, 105, 172,
    207, 241
  field, 37, 40, 42, 49, 58, 72–73,
    91–92, 97, 101–02, 111, 121,
    131–32, 136, 140, 149, 151,
    155–63, 165–72, 174–82,
    185–86, 189–95, 197–98,
    200–03, 210–11, 217, 221,
    224–29
  frontier, 145
  long-term, 78, 82
  pre-field training, 79, 94, 125,
    151, 174, 203, 228, 233
  short-term, 209
Mission Training International
  (MTI), 52, 55
missionary
  call, 78, 82, 97–98, 147, 201
  community, 157, 164–66
  member care, 66, 73, 84–85, 166
  second-career, 221-24, 226-28
  single, 45–48, 51, 56–57, 65,
    67, 70, 75, 77, 79, 101–02
    112–16, 118–19, 121–22, 130,
    142, 157, 159, 163, 168–76,

199, 243, 262, 264
women. *See* women.
Montgomery, Helen Barrett, 27
Montreal, 142
Moon, Lottie, 132
Mormon, 108, 247
motherhood, 8, 12, 112–13, 267
multiple roles, 176–77
Muslim, 137, 145–46, 148–49, 164, 261
Myors, Ruth, 131

N

Nairobi, 125
Naomi, 114
Navigators, 223
Nazi
    concentration camp, 188
needs of missionary women
    interpersonal relationships, 40, 74, 76, 149, 208, 234, 243
    recognize emotional needs, 155–57, 159, 168–69, 174–76, 179–85, 187, 189, 197, 200–03
    self-esteem, 50, 93, 162, 181
    spiritual nourishment, 157, 165
    validation, 41–42, 48, 50, 157, 162–64
New Testament, 24, 211–12, 215, 237, 271
Nicholson, Steve, 254
Nigeria, 11–12
North Africa, 262
North America, 42, 148, 211, 225, 263, 265

O

obedience to God, 233
Oberg, Kalervo, 35, 92
Old Testament, 24, 211, 271
orphans, 28, 71

Orthodox, 26
outreach, 61, 102, 107, 110, 190

P

Pakistan, 259
Palmer Lake, 52
Papua New Guinea, 254
Paraguay, 110
Parrott, Don, 224
Parshall, Phil, 268–69
pastoral care, 98, 165–66
Paul, 23, 40, 155, 235–36, 266
Pentecost, 23
Peter, 23
Philippines, 142, 259, 262
    Filipina, 273
Phoebe, 24
prayer, 24, 48, 80, 117, 127, 130, 145, 181, 183, 187, 193, 196, 202, 218, 231, 236, 243, 248, 252–53, 264, 274
Priscilla, 24
Protestant, 26, 66–67, 113
public vs. private sphere, 10

R

recovery, 35, 93, 96–98
    stages of, 96
Robert, Dana, 147–48, 266–67
role abdication, 135, 140–43
role adaptation, 135, 144
role challenges, 129–30
role coping methods, 136, 140, 144
role insistence, 135–37, 139
Roman Catholic, 26, 117
Romania, 93, 127, 136–38, 140, 143, 145, 150, 264
    Romanian, 127–29, 134, 136, 138–39, 141, 265
Roseveare, Helen, 132
Ruth, 114

S

Sang-Cheol Moon, Steve, 121
Satan, 156, 233–35, 236, 238–41,
    243, 249–50, 253–57
    attacks, 156, 240
    Devil, 216, 234
    Satanic activity, 235–36
Saucy, Robert L., 23, 27
Schrag, Lyle, 88
Scientology, 247
second-career missionaries. *See*
    missionary.
security vs. freedom orientation,
    9–10
self-doubt, 130, 171, 241
self-hatred, 242–43
self-rejection, 242
self-worth, 240–43
sexism, 132, 144
sexual
    abuse, 118, 162
    allure, 13
    attraction, 117
    desire, 95, 116
    discrimination, 1
    experience, 116
    fantasy, 116
    feelings, 116–17, 174
    harassment, 170–71
    impurity, 116
    interest, 118, 273
    intimacy, 95
    involvement, 175
    needs, 173–75, 196
    oppression, 119
    sin, 162
    temptation, 116
sexuality, 14–15, 116–18, 168,
    173–74, 196
shame, 15, 115, 125, 171–72, 232,
    243–44, 251

Sherrer, Quin, 235, 249
Siberia, 263
Singapore, 262
singleness, 41, 168, 170–73, 187,
    194–95, 245
    accepting/embracing singleness,
    111
    affirmation, 157, 162–63
    aloneness, 51
    authority, 111, 119
    intimacy needs, 157–58
    marginality status, 112–13
    safety issues, 193, 261
    single women. *See* missionary.
    symbiotic relationships, 108
social
    changes, 102, 138, 146, 150
    differences, 11
    order, 6
    reform, 137, 139
    status, 9
    structure, 8, 15, 139, 148
socialization process, 12, 116
South America, 111, 117
Spanish, 102–04, 106, 210–11, 234
spiritual, 14–16, 28, 101, 113,
    117–18, 120, 130–31, 145, 151,
    156–58, 165–66, 168, 180,
    187, 200–01, 218, 225, 233–35,
    240–41, 248, 250–52, 254–55,
    257, 263
    bondage, 249
    change, 48, 150
    equality, 21
    gifts, 107, 122, 235
    growth, 37
    power, 15–16, 240, 251, 253
    sensitivity, 232
    warfare, 234–35, 237, 239, 248,
    251–57, 261
status, 6, 8–9, 11–16, 35, 70,

92–93, 102, 111–12, 114,
121–22, 133, 137–38, 143,
146–48, 150, 163, 168, 175
Stephens, Connie, 15
Stockton, Betsy, 102
stress, 25, 34, 37, 44, 46, 50,
53, 57, 58, 60, 68–69, 71–72,
74–75, 81, 83, 92, 128, 137,
142, 156, 176, 180–81, 188,
198, 207–08, 210, 213–18,
227–28, 232–33, 241, 259, 264,
269, 271, 274
Sweatman, Stephen, 55

T

Tannen, Deborah, 6–7
Tavard, George, 26
TenElshof, Judith K., 27
Theological Education by Extension
(TEE), 106, 109–11, 118
theology, 17, 25, 85, 109–10, 172,
207, 266, 273
Tokyo, 184
transitions, 86–87, 114, 160, 185
Trasher, Lillian, 28
trauma, 38, 76, 108
Trinity Western University, 84
Turkmenistan, 261

U

United States of America, 3, 5, 8,
13, 28, 59, 74, 76–77, 127, 186,
211–22, 242
American, 1, 3, 9, 13, 59, 71,
102–03, 131, 136–37, 180,
184, 207, 265
uprootedness, 160
Uzbekistan, 261

V

Van Leeuwen, Mary Stewart, 4
visibility and power, 11

W

West Africa, 15
Western, 1–2, 9, 16, 44, 58, 102,
116, 120, 137–40, 177, 237, 274
society, 1, 8, 11, 50, 251
Wilson, Linda, 50, 141–42
witchcraft, 254
women
as nurturers, 183
gifting, 26, 49, 51
in ministry, 21–22, 24, 26–27,
49–50, 66, 83, 86, 146, 148,
267, 272
in traditional roles, 15, 25,
130, 151
missionary(ies)
special needs of, 48
World Vision, 148
worry, 7, 128, 244–46

Y

YMCA, 179
Youth With A Mission (YWAM), 17,
21, 148, 263